DON CARLO
BOSS *OF* BOSSES
THE TRUE-CRIME CLASSIC, UPDATED WITH NEW MATERIAL

PAUL MESKIL & JAMES PIERRE

Don Carlo: Boss of Bosses by Paul Meskil

Copyright 1973 © Paul Meskil

Second Edition. Released in the United States of America and the United Kingdom.

Ironworks Publishing Company
360 Bloomfield Avenue,
Windsor, CT 06105

http://www.ironworkspublishing.com

Cover Design: Damonza

ISBN: 978-1-7349000-0-2 (Digital)
ISBN: 978-1-7349000-1-9 (Print)

DON CARLO
BOSS *OF* BOSSES
THE TRUE-CRIME CLASSIC, UPDATED WITH NEW MATERIAL

"STILL AT THE SUMMIT OF THE UNDERWORLD IS CARLO GAMBINO, THE UNQUESTIONED BOSS, THE SINGLE MOST IMPORTANT MAFIOSO IN THE COUNTRY."

"Gambino can still stroll unnoticed along Flushing's busy Main Street on Saturday afternoons, squeezing the cantaloupes and depositing bag after bag in the back seat of the inconspicuous dark green Mercury sedan that follows behind.

"Last August 13, when he attended the wedding of a friend's daughter at the Huntington Town House on Long Island, he was, as usual, fawned over by the guests; the musicians even broke into the theme from THE GODFATHER in his honor."

Nicholas Pileggi

April 1972

New York Magazine

ONE MAN'S FAMILY

IT WAS TIME TO TAKE his wife shopping so the old man turned off the radio and got his midnight blue overcoat and dark grey fedora from the hall closet. He put on the coat over a plain gray suit and a tieless gray shirt, and he planted the hat squarely on his silver-haired head with the brim turned up all around.

He walked slowly, carefully, down the stairs from the second floor of the square brick two-story house at 2230 Ocean Parkway, Brooklyn, on a quiet, tree-lined street of middle-class Italian and Jewish families. His wife and daughter-in-law were a few steps behind him.

His face was a web of fine wrinkles and his eyes seemed almost closed. The thin lips beneath his aquiline nose were set in a faint smile, the enigmatic Mediterranean smile of a Mona Lisa. Or a Borgia. He looked like a kindly, gentle grandfather—which, among other things, he was.

He opened the white front door and paused for a

moment in the entranceway alongside a plaster cherub installed by his wife and her sister. The patriarch and the cherub smiling their almost identical frozen smiles.

He stood in the doorway, staring out at the street through his half-shut eyes. Then he came out of the house and a watcher noted it was 1:42 p.m. March 23, 1970.

"Surveillance begun," the watcher wrote on his memo pad.

Pulling up his coat collar against the icy, salt-flavored wind blowing from the nearby Atlantic, the old man walked down the steep brick steps in front of the house and along the walk and through the gate in the iron picket fence bordering the small front yard. The fence was high enough to discourage dogs but low enough to be climbed by almost any agile human, so it was more decorative than protective.

The two women, bundled in fur-trimmed black coats, followed the old man to a gleaming Continental parked at the curb. They all climbed in, locked their seat belts and headed north on Ocean Parkway at a steady 30 miles an hour. A much less impressive car started up a half-block behind them and took off in the same direction.

Eighteen minutes later, the Continental backed into a parking space on 48th St. near 14th Ave. in the Borough Park section of Brooklyn. The elderly couple and their daughter-in-law had planned to visit some stores on 13th Ave., but they never got there that day.

As soon as they emerged from the car, they were accosted by two, serious, efficient-looking men who identified themselves as special agents of the Federal Bureau of Investigation.

"Mr. Gambino," one of them said politely, "you're under arrest."

They frisked him and were not surprised to find him unarmed. He had never been known to carry a gun, not even in the wild wars of the Prohibition era.

His wallet contained a couple of hundred dollars in cash, the car registration and his driver's license. They found nothing else in his pockets but his house and cars keys, a clean white handkerchief and a small bottle of nitroglycerin pills to keep his heart pumping. When they were through frisking him, they snapped handcuffs on his bony wrists. It had been many years since he last felt the cold steel bracelets.

A small crowd gathered to see what was happening. The arrest of a respectable-looking elderly gentleman in this Orthodox Jewish neighborhood was an unusual occurrence, but no one in the crowd recognized Don Carlo Gambino even though his picture had appeared in the *New York Times* a week before along with a story about his accession to *Capo di Tutti Capi*—Boss of Bosses of the American Mafia.

If they had seen the photo and read the story, they would still have found it hard to believe that this frail, mild-mannered man was the most powerful, most feared racketeer in the world. Brooklyn residents know what gangsters look like. Scarface Al Capone and Little Augie Pisano and Big Albert Anastasia and his Murder, Inc. killers were Brooklyn boys. And Carlo Gambino didn't resemble them in the slightest. Still, as one federal agent observed, "you don't get to be a Mafia don by being Mr. Nice Guy."

Throughout his ordeal, while he was searched and

manacled and questioned before gawking strangers, the smile never left his face.

Don Carlo, a basically solemn man, has smiled so many times at so many people for so many reasons that smiling has become as automatic as breathing. His smile can warm the heart or chill the blood, depending on the occasion. Or it may mean nothing at all.

The unsmiling FBI agents took him to their Manhattan headquarters and charged him with supervising a fantastic scheme to steal up to $30 million cash from an armored truck and the fortress-like headquarters of the United States Trucking Corp., which is almost as impregnable as Fort Knox.

If these robberies had been pulled off, they would have been the biggest, boldest heists in the annals of American crime. And even though they never got past the blue-print stage, the conspiracy charges filed against Gambino were the most serious official accusations of his half-century crime career.

At his arraignment in Federal Court, details of the alleged plot were presented by Daniel P. Hollman, a special Justice Department attorney in charge of the Joint Strike Force on Organized Crime in the Southern District of New York.

According to Hollman, a group of minor Mafiosi wanted to try robbing armored trucks but none of them had any experience in this specialized line of work, so they brought in an expert, John J. (Red) Kelley of Boston. He is considered one of the country's top bank and armored truck robbers.

Kelley spent a few weeks casing the various armored

truck firms and finally decided that the U.S. Trucking rigs met his specifications. He observed that one truck left the company garage in downtown Manhattan twice a week to deliver bundles of crisp new bills to Chase Manhattan Bank branches in outlying sections of the city and in suburban Long Island. On these runs, the truck usually carried $3 million to $5 million.

Kelley figured he could take the truck without too much trouble. The big problem, as he saw it, was how to dispose of the new currency without arousing suspicion. The plotters decided to consult Gambino, Hollman said.

He added that Gambino agreed to provide "among other things, autos for the robbery and the means to dispose of the money—at 60 cents on the dollar." Used cash for new. Gambino then took charge of the project, Hollman said, and ordered Kelley to make a thorough survey of the U.S. Trucking security setup.

Kelley did and concluded it would be possible to invade the firm's headquarters, which often had up to $25 million on hand when the Federal Reserve Bank sent huge amounts of cash for distribution to hundreds of banks throughout the city and suburbs.

Before the plot could be put into action, Kelley was arrested in Massachusetts for the $542,000 robbery of a Brinks armored truck in Boston.

Questioned about his frequent trips to New York, he confessed to the U.S. Trucking plot and implicated Gambino, Hollman said. The prosecutor added that Kelley "has been found to be of extreme reliability in connection with federal offenses committed in New York and Massachusetts."

When he heard this testimonial, Gambino appeared

amused. His smile broadened to a wide grin. U.S. Commissioner Earl Bishopp then set bail at $75,000 and Don Carlo's grin faded.

"I won't pay it," he said. "I'll stay in jail. I'm innocent from this accusation. I won't put up five cents for bail."

His lawyer Edward Ennis protested: "You're not well enough to go to jail."

"I stay in jail," the old man insisted.

His oldest son, Thomas, appeared at this point. He embraced his father and kissed him on the lips. They were permitted to leave the court room for a conference. When they returned 30 minutes later, Don Carlo said he had changed his mind and would post bail.

"That's a good idea," Bishopp said. "A man should be free if he can make bail."

Don Carlo nodded, smiled his inscrutable smile, made a courtly bow to the commissioner and strode from the court. A federal grand jury later indicted him for conspiracy to rob an armored truck. But the case was never brought to trial. It's a safe bet it never will be.

Detectives and underworld sources familiar with Gambino's *modus operandi* find it hard to believe he would have discussed mob business with Kelley, an outsider. Such matters are handled by the underboss or a captain. The orders come down from the top but the men who carry them out have no direct link to the boss. In this way, the boss is insulated from just such informers as Red Kelley.

Gambino heads the largest, strongest, and richest Mafia family ever put together. It has more than 1,200 members—more than any three of the city's other crime families combined. The associates work with and for the mob but do not necessarily belong to the Mafia. At least 800 Gambino men are believed to be sworn-in Mafiosi.

The family operates in all of the city's five boroughs and suburban counties. It has branches in New England, New Jersey, Pennsylvania, Louisiana, and Florida.

Besides running his own family, Don Carlo has direct or indirect control over the other four New York City crime clans. The acting heads of these families all owe their jobs to Gambino. He is the godfather of the city's youngest Mafia boss and an old friend of all the others. He also controls the Commission, the Mafia's national policy-making body and high court.

The Mafia family structure is like that of an army. At the top is the *capo* (chief or leader); as the head of the family, he is also called "the godfather." Immediately beneath him in rank are the *sottocapo* (sub-chief or underboss), the administrator who oversees the day-by-day operations of family affairs, and the consigliere (counselor) who advises the boss and is responsible to no one else.

Next in line are the captains or *capiregime* (literally chiefs of regimes of heads of governments), each of whom is in charge of a separate division or mini-mob commonly called a *borgata*. The word originally meant a slum neighborhood.

As the slums of Sicily are ruled by the Mafia, *borgata* became the slang expression for "mob territory" or any unit run by a *capiregime* or other Mafia chief.

Under the *capiregime* are the lieutenants or *capidecina* (chief of 10), each of whom commands a squad of 10 *soldati* (soldiers), also known as "button men," a term deriving from the brass buttons of Italian *carabinieri*, who, like the Mafiosi, were called "men of respect."

"They treat the soldiers lousy," the late Joe Valachi, Mafioso-turned-informer, told the Senate crime committee. "In the old days (the bosses) were all fighting each other and they needed us. In those days everyone wanted you to be a soldier in his family. We were important.

"In the old days, we had to prove ourselves (commit murders). Today, if any of these guys (new members) had to do something, he'd drop dead."

Like soldiers everywhere, the Mafia troops are expendable. But they are the highest paid soldiers in the world. Although there are no set pay scales, some of them have become millionaires without risking in rank. They are expected to obey orders and die if necessary for their commanders. Except for his personal guard and headquarters staff, the family *capo* has even less contact with his *soldati* than a U.S. Army general does with the GIs under his command.

So even if Red Kelley and his Mafia buddies planned to pull the Great Armored Car Robbery, and even if Don Carlo approved the imaginative plot, it seems most unlikely that Gambino would have conferred with the men who were to do the dirty work.

In any event, the arrest and indictment did not appear to worry him. He was still active in 1970, despite a series of heart attacks, and he continued to conduct business as usual.

He drove his wife on weekly shopping trips around Brooklyn. These were the only occasions he was seen behind the wheel of a car. During his other travels around the city and suburbs, he rode in a car driven by one of his relatives or retainers. He never used the same car two days in a row, changing them the way some wealthy men change suits. Some of the cars were owned by his brothers and cousins; others were rented by family members or associates; others were registered in the name of a Gambino-controlled company or a union, such as the International Longshoremen's Association.

Carlo never lacked transportation. In those days, he would drive to Little Italy in Manhattan at least two or three times a week, out to a wholesale meat plant in Queens or a paper trucking firm in the garment district. He would stop for coffee and cake at Ferrara's or lunch at Angelo's or have a hair trim in an East Village barber shop on Second Ave.

As soon as his Lincoln or Caddy entered Little Italy— any Little Italy in the five boroughs—his presence was immediately known. Housewives leaning from their tenement windows or gossiping on the sidewalk, old men sunning themselves outside crumbling buildings, young men lounging on the corners, children playing in the grimy streets—they all knew and the word went out: "The Old Man is here." "Papa's here." "The Godfather's here."

He held court in the cafes and restaurants, always choosing a table in the middle of the room. Never the front or the rear. And the people came in a steady stream. Old men, older than Carlo, with black suits and white mustaches; round-bellied businessmen seeking his approval of a deal; tough young Sicilians in the uniform of truck drivers or the hard hats of construction workers. Nearly all men, though sometimes a nervous, frightened woman.

They would first approach the bodyguards, respectfully asking permission for a moment or two with the don, and then, permission granted, moving to his table, bowing, apologizing for the intrusion, or embracing him and kissing him on both cheeks if they knew him long and well.

A man said his wife needed an operation and he didn't have enough money. Another man wanted a job for his son. A merchant wanted to get his son into an Ivy League college even though his grades weren't good enough. A landlord complained of hippies who had moved into one of his flats but refused to pay rent. A tenant complained that his landlord cut off his heat and hot water in an effort to make him move.

He listened politely to each appeal and grievance, seldom interrupting, smiling his perpetual smile and nodding his white head. When each petitioner was finished talking, the don would usually turn to one of his aides and say, "Take care of this," or "See what can be done."

In those days, Gambino was the most accessible Mafia boss in the country, always willing to grant a request if it was within his power to do so.

"He has good relations with people in all the Italian communities," said a lifelong observer of Manhattan's Little Italy scene. "He always grants favors if he can, so favors are always owed him in return. He can call on thousands of people who owe him favors, in all walks of life and occupations. Not just mobsters.

"He does more for legitimate people than he does for the bad guys. The legitimate person may never be asked to pay back the favor. The bad guy always pays, with interest, for what is done on his behalf.

"Sometimes you're better off if he gets you a job with the Parks Department than if he sets you up as a bookie. The less you want, the less you owe."

When Gambino arrived at a favorite restaurant in Brooklyn one day, he was surprised to find a picket line out front. The owner told him he was being harassed by union goons who were trying to organize his non-union workers.

"Don't worry," Don Carlo said. "They won't be here tomorrow."

The pickets were promptly withdrawn and never returned. Gambino has the power to make picket lines appear and disappear as if by magic. A Manhattan restaurant owner, involved in a similar labor hassle, consulted him and was told he could have peace for a price. The restauranteur replied that he was considering closing his business.

Gambino urged him to think it over.

"Where would this city be," the don said, "if every businessman threw in the towel because of a little unpleasantness?"

Recalling this incident recently, the restaurant owner said Gambino didn't act like a hoodlum. "He was very sympathetic, like Dr. Marcus Welby on TV."

On another occasion, Gambino heard that the gambling was getting out of hand at a church festival in Brooklyn. Besides the charity games being played in the churchyard, some neighborhood gamblers were running their own dice and card games in the nearby streets, jeopardizing the whole celebration. The festival sponsors feared police would shut down the games, including those run by the church for charitable purposes.

A word from Don Carlo and the street sharpies vanished.

When his Mafia peers want to talk to him, they make an appointment through one of his aides and are granted a private audience. Most such meetings have been held in the backrooms of small Italian restaurants and coffee shops, neighborhood places that strangers seldom visit.

A new jersey mob boss, Simone Rizzo DeCavalcante, came to Don Carlo with an unusual problem. The son of one of his members had a fight with a black laborer at a construction site in Elizabeth, N.J. The Mafioso's son lost, suffering broken ribs and a collapsed lung. His father demanded "satisfaction."

In other words, he wanted DeCavalcante to avenge his son by ordering gang members to murder the black man. There were several discussions about how this should be done. One of DeCavalcante's lieutenants said the black man should be shot; another suggested stabbing him "to make it look like a nigger job."

Then DeCavalcante learned that the intended victim was a Black Muslim. If the mob retaliated against him, the Muslims might declare war on the Mafia. Unable to decide what to do, he consulted Gambino.

Gambino carefully explained the Mafia rules. He said the Cosa Nostra member whose son was injured had a right to request satisfaction. "But the *capo* does not have to grant the request if there is a danger that doing so might destroy the *borgata*."

Gambino recommended that any final decision be held up for two or three months. DeCavalcante followed this advice and, during the cooling-off period, the matter was forgotten. Not all the problems laid in Gambino's lap have had such peaceful solutions.

Except for his arrest by the FBI, a humiliating episode which he felt should have been conducted more discreetly, the spring of 1970 was a comparatively quiet time for the supreme *capo*. He was seen strolling along Mulberry St. in Manhattan's Little Italy on numerous occasions, pausing to greet an old friend, shake hands with a well-wisher, pat a baby's cheek. He would shop in neighborhood stores, buying cheese, fruit, sausages and other specialties. All these items were available to him free from his own businesses, but he preferred to buy them from neighborhood merchants.

He walked the streets of Little Italy without a bodyguard, as he had always done, but as soon as he was through shopping, a large car would appear with two or three stone-faced men in it. He would come out of a bakery or cheese store and the car would be there at the curb. Two men would hop out and take his brown paper shopping bag and hold the car door and assist him as he climbed into the back seat.

He walked through Little Italy the way the President walks through small towns in election years, mingling with the crowds, pumping hands and smiling, showing how pleased he was to be out there among his people, but always with the Secret Service men and the big black limousine standing by.

On Mulberry St., Don Carlo is bigger than any President. He is bigger even than Marlon Brando was when he visited the neighborhood, his cheeks stuffed like a squirrel, playing the Godfather. No Hollywood Godfather could ever rate the deference displayed by Little Italy for Godfather Gambino.

He is known to many people for his good works and to many others for his bad works, and between them these activities have made him a multimillionaire. Don Carlo does not flaunt his wealth, but he could raise $10 million cash on a few hours' notice.

He has always lived a simple, though comfortable life. Money has not been as important to him as power.

Early in 1970, investigators learned from informers and electronic surveillance that Gambino had reached the top of the Mafia pyramid. On March 14, nine days before he was arrested, Gambino was described by the chief of the New York City Police Department's Intelligence Division as "the most powerful of all the family bosses in the country."

The *New York Times* reported on March 15 that Don Carlo had been appointed commander-in-chief of the underworld armies. Charles Grutzner, the newspaper's veteran Mafia-watcher, reported: "The long vacant post of 'boss of all bosses' has been reactivated because of trouble and uncertainty of command in several families caused by recent jailings of local leaders, murderous rivalries, and territorial disputes."

In the weeks before and after Gambino's arrest, he received a steady stream of expensively-suited, chauffeur-driven visitors representing all the city's Mafia families and other clans from Boston to Los Angeles. To avoid another Apalachin-type disaster, no single large assemblage was held. Instead, the delegates came singly or in pairs like foreign ambassadors paying their governments' respects to a newly-crowned king.

Gambino's underboss, Aniello (Mr. O'Neill) Dellacroce, also held a series of small but high-level meetings with other Mafia executives in his Little Italy headquarters, the Ravenite Social Club.

When the weather grew warm, Gambino and his wife made their annual move from the "old house" on Ocean

Parkway to the "summer house" at 34 Club Drive, Massapequa, Long Island.

This waterfront mansion is actually a year-round residence, fully insulated against the worst ocean gales. Gambino had planned to make it his permanent residence but his wife didn't want to leave their old Coney Island neighborhood, where she knew nearly everyone. So they compromised.

They would spend the summer at their Long Island "splanch," an architectural mixture of ranch and split-level designs, and the rest of the year at the $50,000 Brooklyn residence.

The white brick Massapequa mansion, on an inlet of South Oyster Bay, is similar to several other houses in this affluent suburban community of weekend sailors and yachtsman. But there are a few differences. The most notable is its complete lack of shade trees.

The only tree that could possibly provide cover for an unwanted visitor is a blue spruce at the edge of the front lawn, a few feet from an electric power pole. The street lamp shines directly on the front of the house, the lawn and the spruce, which is not allowed to grow tall enough to obstruct the view from the upper windows. At the curb in front of the light pole is a Nassau County Police Department sign warning passersby: NO STOPPING.

The front of the house and attached two-car garage, driveway, and front lawn are unprotected except for a white brick wall about two feet high bordering the lawn from the drive to the property line. The side and back-yards are enclosed by eight-foot-high walls starting at the front sides of the house and garage.

Anyone entering or leaving the block can be seen from the house, which was valued at $50,000 when it was built around 1960, and is now worth more than $100,000. In the large backyard are a brick barbeque grill, a tiled patio, flower gardens and vegetable patches where the don raised tomatoes, peppers and beans. He also made his own wine until a few years ago.

Gambino did the cooking at most of his summer barbecues. Steak and lobster usually were the main courses, with plates of blood-red tomatoes, black olives, succulent Long Island clams, red peppers, anchovies, artichoke hearts, sliced sausages, and cheese. He enjoyed taking his guests out for short spins or fishing trips on his sleek white cabin cruiser.

One of his most frequent visitors was his next-door neighbor, Ettore (Tony Russo) Zappi, a mattress manufacturer and Gambino *caporegime*. An old-time gangster, Zappi has been with Gambino for years and supervised the construction of his "summer house." Zappi's long police record includes arrests for assault, robbery, gun possession, and Prohibition violations.

In testimony before a U.S. Senate committee, a New York Police official said, "Zappi is in shylocking and labor racketeering. He is a neighbor and close associate of Carlo. They handle the unions of the Castro Convertible Co. He (Zappi) has influence in those unions."

He was an official of a catch-all union with one of the most imposing titles in the American labor movement: Local 854 of the Television, Radio, Instrument, Business Machine, and Furniture Manufacturing Drivers, Helpers, Warehousemen, and Employes Union of the International Brotherhood of Teamsters.

Zappi used his position in this independent union to organize workers in the Convertible Mattress Co. He later took over the firm. He has other legitimate businesses in New York and Florida. Zappi's business career is mentioned here because it is typical of Gambino executives to juggle legitimate and illegitimate interests in such a skillful fashion that it is often almost impossible to tell them apart.

Carlo Gambino runs the most diversified rackets empire in history. It is a genuine conglomerate, dealing in everything from pizza pies and real estate to narcotics, Wall St. stock swindles, and contract murder. Despite its huge size and tremendously intricate operations, it is basically a family business in which several of the top executives are related by blood and marriage.

For example, Gambino's two brothers, Paul and Joe, and two cousins are listed on FBI charts as captains in his organization and several cousins, nephews and other relatives are among the *soldati*.

"The thing that's different about this group, that makes it different from any other Mafia group in America, is the intermarriage tradition—the incest—that they have," said a law-enforcement official who has traced the Gambino genealogy back through five generations.

Gambino's mother was a Castellano and her family was more affluent than the Gambino clan into which she married. When Carlo Gambino sneaked into the U.S. and joined his Castellano relatives, the clan matriarch was a Castellano aunt who lived into her 90s and served as the family matchmaker. She saw the potential in young Carlo and persuaded him to marry his first cousin, Katheryn Castellano, sister of Paul and Peter Castellano.

"She used to arrange the marriages of cousins with cousins," the official said. "She felt the Gambinos and the Castellanos had the power, or would have it some day, and they should keep it within the family. And they set up this program among themselves for the marriages of first cousins."

It was not unlike the Ptolemaic dynasty of ancient Egypt, in which kings married their sisters and other close relatives. The most famous ruler of this line, Queen Cleopatra, married two of her brothers. As the bloodline grew thin, producing more and more insane and feeble-minded heirs, the dynasty declined.

All of Don Carlo's offspring were normal, but one close relative married a first cousin and two of their children were mentally retarded. One of them eventually was sent to Sicily and married off to another first cousin.

When he was U.S. Attorney General, the late Robert Kennedy spent hours studying the Gambino family tree and its intertwined branches. A devout Catholic, he was shocked by the incestuous marriages. Partly because of his interest in the matter, the FBI contacted officials of the New York Archdiocese and the Brooklyn Diocese of the Roman Catholic Church and told them what was happening. The church agreed not to approve any more of these strange marriages.

The laws of the Catholic Church, several other churches and some states forbid marriages between first, second, or third cousins.

One of the major social events of the closely-knit Gambino family was the annual Fourth of July get-together at Carlo's Long Island retreat. The Independence Day party in 1970 was particularly festive because the guests were celebrating not only the end of British rule over America but the beginning of a new monarchy with the coronation of Carlo I as underworld emperor.

Carlo's friends, relatives, and Mafia peers enjoyed water sports, music, a fireworks display, and a gargantuan barbecue. And none of them had the slightest premonition that the Fourth of July entertainment was Carlo's last big blast.

CHAPTER 1

A SHIP-JUMPER
WITH CONNECTIONS

TO GROW UP IN PALERMO is to grow up with the
Mafia. Its presence is felt everywhere in the ancient Sicilian capital. This has been true for centuries and, despite
countless investigations and purges and mass deportations
of Mafiosi, it remains so today.

When Carlo Gambino was a boy in Palermo, the Mafia
reached its zenith of power. Mafia dons ruled the mountainous, poverty-plagued island and ran the cities, towns,
villages, and farms like feudal fiefs, exacting tribute from
landowners, peasants, merchants, politicians, nobility, even
priests. No one could escape the squeeze.

Carlo was born Aug. 24, 1900 (official reports list different birth dates, but this one appears on some of the
earliest U.S. Government records on Gambino) in a section of Palermo so completely controlled by the Mafia that

police did not go there without special permission. He grew up in the fountainhead of the Honored Society and to him it was just that—not an organization of criminals but a benevolent and protective order of patriots and patriarchs. It was only natural that he should aspire to become a Mafia executive, just as a boy growing up in a blue-collar section of Detroit might dream of becoming president of General Motors.

The stories he heard as a child were not fairy tales but blood-soaked legends of revenge and honor and the Mafia freedom fighters who drove foreign conquerors out of Sicily, returning the island to its own people for the first time in thousands of years. The tale he liked best was the legend of the Sicilian Vespers.

On Easter Monday, in the year 1282, the story goes, a young couple went to a Palermo church to be married. The girl waited outside while her lover entered the church to look for the priest. A drunken French soldier came along, ogled the nubile lass and dragged her into the churchyard where he ravished and killed her.

Her body was found as the church bells tolled the evening vespers. Word of the outrage quickly spread through Palermo and the surrounding countryside. Thousands of furious Sicilians rose up against the French forces occupying the island, killing every Frenchmen they could catch.

"*Morte alla Francia Italia anela!*" the rebels shouted. "Death to the French is Italy's cry."

Nearly all the French troops on the island were massacred and the initials of the rebel slogan—MAFIA—became the name of a guerilla army formed to fight the heavily-armed French soldiers sent to avenge the slaughter.

The Sicilian Vespers uprising actually occurred. But whether the Mafia was formed at this time, which would make it nearly 700 years old, no one knows for sure. Another theory is that it began with the feudal practice of hiring brigands to protect the estate of the landed gentry from the wrath of their starving serfs. Eventually, these strong-arm thugs formed a sort of trade union and began shaking down both rich and poor.

The situation in Sicily during the first 20 years of the 20th century was described in a 1931 report by the Procurator-General of Palermo, who was appointed by Dictator Benito Mussolini with explicit orders to stamp out the Mafia:

"The Mafia dominated and controlled the whole social life; it had leaders and followers; it issued orders and decrees; it was to be found equally in big cities and in small centers, in factories and in rural districts; it regulated agricultural and urban rents, forced itself into every kind of business, and got its way by means of threats and intimidation or of penalties imposed by its leaders and put into execution by its officers. Its orders had the force of laws and its protection was a legal protection, more effective and secure than that which the State offers to its citizens, so that owners of property and businessmen insured their goods and their persons by submitting to pay the price of the insurance."

Carlo Gambino's boyhood idol was the uncrowned king of Sicily, Don Vito Cascio Ferro. An intelligent though uneducated and completely unscrupulous man, he had emigrated to America as a youth and was one of the original Black Hand terrorists who extorted hard-earned money from thousands of Italian immigrants. Returning to Sicily around the turn of the century to beat a murder rap in the U.S., he became head of the Sicilian Mafia.

He also became the toast of Sicilian society. Though he could scarcely read or write and had been accused of some 20 murders and at least 50 other major crimes, he dined with aristocrats, bankers and judges. No important social function was complete without his presence. Authors, artists, and actors sought his patronage.

To Carlo and other Palermo children, he was a Sicilian Santa Claus who rode through the city's poor neighborhoods in a gilded carriage every All Soul's Eve, distributing little cakes and candies. He also distributed favors to adults of all classes.

But there was a trick in every treat—a price that was never mentioned but eventually would have to be paid. Carlo Gambino remembered all he heard and read about Don Vito and based his own crime career, consciously or not, on the life of the Mafia monarch.

When Carlo was eight, an event occurred that made a lasting impression on him and proved to the outside world that the Sicilian secret society was all-powerful on its home turf.

A portly, middle-aged man in a dark suit and black derby arrived in Palermo from Rome on February 28, 1909. He spoke perfect Italian, which was his native tongue, but his clothes and luggage marked him as an American. He checked into the Hotel de France, signing the register, "Guglielmo DeSimoni," and spent the next two days in his room, recovering from an attack of influenza.

He was confident no one had recognized him as the famous Detective Lt. Joseph Petrosino of the New York

City Police Department. But he was wrong. As soon as he sailed from New York in late January, a telegram was sent to Don Vito. Petrosino's arrival in Palermo was expected, observed, and reported.

Petrosino had been waging a one-man war on the Mafia's New York colony. As a direct result of his crime crackdown, scores of Mafiosi had been sent to prison and hundreds had been booted back to Italy. His work had received international acclaim. He had been praised by American Presidents and consulted by the chiefs of every major law-enforcement agency in the U.S. and Italy. The Italian government had presented him with a gold watch, his proudest possession.

He consulted the vest-pocket watch on the evening of March 12, 1909, as he left a restaurant near the Piazza Marina in downtown Palermo. The time was a few minutes before nine o'clock. Petrosino started back to his hotel.

As he strolled through the square in front of the Garibaldi statue, two well-dressed men came up behind him. One of them drew a large, expensive Belgian-made revolver and shot him in the head and back, killing him instantly. Petrosino's own gun, a Smith & Wesson Police Special, was still in his suitcase.

The murder made headlines throughout the world, triggered new probes of the Mafia, and supplied the citizens of Palermo with another chapter of Mafia folklore. Though there was loud indignation in New York, Rome and other places, few Sicilians shed any tears for Petrosino. He was, after all, a foreigner, even though he was born in Salerno, near Naples.

He had come to Palermo to look into the ties between

the Sicilian secret society and the New York underworld. So far as Palermo was concerned, this was none of his business.

Officially, the cold-blooded killing was never solved. But almost everyone in Palermo, including young Carlo Gambino, knew the American detective was gunned down by Don Vito himself. Ferro, in fact, openly claimed credit for Petrosino's death and boasted that he drove to and from the murder scene in the private carriage of a member of Parliament who served as his alibi, swearing Don Vito was at his home during the shooting.

Carlo and some of his schoolmates made a special trip to the Piazza Marina to see the spot where Mafia history was made. In their eyes, Don Vito had become more of a hero than ever.

Three years later, when Sicily adopted universal suffrage, the Mafia grew even stronger. Peasants about to cast their first ballots were bribed, cajoled, and coerced into voting for Mafia-backed candidates. For the Mafia dons, ballots worked better than bullets.

Exactly when Carlo Gambino joined the Mafia is not known to any outsiders. Investigators who have checked his background as thoroughly as possible believe he took the blood oath before he left Sicily in 1921.

Several members-turned-informers have described the traditional initiation ceremony—the Mafia is the only crime organization that swears in its members—and it must have been the same for Gambino. A long table surrounded by grim-faced men in their Sunday suits. On the table, a flickering candle, a paper effigy of a saint (perhaps St. Jude), a dagger and sometimes a loaded revolver.

The initiate's Mafia "godfather" or sponsor takes the

dagger and pricks the young man's right index finger, which is then held over the paper statue until the saint is drenched with blood. Then the paper is set afire. The initiate holds the burning image in his hands and swears everlasting loyalty to the Mafia.

"This is the way I will burn if I betray the brotherhood."

As one born in the very womb of the Mafia, Carlo Gambino took the oath with the utmost seriousness. He had been selected as a prospective Mafioso while in his mid-teens. It was noted that he was respectful of his elders, a good son, a diligent worker at the odd jobs he obtained after school. A youth whose quiet strength of character indicated that he was a natural leader. There was some doubt as to whether he was bloodthirsty enough for the society's killer corps, but it was expected that he would faithfully obey all orders, no matter how dark the deed.

It was the practice then for Mafia dons to recruit promising young men in much the same way that American industries now recruit bright college students. Only the brotherhood oath is much more binding than any mere employment contract. The Mafia recruit signs up for life.

Carlo picked a good time to leave Palermo. Jobs were scarce in the years following the first World War. The dons who owned Sicily made millions, but their young followers got only a few scraps. There were many more openings for ambitious Mafiosi in America than on their home island. The society had established branches in New York, New Orleans, Chicago and several other U.S. cities and there were opportunities galore for the reckless and ruthless.

Furthermore, Mussolini and his black-shirted Fascisti were on the march in Italy. Soon after he seized power in

1922, Il Duce sent an army of policemen and soldiers to Sicily to stamp out the Mafia. Thousands of Sicilians fled to the United States, jumping ship in American ports and pouring across the borders from Canada and Mexico.

Gambino beat the rush by boarding a freighter that docked at Norfolk, Va., on Dec. 23, 1921. He was the only passenger and his presence on the cargo-laden ship was not reported to American authorities. The captain had been well paid to keep quiet and the crew suspected the stranger in their midst was someone they should not discuss.

A short, chunky man, 5 feet 7 and about 160 pounds, with brown eyes, bushy black hair brushed straight back from his forehead and a nose like an eagle's beak, Carlo was not particularly handsome but he seemed sincere. Men felt he could be trusted, although this impression was often misleading. Beneath a warm, friendly personality, with considerable charm, lay a dark pit of guile.

When he left the SS *Vincenzo Floria* on the night of December 23, he wore a black, wide-brimmed fedora, stiletto-toed shoes, and a brand new suit from the best men's store in Palermo. He carried his father's heavy, old-fashioned watch in his vest pocket.

Fog shrouded the waterfront as he came down the gangplank and a chill winter wind off the ocean set his teeth chattering. At the foot of the gangplank, he paused and looked up and down the deserted street. Through the fog, he could see the red and green lights of Christmas decorations in the windows of dockside cafés.

A car's headlights flashed on and off about 50 yards from the freighter. Carlo walked to the car and peered inside, recognizing the swarthy face of a relative he had not seen in years. The two men embraced and kissed each other on the cheeks. Then they drove away.

Shortly thereafter, Gambino arrived in New York and moved into a flat on Navy Street in Brooklyn, in the heart of a brawling, boozing neighborhood frequented by sailors, prostitutes and Italian and Jewish gangsters. Residents were so accustomed to body-littered pavements that they seldom bothered to determine whether the prone persons were drunk or dead.

Unlike most other ship-jumpers, Gambino did not have to worry about where to obtain food, lodgings, and employment. He already had important connections in America and his future success was guaranteed so long as he was willing to work hard and do what he was told. He had not one but two families to look after him—his own and the Mafia.

Several blood relatives were living in the New York metropolitan area and New England, including members of the Castellano and Masotto clans. His first cousins, Peter and Paul Castellano, gave him a job in their small trucking firm. Another first cousin, Thomas Masotto, whose mother and Gambino's mother were sisters, became one of his closest companions. Down through the years, his cousins assisted Gambino in nearly all his enterprises, legitimate and otherwise. And he made them all wealthy.

He also took care of his brothers, Paolo (Paul), born in 1904, and Giuseppe (Joseph), born in 1908. He sent for them as soon as he could afford their passage and they became fronts for Carlo's various businesses.

And he had the help of his *paisans*, men from his hometown who had known him or his family in Palermo. Chief among these was his childhood friend, Gaetano Lucchese, also known as Thomas Lucchese, Tommy Brown, and by a nickname he loathed, Three -Finger Brown. When they met in New York, Tommy didn't mention his recently-acquired handle, and Gambino didn't hear of it until he read it in the newspapers some years later.

Lucchese, eight months older than Carlo, moved from Palermo to New York with his parents in 1911. The family settled in East Harlem, then a solidly Italian section. At 16, Tommy became a plumber's helper. He later went on to work as an apprentice machinist. He quit his job in 1919 after losing his right index finger in a machine shop accident. The mishap convinced him there must be an easier way to make a buck. Prohibition provided the route he was looking for.

Soon after the Volstead Act shut down the saloons in 1920, thousands of speakeasies opened and racketeers rushed to cash in on the public's unquenchable thirst for illegal alcohol. Lucchese joined an East Harlem bootleg gang that was one of the many underworld enterprises masterminded by a fellow Sicilian, Salvatore (Little Caesar) Maranzano.

In 1921, a few months before Gambino arrived in America, Lucchese was caught in a stolen car he had driven to a bootleggers rendezvous in eastern Long Island. He was arrested for auto theft.

The cop who took his fingerprints in the police station at Riverhead, L.I. was a fan of baseball star Mordecai (Three-Finger) Brown, the Chicago Cubs pitcher. When he noticed Lucchese's missing digit, the playful policeman wrote down "Three-Finger Brown" on the finger-print card, under "aliases." The nickname stuck to Tommy for the rest of his life, although none of his associates ever called him that to his face.

Lucchese was out on bail when Gambino landed and he tried to find a spot for his pal in the Maranzano organization. But before these arrangements could be completed, the auto theft case came to trial. Tommy was convicted and sentenced to 3-to-10 years in prison. He spent the next three years behind bars.

While he was away, Gambino joined the Brooklyn branch of the city's largest gang, headed by Giuseppe (Joe the Boss) Masseria. Top gun of this citywide mob was Salvatore Carlo Lucania of Lercara Friddi, Sicily. He was known to police and most of his associates as Charlie Luciano.

Charlie was a big dealer in bootleg booze and narcotics. One night, a rival gang kidnaped him, took him to Staten Island and tortured him in an effort to find out where he had stashed a shipment of heroin. They beat his sallow face to a bloody pulp, slashed him with knives, burned the soles of his feet with cigarettes. But Charlie remained mute, so they left him for dead, hanging by his fingers from a tree limb on a country road. Charlie survived and from then on was known as Lucky Luciano.

His boss, Giuseppe Masseria also was a lucky man. Around noon on August 9, 1922, he was ambushed as he left his home at 80 Second Ave. on Manhattan's Lower East Side. One gunman ran onto his front steps to prevent him from returning to the house. Another chased him into a millinery shop next door.

The pursuing thug fired six shots at him while Joe the Boss ducked, dodged, and danced around the store in an amazing display of twinkle-toed dexterity. When his pistol was empty, the torpedo fled in a getaway car driven by his companion. As the car roared around the corner onto Fifth St., it was blocked by a crowd of workers who had just left a meeting of the International Ladies Garment Workers Union.

The workers tried to stop the car and the gangsters opened fire, shooting five union members—one fatally—and bowling over two more with the auto.

Joe the Boss was tired but unhurt. He immediately surmised that the assassins were sent by a rival bootlegger named Umberto Valenti. So he invited Valenti to a peace conference held in a spaghetti house on East 12th St. They embraced, broke bread together, sipped some wine and agreed to settle their differences amicably. And when they left the restaurant, two Masseria mobsters emptied their guns into Valenti's back. He staggered to a taxi, opened the door, and dropped dead.

In those days, the majority of Americans have never heard of the Mafia. But the public had become aware that some sort of Sicilian secret society existed and that it was not like the Elks or Masons. Traditionally, at home and abroad, the Mafia has tried to pretend there was no such organization. It has attempted to divert investigators by giving different names to Mafia branches, or even publicizing alleged crime groups that are pure fantasies.

Take the so-called Black Hand Society, for example. At the turn of the century, the Black Hand menace pervaded every Little Italy in America. Shopkeepers, restaurant-owners, and other victims would receive an extortion note signed with a crude drawing of a black hand, usually clutching a knife.

If a victim refused to pay for "protection," he could expect to be beaten by goons, or his business would be bombed, or his wife and children would be threatened.

Lt. Petrosino's lengthy investigation of the Black Hand proved there had never been any such "society." The Black Hand terrorists consisted of several small, unaffiliated gangs and individuals, acting independently of each other. The group most of them belonged to was not the Black Hand, but the Mafia.

The furor that followed Petrosino's murder persuaded the extortionists to give up their particularly nasty racket. And as they went into other illegal enterprises the name Black Hand disappeared from the headlines, being gradually replaced by such impressive titles as the Italian Society, Union Siciliano and, in recent years, Cosa Nostra (Our Thing). But no matter what the crime conglomerate is called, its origins can be traced directly to the Sicilian Mafia and its current directors are all Mafiosi.

As the Procurator-General of Palermo observed in his 1931 report: "It not infrequently occurred that in the same commune there were two Mafias, either deliberately created, spontaneously generated, or born of some dispute over the booty, contending for supremacy. The result of this was a bitter struggle involving the deaths of leaders and more influential members of the executive and their respective families."

He was talking about what happened in Sicily, but it also happened in New York, Chicago, and elsewhere during the roaring 20s. And Carlo Gambino was near the center of the action when the New York gangs went to war. His boss was Lucky Luciano and he worked alongside such up-and-coming hoods as a Vito Genovese, Francesco "Frank Costello" Saveria, and Ciro Terranova, the Artichoke King.

Carlo was assigned to the Masseria gang's bootlegging business. He learned every phase of the operation from distillery to distribution, from smuggling ship to speakeasy. He worked in the moonshine stills and on the trucks. He learned where the rum fleet anchored, how to dodge the Coast Guard and hijackers, the best spots to grab a rival mob's shipments, and how to persuade speakeasy owners to buy Masseria potables.

Gambino's brand of persuasion was something new to the New York underworld. Soft-spoken, polite, and friendly, he greeted potential customers with a smile instead of a growl. He preferred to use a handshake instead of a gun or a blackjack. His unique approach to underworld enterprise aroused considerable suspicion at first, but eventually won him many friends on both sides of the law.

"He doesn't look or act like a gangster," people often observed on meeting him for the first time. But he thought like one, although he was far shrewder and more subtle than most of his peers.

In 1930, the young mob executive found his career temporarily threatened by open warfare between the Masseria and Maranzano armies. He decided to stick with Joe the Boss, but only so long as Joe looked like the probable winner.

Maranzano and several of his henchmen, including the future gang boss Joseph (Joe Bananas) Bonanno, came from the Sicilian town of Castellammare Del Golfo. For some unexplained reason, Masseria hated all Castellammarese gangsters in general and Maranzano in particular. Maranzano, in turn, was determined to succeed Joe the Boss as crime king of New York. Their feud exploded into an extermination contest that was called the Castellammarese War.

"All the Castellammarese were sentenced to death (by Masseria)," gangster Joe Valachi explained to the Senate Investigation Subcommittee years later. Valachi had good reason to remember the bloodbath, for he married the daughter of its first victim, Tom Reina, a gang boss who was backing Maranzano.

At 8:10 p.m. on February 26, 1930, Reina and a female friend, Marie Annise, left her Bronx apartment and were greeted by a Masseria emissary who fired both barrels of a sawed-off shotgun into Reina's body, almost blowing him in half.

The Maranzano forces struck back six months later by fatally shooting Masseria mobster Peter Morello in his East Harlem headquarters and also killing a visitor to the office, Giuseppe Piranio.

Meanwhile, Masseria installed one of his lieutenants, Joseph Pinzola, as head of the Reina outfit. An old Black Hand terrorist, Pinzola was described by Valachi as "a greasy-looking guy" who wore a handlebar mustache and "threw a lot of bombs" in his day. He also ran a food firm called California Dried Fruit Importers. The Reina regulars resented his appointment as their chief and they informed Maranzano of their discontent.

Pinzola's body was found at 9 p.m., September 9, 1930, on the floor of his 10th-floor office in the Brokaw Building, 1487 Broadway in Times Square. He had been shot in the heart and neck. Pinzola had leased the premises from Carlo Gambino's buddy, Tom (Three-Finger Brown) Lucchese.

On September 11, Lucchese was charged with Pinzola's murder. He was arraigned in court and held without bail, but a grand jury later refused to indict him due to insufficient evidence.

While Three-Finger Brown was awaiting the disposition of the homicide charge, Gambino was arrested for the first time. He was picked up in Lowell, Mass., on November 13, 1930, as a suspicious person. But his Old World manners convinced the judge that he wasn't really a no-good. The case was dismissed.

Gambino was a frequent visitor to the Commonwealth of Massachusetts in those days. He may have gone there on gangland business, to visit relatives, or simply to avoid the flying bullets of the Castellammarese War.

The war was still on when he returned to New York, but he kept out of it and eventually received an unexpected invitation to switch sides. It came from Little Caesar himself, and Gambino accepted without even bothering to send a note of resignation to Joe the Boss. It was not the most loyal thing to do, but it was the wisest.

More than 60 gangsters, mostly Masseria troops, were killed in the first year of the conflict. Though the Castellammarese were outnumbered and outgunned at first, Maranzano received financial aid and firepower from several other mob leaders. The entire Reina gang joined him and it's underboss, Tom Gagliano, contributed $140,000 to the war chest. Stefano Magaddino, Mafia chief of the Buffalo-Niagara Falls area, sent soldiers and $5,000 a week.

Chicago mobster Joe Aiello also sent $5,000 weekly until Al Capone had him killed.

Maranzano's Army commanders included Three-Finger Brown, Joe Bananas, Joseph (Joe Adonis) Doto, Albert Anastasia, and Joe Profaci, all future gang chiefs. The Masseria troops were led by Lucky Luciano and Vito Genovese, whom Carlo Gambino would one day succeed as "boss of all bosses."

As more and more Masseria supporters wound up in the East River or on slabs in the morgue, Maranzano sent a brief message to Luciano: "Get rid of Masseria or we'll wipe out the whole mob." A secret meeting followed at which plans for Joe's exit were made.

Masseria was then living in a heavily-guarded, ornately-furnished penthouse on Central Park West, overlooking Central Park. Luciano picked him up there on April 15, 1931, and drove him to Coney Island for lunch at Scarpato's restaurant. They lingered over there hearty meals and espresso cups until all the other diners had left. Then Lucky suggested a game of cards.

The house provided a deck and they played and chatted until 3:30, at which time Lucky excused himself and went to the men's room. Seconds after he left the table, four gunmen charged into the restaurant and blazed away at Joe the Boss, shooting him six times in the back and head. And when Lucky emerged from the john, he was the new head of the Masseria family.

The Italian Society, which Masseria founded, died with him And the Unione Siciliano was born, a brain-child of Lucky Luciano. Masseria's executioners were never identified officially, but Valachi claimed they were Vito Genovese,

Ciro Terranova, Joseph (Joe Stretch) Stracci and another Masseria mobster called Cheech.

Masseria was buried in a $15,000 coffin and Maranzano called the biggest crime convention ever held in New York City. More than 500 high-ranking hoodlums from all over the nation gathered in a Bronx meeting hall decorated with religious pictures. A large, gold-colored crucifix hung over the platform where Maranzano was seated. A dignified man, who looked more like a banker or diplomat than a gangster, he addressed his audience in a deep voice charged with evangelistic fervor.

"Whatever happened in the past is over," he said. "There is to be no more hatred among us. Those who lost someone in the war must forgive and forget. Even if your own brother was killed, don't try to find out who did it or take revenge. Those who do will pay with their lives."

Then he proclaimed himself "boss of bosses." He also announced a new deal for the New York gangs, a reorganization that would divide the city and suburbs among five Mafia families.

His plan didn't consider the Irish and Jewish gangs and other ethnic groups that were not about to give up their territories without a fight. Maranzano was concerned only with the Italian outfits and old-fashioned Mustache Petes who ran them.

Under the new setup, Maranzano retained his palace guard of Castellammarese gunman and supervised the activities of all five crime families, taking a percentage of their earnings from every project. Two of his henchmen, Joe Bananas and Joe Profaci, were placed in charge of their own Brooklyn gangs. Luciano ran the old Masseria outfit and Tom Gagliano commanded the old Reina crew. A fifth gang was headed by brothers Vince and Phil Mangano.

The Maranzano blueprint worked so well in New York that it was adopted by other crime groups around the country. The same basic structure exists today.

CHAPTER 2

PURGE OF THE MUSTACHE PETES

EARLY IN 1931, ABOUT THREE months before Joe the Boss was dethroned, Maranzano decided to get rid of a bothersome bootlegger, Joseph (Joe Baker) Catania, who had been hijacking his alcohol trucks.

Maranzano gave the death contract to a lieutenant, Nick Capuzzi, and Capuzzi assigned soldiers Joe Valachi and Steve Rinelli to take care of the matter. Baker, a nephew of the infamous Ciro Terranova, lived in the Bronx but could usually be found at his headquarters in Brooklyn.

Valachi told the Senate Investigations Subcommittee, 32 years later, how he bungled his first contract and thereby helped Carlo Gambino get a new job.

"So now one day, Steve Rinelli and I were riding through Flatbush Ave. in the (Brooklyn) neighborhood where Joe the Baker hung out, near the office, and on the way over Steve spots another man, and he tells me to swing around," Valachi recalled.

"I said, 'Who is that?' and he said, 'He is a big boss.' So I swung the car around and I went up and pulled up to the other car, which was, I think, a Lincoln. Let us say it was a Lincoln. So when I pulled up to him and I put him right alongside the other car, Steve Rinelli fired one shot at him and I saw this man go with the shot.

"I didn't know him at the time but I later found out his name was Paolo (Paul) Gambino. Half his ear was shot off.

"So I tried to tell Steve, but he got panicky after the first shot, and he started yelling, 'Step on it! Step on it!' So I pulled away, and as I pulled away I felt I was pulling something. My rear bumper got stuck with his (Paul Gambino's) front bumper, so I was pulling and pulling, and about half a block I broke loose."

Valachi then drove Rinelli back to the Bronx, let him out on Southern Boulevard, and proceeded to a house where Maranzano was staying in suburban Yonkers, just north of the New York City line.

"Maranzano was waiting for me in front of the door and he said to me as soon as I came—he seemed to know already what happened—and he said to me, 'Did he (Rinelli) tell you who this guy was?' and I said, 'He told me he was a big boss,' and he started cursing. He said the guy is not even a member (of the Mafia).

"Well," I said, 'Look, I don't want to work with him then, as long as you feel that he (Paul Gambino) wasn't to be touched, don't worry about it because I don't think that he got hit.'

"With that, as I am talking, the phone rang."

Maranzano took the call, then told Valachi that Paul Gambino was not seriously wounded. "He got off the car and he walked away."

"This thing turned out for the better," Valachi told the Senate crime probers. "Carlo Gambino is Paul Gambino's brother, and Carlo Gambino was a member, and Maranzano explained that that brought this new group in with us, and that is why it turned out for the best."

A bit confused by his explanation, Sen. John McClellan, the committee chairman, inquired: "As a result of the shooting, Gambino came in with you folks?"

"Yes sir," Valachi replied.

As for Joe Baker, the Maranzano gang learned that he stopped at a bail bondsman's office in the Bronx every weekday morning to pick up a bag of money which he took to a bank. He left the office at 11:43 p.m. on February 3, 1931, accompanied by his attractive wife. He kissed her goodbye in front of the office and started to walk towards his car. As his wife watched in helpless horror, three gunman appeared, pumped six shots into Joe Baker's head and body, then roared off in a car driven by Joe Valachi.

Baker died a few hours later in Fordham Hospital and was given the most fabulous funeral ever seen in the Bronx. At least 20,000 lined the streets to watch the cortege go by. Nearly 100 gleaming black limousines, 40 of them filled with floral tributes, followed the hearse bearing his $15,000 bronze casket.

By this time, Carlo Gambino had accepted Maranzano's apology for the mistaken-identity shooting of his younger brother. He had also accepted the offer of a lucrative post in the Maranzano crime combine.

Carlo realized that the tide of battle was running against Joe the Boss. Masseria had lost so many men through sudden death and defection that he no longer held a numeric supremacy over his foes. So Carlo switched to the winning team and, as things turned out, he made his move just in time to share the spoils of victory.

Carlo's association with the new "boss of bosses" lasted less than eight months but he learned a lot from Little Caesar. The first American Mafia chief with a college education, Maranzano had studied for the priesthood and spoke six or seven languages.

He was an authority on Julius Caesar and the Roman Empire. His home library contained more than 200 books about Caesar and busts of his idol decorated his house and office. Maranzano claimed to have built his crime empire on Caesar's plan for world conquest. He thought of his gun-slinging goons as the modern equivalent of Caesar's legions.

The non-Italian gangs were the barbarian hordes, too undisciplined to take seriously. Maranzano curtly rejected Luciano's suggestion that the Mafia mobs form a working alliance with their Irish and Jewish counterparts. He didn't even trust Neapolitans.

When Maranzano took over the New York families, Mussolini's purge of the Sicilian Mafia was in full swing. So Maranzano offered sanctuary to all Mafiosi who had to leave Sicily in a hurry and could afford to pay for his relocation services.

Little Caesar became the biggest alien-smuggler in American history. He imported an estimated 8,000 Italians to the U.S., sneaking them in without immigration or customs formalities and collecting millions of dollars in fees. Many of them went to work for his mob and the businesses he controlled. Maranzano knew more about the U.S. immigration laws than the men who wrote them. The bookshelves lining his office walls contained just about everything ever written on these laws—and their loopholes.

Carlo Gambino, an illegal alien himself, studied the smuggling operation carefully. The knowledge he acquired would come in handy in future years when he ran his own Italian-importing business and used all the legal loopholes in an effort to escape deportation.

In the summer of 1931, friction developed between Maranzano and a few of his junior executives. They complained he was taking too large a share of the profits they earned and that he had given the juiciest rackets to the conservative old Mustache Petes. Maranzano promised to consider their grievances.

Then he prepared a death list containing the name of a dozen mob leaders he believed were plotting against him. The list was headed by Lucky Luciano and his underboss, Vito Genovese. To ensure secrecy, Maranzano handed the Luciano-Genovese contract to a hired killer from outside the Mafia—Vincent (Mad Dog) Coll. It was decided that Maranzano would summon Lucky and Vito to his office and Coll would ambush them as they left.

The meeting was scheduled for the afternoon of September 11, 1931, in Maranzano's legitimate business front, a real estate firm called Eagle Building Corp. The firm occupied a suite of offices on the ninth floor of the Grand Central Building, on Park Ave. behind Grand Central Terminal.

But Lucky and Vito failed to keep the appointment.

Instead, four husky strangers barged in, flashed what appeared to be police badges and announced that the premises were being raided. Fearful of just such a happening, Maranzano had instructed his minions not to wear guns at his headquarters. So none of the seven Maranzano mobsters in the outer office were armed when the "detectives" arrived.

The seven hoods and a secretary were lined up against a wall of the waiting room. While one of the raiders kept a revolver trained on them, his three companions invaded Maranzano's inner sanctum and emptied their pistols at him as he sat behind his enormous desk. Then, to make sure he was dead, one of the assassins leaned over Little Caesar's twitching corpse and calmly slit his throat.

On their way out of the building, the execution squad met Mad Dog Coll coming in. They waved to him, indicating he should get out fast, and he took their advice. Investigators later learned that the quartet consisted of three Jewish gunmen, loaned to Lucky Luciano for the occasion by his good friends Bugsy Siegel and Meyer Lansky, and an Italian who went along to identify Maranzano in case he was not in his office.

The Maranzano murder was a signal for a coast-to-coast massacre of Mustache Petes. During the next 48 hours at least 40 more mob chiefs were killed, nearly all of them Mafia dons who shared Maranzano's dream of an Unholy Sicilian Empire.

Luciano, who planned the purge, emerged as the new crime czar. But instead of appointing himself "boss of bosses," he formed a national crime syndicate whose directors represented all the major mobs—Italian, Irish, Jewish, etc. And he established a 12-member Commission, all of whose members belonged to the Mafia, as the Supreme Court of the underworld. The family structure was retained, and he added the new position of *consigliere*, clan counselor.

Among other things, the Maranzano rubout caused a federal roundup of illegal aliens. More than 1,000 Italians, many with criminal records, were deported. But Carlo Gambino remained secure in Brooklyn, undisturbed by the immigration authorities or the staccato stutter of gangland artillery.

He pledged allegiance to Lucky Luciano and joined a South Brooklyn gang bossed by Phillip and Vincent Mangano. The brains and brawns of this outfit were supplied respectively by underboss Joe Adonis and Albert Anastasia. Gambino was made a *caporegime*, in charge of his own *borgata*, or Cosa Nostra cell.

A less likely combination than Adonis, Anastasia, and Gambino would be impossible to imagine.

The flamboyant, luxury-loving Adonis wore hand-tailored suits and diamond jewelry. He hung out in the most expensive clubs and slept with Broadway showgirls. His dinning and drinking buddies included police officials, judges, and politicians. He had made a fortune in the bootlegging, narcotics, and gambling rackets and he seemed determined to spend it all.

Anastasia, a scowling, sadistic gorilla took to maiming, mayhem, and murder the way some men take to golf. He enjoyed killing with his bare hands, though he usually used a gun. His trademark was a single bullet in the skull, which is why he was called the Mad Hatter. He ran all the rackets on the Brooklyn waterfront, engaged in dope smuggling and eventually was immortalized by the press as the "lord high executioner of Murder, Inc." a title he justly deserved.

His first wife vanished without a trace and he remarried shortly thereafter, leading the underworld to conclude that he was a self-made widower.

Adonis and Anastasia were living models for a generation of gangster films. The shadowy Gambino had almost nothing in common with them but their mutual greed and Mafia membership. Yet they got along well. So well, in fact, that Anastasia trusted Gambino to the very end, never guessing the quiet, courtly Carlo would double-cross him after they worked together for 26 years.

An underworld joke concerned a meeting at which Adonis, Anastasia, and Gambino confronted each other, reached inside their coats and whipped out snapshots. Adonis displayed some nude photos of a sexsational chorus queen. Anastasia showed a newspaper picture of a bloody corpse, his latest victim. And Gambino exhibited pictures of his children.

One of the major gangland social events of 1932 was the wedding of Mildred Reina, daughter of slain gang boss Tom Reina, and Joe Valachi. It took place September 18 in a chapel crowded with mob luminaries and their wives.

After the ceremony, the newlyweds were toasted at a party in the Palm Gardens, a Manhattan hall on 52nd St. near Broadway. The guests consumed thousands of sandwiches, hundreds of beautifully-decorated pastries and—though it was still Prohibition—uncounted gallons of "straight off the boat" whiskey and wine, plus 25 barrels of the best available beer.

Mafia chiefs lined up to kiss the bride, congratulate the groom, and present white envelopes stuffed with cash. Lucky Luciano couldn't make it, but he sent an envelope anyway.

Several bosses and underbosses were there. The Mangano family was represented by boss Vince Mangano, underboss Albert Anastasia, and *caporegime* Carlo Gambino. The honeymooners collected more than $6,000 that day.

Carlo's own wedding to cousin Kathryn had been a much quieter affair, attended by a score of relatives and a few close friends such as Tom Lucchese. After the honeymoon, Carlo and Kathryn moved into a new two-family house on Ocean Parkway, not far from the match-making aunt, and there they raised four children—a daughter, Phyllis, who married a prominent New York City physician, Dr. Thomas Sinatra; and three sons, Thomas, Joseph, and Carl. The oldest son, Thomas, was named for his godfather, Tom Lucchese, and he married Lucchese's Vassar-educated daughter, Frances.

Gambino's sons went to work for the family businesses, but did not join the Mafia family and never were in trouble with the law.

For a Mafia don, Carlo's criminal record is unusually mild. He has been arrested about a dozen times, mostly for violations of federal liquor and immigration laws, and has two bootlegging convictions. His New York Police Department file is No. 8-128760; his FBI file is No. 334450.

There are voluminous dossiers on him in the files of the Immigration and Naturalization Service, the Internal Revenue Service, the Federal Bureau of Narcotics and Dangerous Drugs, the Waterfront Commission of New York Harbor, the New York State Investigation Commission, the U.S. Senate Investigations Subcommittee, the Joint Task Force on Organized Crime and other law-enforcement agencies.

Two years after his first arrest, he returned to

Massachusetts and was arrested at Brockton on December 8, 1932, for swindling a local citizen out of $1,000 in what was described as a "handkerchief and pill game." Released on bail, he left town. The Brockton charge was dropped when he paid back the money two years later, following his arrest in New York as a fugitive from Massachusetts.

Vito Genovese, underboss to Lucky Luciano, also became a fugitive around this time. Sought for his gangland bumpoff of a Brooklyn thug named Ferdinand (The Shadow) Boccia, the ferocious Genovese vanished from his New York haunts late in 1934, taking $750,000 in gangland funds with him. He surfaced in Italy, where he became a pal of Dictator Mussolini, and remained there until after World War II. As Vito came from Naples and contributed generously to the Fascist cause, Mussolini overlooked the fact that he was a high-ranking Mafioso.

His boss, Lucky Luciano, was sent to prison in 1936 for running a prostitution ring. He remained behind bars until his mysterious release and deportation in 1946 under circumstances never credibly explained. With Luciano and Genovese both removed from the underworld scene, Frank Costello took over Lucky's mob and ran it for a prosperous and comparatively peaceful decade.

While Lucky's arrest and trial were making headlines, Carlo Gambino was quietly acquiring a chain of whiskey stills that eventually stretched from Brooklyn to the Catskill Mountains and from eastern Long Island to New Jersey, Pennsylvania, and Maryland.

When Prohibition ended, most bootleg barons began scurrying around for new sources of revenue. Many of them got into gambling and narcotics, which were to become the Mafia's biggest and most profitable rackets. But Gambino believed the alcohol business wasn't dried up yet, even though liquor was legal.

He figured there was still a large market for low-priced, high-proof hooch. So he bought more distillery equipment, trucks and vast quantities of alcohol, all at bargain prices from fellow racketeers who were winding up their joy juice ventures.

Within a few years he had virtually cornered the moonshine market in the Northeastern United States. "Carlo used to tie up the alcohol," Joe Valachi recalled years later. "Every still that operated, he would buy off of, see, and stack it up in the warehouse and then make his own price.

"For instance, say he bought at fifteen dollars a tin—a tin consists of five gallons. By the time he gets through with it and ties it up, he controls the market. He can sell it for fifty dollars a tin when he is ready to release it."

He bought out every still within 100 miles of New York City and when their alcohol stocks were depleted he gained control of several legitimate business firms that used alcohol commercially, such as a Brooklyn varnish firm from which Gambino and his partners diverted tank carloads of pure alcohol.

The methods used by the bootleggers to "clean" the commercial alcohol and make it fit for drinking purposes were so crude that many of their customers were poisoned. It is almost certain that some fatalities resulted, but no alky deaths were directly attributed to the Gambino gang.

In 1937, a federal grand jury in Brooklyn indicted Gambino and 41 other moonshiners on charges of conspiracy to defraud the U.S. Government out of more than

$300,000 in liquor taxes. Assistant U.S. Attorney James Saver said the gang had obtained about 114,000 gallons of denatured alcohol from commercial firms. The alcohol was stored in various warehouses throughout the city, then distributed in small lots to stills scattered over Brooklyn, Staten Island, Long Island, upstate New York, and New Jersey. Raids on these stills disclosed that the alcohol "had been treated so inefficiently as to be poisonous," Saver said.

The trial was held in Federal Court at Philadelphia and Gambino was convicted of tax-dodging. On May 20, 1939, he received the most severe shock of his criminal career—a $2,500 fine and a sentence of 22 months in Lewisburg Federal Prison.

Eight months later his conviction and the original indictment were thrown out because of a Supreme Court ruling that evidence obtained by wiretaps could not be used in a trial. The Government admitted its case against the Gambino gang was based on electronic eavesdropping. So Carlo and his merry men went free.

Three weeks after the indictment was dismissed, a Federal Grand Jury in Brooklyn returned a new indictment charging Gambino and nine others with operating illegal stills that allegedly beat Uncle Sam out of $3 million in taxes. The Government later sued Carlo and Paul Gambino and four other men for $1,365,000 in unpaid alky taxes.

Revenue agents and prosecutors tried valiantly to send Carlo away for a long sojourn in the slammer, but their long and costly efforts were wasted. On his second bootlegging conviction, Gambino only got 30 days in jail.

He was never locked up again for longer than overnight. In a crime career that has spanned half a century, he has been virtually untouched, or at least unbruised, by the law. The New York City Police Department has had him under surveillance off and on for years. He has been hauled in for questioning about numerous murders and other atrocities. But the New York cops and the city's five district attorneys have never charged him with anything more serious than consorting with known criminals, a misdemeanor about as serious as mopery or jay-walking. In fact, New York justice often tends to treat jay-walkers more harshly than Mafia dons.

John F. Shanley, a former top NYPD official who knew as much about Gambino as any cop alive, gave the Senate Investigations Subcommittee a brief summary of Gambino's underworld activities:

"Carlo Gambino is considered to be the boss. He is suspected of being active in narcotics. He is in gambling, shylocking, labor racketeering, vending machines, criminally receiving (of stolen property) and alcohol tax violations. He has been arrested 16 times and he has six convictions (not true).

"He is related to Tom Lucchese through marriage. He entered the country sometime around 1921 as a stowaway at Norfolk, Va. He was suspected of being involved in smuggling aliens."

But neither Shanley nor any other New York police official has ever explained why the entire 30,000-member force was never able to catch Carlo Gambino committing a single felonious act.

Federal agents made a bit more headway than the city cops. On December 26, 1940, after spending a joyous Christmas in the bosom of his family and perhaps celebrating the 19th anniversary of his entry to the U.S., Gambino was finally picked up as an illegal alien.

He could afford the best legal help, so it was a simple matter to stall deportation proceedings for a year. And by then the United States was engaged in World War II, so it was impossible to ship Carlo back to Sicily even if an order for such action was issued, which it was not.

The case of Carlo Gambino, illegal alien, was stuck in the files of the Immigration and Naturalization Service, where it moldered for more than a dozen years before being dug out, dusted off, and gingerly reactivated.

CHAPTER 3

A LEAK IN SAM THE
PLUMBER'S PIPELINE

WORLD WAR II WAS THE best thing that ever happened to Carlo Gambino. It not only prevented his deportation but also made him a millionaire.

The wartime rationing of gasoline, meat, and groceries opened a nationwide black market that the American public patronized as eagerly as it had once bought bootleg booze. And Carlo Gambino, who had cornered the post-prohibition moonshine market, was right there to give the people what they wanted: ration stamps.

These stamps were, or course, much easier to handle than tank carloads of alcohol. They could be obtained and disposed of with none of the effort that went into the manufacture and distribution of illegal whiskey. And, from the consumer's standpoint, it was far safer to use black market stamps than to drink the product of Gambino's stills.

Carlo went into the stamp-collecting business with his brother Paul and New Jersey mobster Settimo (Big Sam) Accardi. At first, they sent teams of safecrackers to steal ration stamps from the vaults of the Office of Price Administration. Then they purchased the stamps directly from dishonest OPA officials, thereby reducing the risk involved to practically zero. They acquired many millions of stamps, selling them to underworld distributors but being careful not to sell too many to any one customer. In this way they made sure that the market would not be flooded with stamps which would have made the price drop.

"When the ration stamps became a money-making proposition, he (Carlo) was one of the wealthiest," Joe Valachi, the Cosa Nostra canary, told the U.S. Senate hearing on organized crime. "Sam himself told me they made over a million dollars on one deal alone."

"I made about $150,000 myself.

"They were genuine stamps, not counterfeits. They came out of the OPA. In the beginning, they (the Gambino group) were robbing safes, the burglars. Then the OPA members themselves were sneaking them (stamps) out and selling them as individuals."

Valachi was asked if Gambino had engaged in other businesses.

"Gambino had been in every kind of business," Valachi answered. "Butcher business. Italian lottery (a gambling racket like policy). Shylocking (loaning money at usurious rates of interest, usually 20 percent a week)."

"Has he been in any legitimate business?"

"Legitimate business," Valachi replied, "I don't know much about."

But Carlo Gambino does. He has been, as Valachi observed, in every kind of business—legal, illegal, and in-between. Anything and everything to make a buck.

With the money he made in alcohol and ration stamps, plus the proceeds of many worse rackets, he invested in meat markets (wholesale and retail), fat rendering firms, supermarkets, imported provisions (olives, olive oil, cheese, etc.), bakeries, restaurants, nightclubs, laundries, a linen-supply service, paper products.

Also insurance and real estate companies, a labor relations firm, construction, fuel oil distribution, dress factories. He gradually built up large chains of fruit and vegetable markets and pizza parlors. And his truck lines haul everything from A (air freight) to Z (zucchini squash). Plus mountains of G, for garbage.

There's a lot of green in garbage. As recently as 1965, New Jersey racketeer Simone DeCavalcante told an associate that Gambino controlled private garbage disposal in "all the boroughs" of New York City. Since then, investigators have uncovered Gambino garbage contracts in suburban Westchester County, Long Island, and New Jersey. And several gangsters who played against Carlo in the garbage game have wound up on the rubbish heap.

Gambino's name almost never appears as the owner or partner of a business (a notable exception to this rule SGS, will be discussed shortly). Many of his enterprises are officially owned or controlled by his brothers or first cousins, the Castellano brothers or Tom Masotto. Others appear to be owned by men who have no criminal records and no apparent ties to the Gambino crime family.

Carlo usually holds onto those businesses which are

steady moneymakers. The shaky ones are squeezed as dry as possible, then dumped into bankruptcy with a load of uncollectable bills. How Gambino acquires and bleeds a legitimate firm is illustrated by the case of the Murray Meat Packing Co.

When the owners got into financial difficulties, they borrowed money from a loan shark. They were unable to meet the payments, so a deal was worked out whereby they acquired a new partner, a relative of Gambino. He milked the firm of $175,000, forcing it into bankruptcy.

For 10 years, Gambino was a partner in SGS Associates, Inc., a labor relations firm that attracted many large business and industrial companies as clients. The other partners were Henry H. Saltzstein, a convicted burglar and bookie, and George Schiller, a Russian-born mystery man.

The name "Carlo Gambino" appeared in gold letters on the office door, between the names of Saltzstein and Schiller and under the legend "SGS ASSOCAITES PUBLIC AND LABOR RELATIONS."

Though the firm's small tenth-floor office at 141 E. 44th St. did not look very impressive, a list of its clients certainly was. They included Wellington Associates, the real estate giant that owned the Chrysler Building and other Manhattan skyscrapers; builder William Levitt; Flower and Fifth Ave. Hospital; Bond Clothes; Howard Clothes; and the Concord Hotel, a popular resort at Kismesha Lake, N.Y.

From these and other clients, SGS made an estimated $500,000 a year. Levitt, who prefers to use non-union labor on his building projects, reportedly paid $7,000 a month.

Flower and Fifth Ave. Hospital hired SGS during a strike of non-medical employees. The strike was promptly settled. Several clients agreed that a contract with SGS was a virtual guarantee of labor peace. Union officials claimed that SGS sent pistol-packing goons to break up a strike of service and maintenance workers at the Chrysler Building.

The labor relations firm finally folded in 1965 in the heat of investigations by the FBI, two Federal Grand Juries and other federal, state, and local agencies. It was the last time Gambino's name ever appeared on an office door.

But Carlo still works both sides of the labor market, pocketing commissions from employers and union representatives, putting the squeeze on contractors, dipping into the dues and pension funds of the unions he controls.

No labor union, no industry, no business is too large or too small to escape Gambino's attention. Over the years, his men have held key positions in such giant labor organizations as the Teamsters Union, the International Longshoreman's Association, and the unions involved in the city's billion-dollar construction industry.

He gets a piece of all the rackets at John F. Kennedy International Airport, where air freight worth millions of dollars is handled by a mob-run union, and on the New York and New Jersey waterfronts.

He even managed to cut in on the city's cutlery-grinding business, at a cost to honest grinders of nearly $650,000.

Paul Gambino, who had no experience in this field but plenty of expertise at muscling into legitimate businesses, set up a grinding service to compete with the reputable 30-year-old New York Grinders Association. Within three years, association members lost an estimated 2,000 customers and $475,000 worth of business.

One of the first customers to change grinders was Price

Meat Supermarkets, in which Peter Castellano, Carlo's cousin and brother-in-law, reportedly had a substantial interest. Then the large supermarket chains—several of which bought meat and other items from Gambino-controlled firms—fell in line.

Sam Maturi, president of the Grinders Association, and his brother Frank told investigators they lost the Trunz chain because Trunz does a big business in pork supplies, which are largely controlled by Gambino fronts.

Robert Trunz, executive vice-president of Trunz Meat Co., denied this but admitted one of his meat stores went out because its prices were consistently undercut by the Blue Star meat chain, reportedly owned by Paul Gambino.

Officers of the Grinders Association said Paul finally offered to remove his nose from their grindstone for $300,000. They turned him down and he finally accepted $175,000 to quit the business. He also turned over his grinding equipment to the association, but Sam Maturi said it was "garbage and junk" which had to be sold at auction for $4,000.

Not that there's anything wrong with garbage and junk. The Gambino clan has made millions from these commodities. Their trucks collect garbage from commercial customers all over the New York Metropolitan area and their junkyards have been used for all sorts of sinister purposes, from the refurbishing of hot cars to the disposal of corpses.

Vincent James (Jimmy Jerome) Squillante knew all the dark secrets of the garbage and auto dumps. And despite this knowledge or perhaps because of it, he wound up in one of them.

A peanut hood, only 5 feet 2 and 130 pounds, he rose from smalltime stickup man and dope-pusher to the hierarchy of the Gambino crime combine. He became a Gambino *caporegime*, specializing in the carting and labor extortion rackets.

He was a sharp dresser and he wore large horn-rimmed glasses that made him look like an undernourished owl. Notwithstanding his diminutive size and somewhat scholarly appearance, he was greatly feared by the businessmen whom he persuaded to sign garbage-hauling and labor contracts. He never let anyone forget that his Mafia godfather was the homicidal Albert Anastasia.

The Federal Narcotics Bureau called him "a major source of supply for narcotics dealers." The NYPD said he was a big man in all kinds of junk. Newspapers proclaimed him "garbage czar of Long Island" and reported that he had tied up a major part of the garbage-hauling industry in the metropolitan areas for Carlo Gambino.

Squillante vanished from his baronial Bronx home in September 1960. His family did not report him missing, but detectives and federal agents heard persistent reports that he had been murdered and his corpse dispatched to a garbage disposal plant or an auto junkyard. One theory held that he was placed in the trunk of a stolen car that was smashed into a metal cube by a huge hydraulic press known in the trade as a "crusher."

The late Robert F. Kennedy, then U.S. Attorney General, told Senate crime probers: "Squillante was taken up to Connecticut, tortured, chopped up into little pieces and burned, according to our information. That's why they never found him."

Investigators never determined why he was killed or who gave the order. According to Joe Valachi, Squillante was "a pervert who abused other Cosa Nostra members' wives," which would have been as good a motive as any.

Another big man in garbage, although not nearly as big as Jimmy Jerome, was ex-convict Joseph (Joey Surprise) Feola. Barred from the carting business in New York City because of his prison record, he started a trash-haul business in suburban Westchester, one of the nation's most affluent counties.

Feola vanished in 1957 when the Senate crime committee sought to question him. As soon as the committee wound up its New York hearings, he reappeared at his Yonkers home. Nine years later, a Federal Grand Jury tried to find Feola for questioning about the multi-million-dollar Westchester carting industry and its ties to New York mobdom. But Feola was missing.

FBI agents believe they know what happened to him. They believe he went the way of so many others who have displeased kindly old Don Carlo.

The unwitting source of this theory was Carlo's old pal, Simone Rizzo (Sam the Plumber) DeCavalcante, head of a large plumbing and heating company and Mafia boss of New Jersey. The FBI had installed an electronic listening device in DeCavalcante's private office in the one-story, cinder-block building at Kenilworth, N.J., that housed his Control Heating Corp., and other firms owned by Sam and his partner.

From 1961 through 1965, G-men listened to and recorded every conversation that took place in Sam's office. Early in 1965, Sam told his lieutenants that he and Gambino were planning to acquire a garbage-dumping site near Sayreville, N.J. Sam said he had discussed the matter with Gambino at a meeting in New York. He added that Carlo took "an active personal interest" in the venture, which eventually should bring in a gross profit of about $500 a day.

Gambino sent two of his men, Nicola (Nick Nelson) Mellilo and James (Jimmy Brown) Failla, to Sam's office on February 26, 1965. They conferred with Sam, his underboss, Frank Majuri, and one of his captains, Louis Larasso, on the garbage dump deal.

"They opposed enlarging the partnership beyond DeCavalcante and Gambino," says an FBI report on the conference. "All were agreed that there is considerable money to be made here and spoke of a volume of one-hundred and two-hundred loads a day."

DeCavalcante, Gambino, and their lieutenants held several more meetings on the same subject. On one occasion, Larasso went to New York to confer with Nick Mellilo. When he returned to Kenilworth, Larasso told Sam he was worried about the possibility of other mobsters getting in on the garbage deal.

An FBI report on this conversation states:

"LARASSO said NICK told him that JOE BANTY (Gambino's underboss), JOE ZINGARO (another Gambino gangster), and JOE FEOLA would be included in the partnership with Gambino and DECAVALCANTE. LARASSO suggested that DECAVALCANTE check with GAMBINO to verify this, noting that it might be better for them (Sam's bunch) if CARL learned it from them than on his own. DECALVACANTE indicated that he would do so.

"LARASSO told DECAVALCANTE that he had

been repeatedly contacted by FEOLA concerning a garbage deal FEOLA wants to arrange between his brother (or brother-in-law) and LARASSO. FEOLA claimed to have made progress towards securing the Ford Motor Co. in Metuchen, N.J., as a lucrative garbage stop. LARASSO's part in the deal was to find a suitable dumping site.

"LARASSO said he had been stalling FEOLA pending instructions from DECAVALCANTE. DECAVALCANTE told LARASSO he would inform GAMBINO of FEOLA's proposition and in the meantime LARASSO should continue to stall FEOLA.

"DECAVALCANTE notes that he has heard that FEOLA is in trouble with GAMBINO, having been accused of stealing garbage stops from JOE COLOMBO.

At a meeting with Gambino in New York next day, Sam asked if Carlo knew his underboss and Joey Surprise were planning to cut themselves in on the garbage dump deal. Carlo said it was news to him.

He said he would speak to Banty about it. He also had a suggestion or two about what should be done with Feola, who was trying to make deals with Gambino and DeCavalcante capos behind their bosses' backs. Carlo also mentioned Feola's invasion of Colombo's trash territory— a matter which concerned him because Colombo was his protégé and had saved his life.

On the morning of April 19, 1965, Sam and Larasso had another discussion about the garbage deal and related matters. They spoke in low voices and the radio in Sam's office was on, so the FBI was unable to catch everything that was said. However the eavesdropping agents heard enough to convince them some skullduggery was afoot.

Larasso mentioned Joe Banty and "the *caporegime*." Sam mentioned $100,000. They talked about getting a rope, burlap and a Ford station wagon. Larasso said he was going to meet someone at 6 p.m. that day and that it would take "about half an hour for him to get there."

They decided that the person Larasso was to meet should be told to bring 75 percent of $10,000, or $8,100 cash. Sam said he would inform Gambino of this arrangement.

Around 10:30 a.m., Sam held another whispered conversation with his cousin and lieutenant, Robert (Bobby) Basile. They discussed a hunting lodge near Toms River, N.J., and "that place in Jersey City."

"This other place would be better," Sam said.

The listening agents assumed they were trying to find a safe hideout for a gang member who was on the lam.

At 5:20 p.m. that day, Bobby Basile returned to Sam's office and an even more mysterious conversation ensued. This is what was said:

BOB: "Frank and I will take Louis back to his car, okay"

SAM: "Yeah."

BOB: Then I'll come over there."

SAM: "Where?"

BOB: "Harriet's."

SAM: "Well, you have to take him home… All right, bring him there. Are you gonna put it in the garage?"

BOB: "Oh yeah, I'll get it in."

SAM: "Have you got enough room to work in?"

BOB: "If everything is ready, I don't even have to bring it all the way in."

SAM: "You haven't got it all the way in?"

BOB: "I won't pull it in now, Sam. After, I'll pull it in."

SAM: "You should have it in there."

BOB: "Doesn't it look funny if a car is in there?"

SAM: "Why?"

BOB: "This guy, hasn't he got any suspicion about anything?"

SAM: "No. Have the hood up, like you're putting oil or something in there. Understand? This way you know it fits in there and all."

BOB: "Oh, it fits in. Don't worry about it."

SAM: "Did your guys get back?"

BOB: "Not yet. Don't worry about it. If they come back, I'll work it out. Frank and I figured it already. I'll have him in the office and I'll just tell the boys… I've got a meeting going on. How long will it take you to get to Harriet's?"

SAM: I'll go down there after…"

BOB: "Okay. We'll drop Louis off and we'll come back. By the time I change the plates and everything…"

SAM: "Got the pliers and everything?"

BOB: "Frank is back there now."

SAM: "Does he know the way all right, that Lou?"

BOB: "Yeah."

SAM: "Now make sure, Bobby…"

BOB: "Yeah… I'll take the money and whatever else he brings. And I'll give Louis the clothes and shoes…"

SAM: "Bob, for God's sake don't get took. This is all gonna… You and Frank keep… Everybody's gonna watch each other. You can expect me. I'm gonna wait for the phone call. You can drive in ten minutes."

BOB: "We'll put the car outside, all right? We'll leave the keys in the ignition and he just has to take it away."

SAM: "Okay. That's a little bit fast. Tell Frank not to be a cowboy. Make sure… (whispers)"

BOB: "Don't want to use rope? You don't want to use rope?"

SAM: "(inaudible whisper)"

BOB: "He said he feels (or kills) better with his arm. He can handle it better with his arm."

SAM: "Well, you have a rope ready anyhow."

BOB: "That's right. He showed me. He near wrecked me."

SAM: "Make sure, Bob. Make sure they don't touch nothing out of…"

BOB: "Sam, don't hold me responsible."

SAM: "You make sure they don't take nothing!"

BOB: "But Sammy, this guy's supposed to have a lot of money on him. All right, let me go put that car in, all right?"

SAM: "All right. Have you got a New York license?"

BOB: (reply inaudible)

SAM: "Are your pistols registered over there?"

BOB: "Yeah, that's why I don't want to use them unless I really have to, because the SOB is registered."

SAM: "Okay. Everything now. Make sure everything is done when it is done. Pull that car right in now.

BOB: "That's what I'm going to do."

At this point, Bob departed. Sam waited nervously in his office. One or two unidentified men came in and Sam said, "Put the light out! Put the light out!"

Louis Larasso entered the office at 7:20 p.m. and informed **Sam:** "I was very careful. You know. In the bedroom. I got lights, but once in a while I put the hangar (phonetic) up there, right? So I'm conscious of putting the lights on, and I went right through it."

Sam replied: "Come on. Get over here. Let me play you some gin. Quarter a game."

Bob Basile returned around 9:25 p.m.

SAM: "Where'd they go?"

BOB: "They're outside."

(Sound of drawer being opened, paper rustling.)

BOB: "Hey, that's a nice one. Frankie's got the same thing… The lousy permit didn't come through (apparent reference to a gun)."

(Sound of drawer closing)

BOB: "All right, Sam, I'm gonna go then, huh?"

SAM: "Yeah."

BOB: "Take care of yourself, Sam."

After studying tape recordings of the conversations between Sam and his lieutenants and other evidence, FBI agents prepared the following report.

"An analysis of this material leads to the belief that DECAVALCANTE and his associates eliminated someone, although the victim's name is nowhere mentioned. It appears that GAMBINO was to be advised of whatever action was to be taken. In an effort to find an explanation common to GAMBINO and DECAVALCANTE, the following is submitted:

"On 3/9/65, NK 2461-C (code number identifying an FBI agent assigned to the DeCavalcante surveillance) reported that LARASSO was with DECAVALCANTE. He said he heard that CARL (GAMBINO), JOE BANTY (BIONDO), JOE ZINGARO, NICK (MELILLO) and JIMMY (FAILLA) were in partnership in the "Mount

Vernon thing" (garbage business). Included with them was one JOE FIOLO (phonetic). DECAVALCANTE said he was aware of this and planned to ask Carl if he knows BANTY, ZINGARO, and FIOLO are connected with the deal. LARASSO expressed some resentment, saying that if true, the GAMBINO participants far outnumbered those from DECAVALCANTE's family. He said they should be watchful that they are given their fair share of the deal.

"According to the source, LARASSO told DECAV-ALCANTE that JOE FIOLO has repeatedly telephoned him concerning a garbage deal. FIOLO has a brother or brother-in-law in the garbage business in New Jersey and wants LARASSO to enter a partnership with this person. FIOLO has been contacting the Ford Motor Company in Metuchen, New Jersey, and eventually expects to secure this stop for LARASSO and FIOLO's relative. FIOLO expects LARASSO to locate a suitable dumping site. LARASSO has been putting FIOLO off until he can consult with DECAVALCANTE. DECAVALCANTE told LARASSO he would see GAMBINO about FIOLO's proposition and in the meantime LARASSO should continue to stall FIOLO diplomatically.

"DECAVALCANTE said he has heard that FIOLO is in trouble with CARL GAMBINO since he has been accused of stealing garbage customers from JOE COLOMBO.

"The information above is set forth because it suggests that FIOLO may have angered GAMBINO sufficiently to cause the latter to authorize his elimination, and that DECAVALCANTE has accommodated him.

"New York (FBI office) is requested to identify JOE FIOLO (phonetic) if possible, and to evaluate him as the possible victim. In this regard it might be useful to recall LARASSO's remark concerning JOE BANTY and the Caporegime. This could indicate that JOE FIOLO is a member of a regime within the GAMBINO family, possibly that of JOE ZINGARO."

Subsequently, investigators identified "Joe Fiolo" as the aforementioned Joseph (Joey Surprise) Feola, a convicted cop-killer. He was sentenced to the electric chair in 1939 for the 1931 murder of Police Sgt. Timothy Murphy, but managed to escape the hot seat through a series of legal maneuvers. During his fourth trial for the Murphy murder, he pleaded guilty to manslaughter and received a prison term of from 7 ½ to 15 years.

Paroled in 1948, he entered the garbage game as a henchmen of Vincent Squillante. And when FBI agents called at Joey Surprise's suburban home on a fine spring day in 1965, they were not at all surprised to find that he was missing.

This time, the surprise was on Joey. He had gone to keep an appointment on the evening of April 19 and he had never returned. According to underworld rumors, he was compacted in one of his own garbage-compacting machines. His disappearance was not reported to police and did not become public knowledge until the Federal Grand Jury began looking for him nine months later.

The FBI picked up this medical footnote to the Feola file:

On the morning of April 20, the day after Feola vanished for the second and last time, Sam the Plumber complained of rectal hemorrhaging and visited a doctor. On his return to the office, he described his affliction to his associates and said it was caused by "too much excitement."

CHAPTER 4

THE BARBERSHOP QUINTET AND ITS APALACHIN AFTERMATH

CARLO GAMBINO'S FIRST TWO MOB bosses, Masseria and Maranzano, died within five months of each other in 1931. Twenty years later, he lost two more bosses almost simultaneously.

Phil Mangano was shot three times in the head and dumped in a swamp in the Bath Beach section of Brooklyn near Jamaica. He was found sprawled face down in the mud, almost hidden by the tall grass of the marshland, on the morning of April 19, 1951. Residents of the area recalled that the strangled body of a policemen's wife had been found in the same spot two years earlier.

Police tried to break the sad news to Phil's brother, Vincent, a power on the Brooklyn waterfront and in the Brooklyn Democratic Club. Failing to find Vince at home, the cops concluded he was in Florida, where he rented a Miami mansion for two or three months every year.

But when Vince failed to show up for Phil's funeral, the authorities concluded that there was a better than even chance that the brothers were together at that great crap game in the sky, or wherever deceased Mafiosi congregate.

Phil's passing was routine, a ho-hum thing completely lacking in imagination. But Vince's departure was arranged with such thoroughness that no trace of him was ever found. The feds searched for him in vain, even requesting Interpol to look in some of the more exotic corners of the world. And when a decade passed with no words of his whereabouts, he was formally declared dead. According to one unconfirmed report, he was shot on the same day Phil was killed, and buried in the wet cement of a Brooklyn housing project's foundation.

Some underworld observers suspected that the Mangano brothers were done in by their underboss, Albert (Mad Hatter) Anastasia, for he was the one to benefit most from the double hit.

Although Joe Adonis became the new head of the Mangano group, he was in deep trouble with the law. His long police record already included arrests for assault, kidnaping, robbery, smuggling and other crimes. And now the Government was trying hard to tuck him away in an iron cot for the rest of his life.

Anastasia knew Joe A. couldn't last long. And when Adonis left, Anastasia would be the boss. And Carlo Gambino would be second in command.

It was reported that Anastasia told Gambino he intended to get rid of the Mangano brothers, and Gambino agreed not to interfere. According to this story, the plot was approved by the current heads of the city's other crime families—Joe Bananas, Joe Profaci, Vito Genovese, and Gambino's old *paisan*, Tom Lucchese. But if this is true, it was one of the best-kept secrets in Cosa Nostra history.

Anastasia certainly had the means to murder his bosses. As chief executioner of the Murder, Inc. mob, he had dispatched killers all over the country. They had carried out their contracts with gun, knife, icepick, garrote, bludgeon, hatchet, poison and any other instrument that struck their fancy.

Murder, Inc. served as the enforcement arm of the national crime syndicate and employed such celebrated butchers as Pittsburgh Phil Strauss, Blue Jaw Magoon, Happy Maione, Dasher Abbandando, and Kid Twist Reles, who turned informer and was hurled to his death from the Brooklyn hotel where he was under police guard.

The killer corps was not part of the Mangano crime family, although the Mangano's sometimes used Murder, Inc. specialists and the two Mangano underbosses, Anastasia and Adonis, were top executives of the murder mob.

Adonis probably outranked Anastasia in this unique organization. The suave, fun-loving Joey A. could be considered the crime syndicate's vice-president for enforcement. Albert was the supervisor who gave the assassins their assignments.

With the abrupt departure of the Mangano's, Adonis succeeded Vincent on the Mafia's national Commission. He had close connections with mob leaders in Chicago, Detroit, Miami, New Orleans, Los Angeles and elsewhere. His gambling interests extended from New York City to

Saratoga, New Jersey, Florida, Nevada, and Cuba. He even had a government-guaranteed monopoly for transporting new cars from the Ford Motor Co. plant at Edgewater, N.J.

But the publicity he received in numerous probes of the New York underworld brought the Immigration Service and other federal agencies down on him. He left the U.S. voluntarily on Jan. 3, 1956, while deportation proceedings were pending against him, and returned to Italy where he died several years later.

He was the only boss Carlo Gambino ever had who met a natural death.

Gambino's name was never mentioned in connection with the coast-to-coast carnage of Murder, Inc. But he must have known his two immediate superiors in the Mangano organization were Murder, Inc. executives. And he must have been aware they were largely responsible for the nationwide epidemic of unsolved murders, including more than 200 in Brooklyn alone.

None of the probers and prosecutors who investigated Murder, Inc. bothered to ask Gambino if he knew what Adonis and Anastasia were up to. But it wouldn't have done them a bit of good if they had.

Now, in 1956, Albert Anastasia became a boss. The head butcher had emerged from the meat department to assume full control of the store. Gambino, who rose with him from *caporegime* to underboss, shook his hand and wished him well. So did Frank Costello, who was as close to the terrible Albert as anyone in the Mafia hierarchy.

Frank Costello, gravel-voiced and distinguished-looking, had also come a long way since the bloody days of the Castellammare War. But, unlike Albert A., he had passed the peak of power and was starting to slide down the other side, with a push from Vito Genovese.

Genovese sat out World War II in Italy, where he first buttered up Mussolini and then conned the Allied Military Government, stealing army supplies from under the noses of U.S. officers and running the country's biggest black market. Finally arrested by Army CID Agent O.C. Dickey, he used his military and political pull to avoid being shipped back to the States until after a key witness in a murder case against him had been fatally poisoned in a maximum security cell at the Brooklyn jail. Then he graciously consented to go back to New York, at the taxpayers' expense.

With the witness dead, the murder case collapsed and Don Vito was free to resume his mob leadership. Frank Costello, who had been running the family in the absence of Genovese and Lucky Luciano, was brusquely told to step down.

Costello, known to gangland as the Prime Minister, didn't mind too much for he had plenty of outside interests to keep him occupied, such as slot machines in New Orleans, gambling casinos in Havana, a piece of the action in Las Vegas and Reno. A firm believer in the free enterprise system, he had carefully constructed a gambling empire that was independent of the Luciano mob. In fact, some members of the family grumbled that Costello had neglected the family rackets and had removed himself from the routine chores—extortion, hijacking, armed robbery, contract murder, etc., that had to be done.

Costello's gambling partners included Joe Adonis; Meyer Lansky, now ensconced in Miami; Carlos Marcello, crime czar of Louisiana; Dandy Phil Kastel; Frank Erickson, a financial wizard known as the bookmaker's bookmaker, and other top underworld figures. A behind-scenes power in City Hall, he gave orders to city officials, judges and a few Congressmen. When Frank Costello growled, important people jumped. But to Vito Genovese, he was just an uppity underling.

After Vito assumed control of the old Luciano outfit, Costello was reduced to *caporegime*. For all his political clout and international interests, he now held the same rank as Anthony (Tony Bender) Strollo, Gaetano (Tommy Ryan) Eboli, Gerardo (Jerry) Catena and the *consigliere*, Mike Miranda. In fact, Genovese delegated much more authority to Tony Bender than he did to Don Francesco.

Then the Senate rackets committee summoned Costello to testify at its most sensational crime hearings. Millions of TV viewers watched the Prime Minister squirm and heard his hoarse voice invoke the Fifth Amendment. The Senate probe set off a barrage of legal armament that riddled Costello's remaining power.

His pals in Tammany Hall and congress ducked for cover. Costello was hit with one prison term for refusing to answer the Senate crime-buster's questions and a second sentence for income-tax evasion. The Government also began denaturalization and deportation proceedings, claiming he lied about his criminal past when he obtained U.S. citizenship.

In November 1956, Genovese called a crime convention to decide Costello's fate. Held at a Mid-Manhattan hotel, it was attended by 42 mob bosses, including 11 of the 12 members of the national Commission. All 26 Mafia families in the U.S. were represented. By a narrow vote and after much argument, the delegates removed Costello from the Commission seat he had held since Luciano was deported.

Costello could not speak for himself at the mob parley because he was in prison. He got out in March 1957. Stripped of all his power and prestige, he still had his gambling interests but the vulturine Vito suggested that he might like to split these with his old gang. Costello declined and obtained support from Albert Anastasia, the one mob leader who was not afraid of Genovese.

Costello dined with friends at an elegant East Side restaurant on the night of May 2, 1957. Then he stopped for a nightclub nightcap and returned home to the Majestic Apartments, Central Park West at 71st St., around 11 o'clock.

A black Cadillac pulled up behind his taxi and, as Frank paid the cabdriver, a mountainous man heaved his belly out of the Caddy and waddled into the apartment house. Frank followed by a few seconds, nodding to the doorman. The hulking hoodlum was waiting in a small foyer between the entrance and lobby.

"This is for you, Frank," he said, whipping out a snub nosed revolver and firing at Costello's neatly-barbered head. The Prime Minister hit the foyer floor, blood spurting from behind his right ear. Believing his mission accomplished, the heavy hitter waddled back to the Caddy and was driven away.

But Costello suffered only a scalp wound. A Genovese thug, Vincent (The Chin) Gigante, was charged with the shooting. Because Costello refused to identify him, the gigantic Gigante was acquitted at his trial for attempted murder. However, police are convinced that he was the shooter and that his chauffer that night was Genovese underboss Thomas (Tommy Ryan) Eboli.

Six weeks after Frank's skull was creased, two more accurate marksmen walked up to a fruit store in the Bronx and shot Frank Scalise to death as he emerged, munching a peach. Scalise, 64, was even closer to Albert Anastasia than Costello. Known as Don Cheech, he was an Anastasia underboss, as was Carlo Gambino, with whom he had risen through the Mafia ranks.

Scalise was one of the country's biggest importers and distributors of narcotics. He dealt directly with the heroin factories of Marseilles and the Sicilian Mafiosi who arranged shipments.

Not satisfied with the fortune he made from poppy products, he had been selling Cosa Nostra memberships to gangsters who were of Italian heritage but did not belong to the Brotherhood. A Union card signed by Scalise reportedly cost about $40,000.

Appalled that a fellow Mafioso would attempt to turn "our thing" into a commercial venture like buying a seat on the Stock Exchange, Genovese ordered his pistoleros to put Don Cheech away.

It was the second indignity inflicted on Anastasia by Don Vito within two months, and Big Albert did not intend to sit still for a third. But he did.

At 10:15 on the morning of October 25, 1957, Albert strolled into the barbershop of the Park Sheraton Hotel at Seventh Ave. and 55th St. He hung up his gray hat, blue topcoat and the jacket of his brown suit. Then he greeted the shopowner and staff before settling his beefy frame into Chair 4, facing the window.

The chauffeur-bodyguard who usually accompanied him was not there that day. He had gone to a nearby store "to get some cigars," leaving the unarmed Anastasia unprotected. There were two other customers, five barbers, a manicurist, a brusher and two bootblacks in the shop.

As his favorite barber applied the clippers to Albert's gray-streaked brown hair, two men came in through a door off the hotel lobby. Their hat brims were pulled down, their coat collars were pulled up, and they wore large, pilot-type sunglasses. Approaching Anastasia from the rear, they brushed the barber aside with a gun muzzle and blasted the gang chief out of his chair with five slugs in his head and back.

The executioner's execution stunned most of his family members. But underboss Gambino was as unruffled as usual. His voice remained calm; his eyes were unblurred by tears.

A week or two before the murder, Gambino had a secret meeting with Vito Genovese. They were old friends. Vito had always liked Carlo and respected his ability. Now he took Carlo into his confidence and explained that it would be necessary to kill Carlo's boss.

He had compiled a list of grievances against Anastasia. One was that Big Al was trying to muscle in on the rackets of other families. Another was that he had "dishonored" Cosa Nostra by allowing Scalise to sell memberships. Genovese even suspected Albert had done some membership-peddling himself.

Furthermore, Vito pointed out, Albert had sworn to avenge the shootings of Scalise and Costello. Any such move might trigger an all-out war that would seriously weaken the Anastasia and Genovese gangs, the city's two largest rat packs, and would lead to their eventual dominance by one or more of the other families.

Genovese also mentioned Albert's heavy-handed efforts to take over Cuban gambling casinos run by Santo Trafficante, Mafia boss of Florida and Havana. Trafficante, a friend of both Vito and Carlo, had complained to Lucky Luciano, who relayed the message to Genovese.

To clinch his arguments, Genovese noted that Gambino would succeed Anastasia as gang boss and would inherit all his rackets, not to mention those left behind by Don Cheech. He hinted there might even be some gambling concessions up for grabs, since Costello had finally agreed that he needed them like a hole in the head.

Gambino promised to give Vito's plan careful consideration. Soldiers were expected to die, but the assassination of one gang boss by another was an extremely serious matter. He had to weigh all the alternatives before deciding what to do.

As underboss, his duty was to warn Anastasia. But if he did that and Albert got hit anyway, then Carlo would surely be next. Tipping off Albert would not improve his own position. Bumping off Albert, on the other hand, would make room at the top.

"With Albert out of the way," Vito had stressed, "you'll be boss and our families can work together in peace."

Gambino conferred with another old friend, Joe Profaci, an olive-oil importer who bossed the most powerful gang in Brooklyn. Profaci found Genovese's arguments reasonable and offered to handle the arrangements for Albert's demise. Then he gave the contract to three of his most trigger-happy followers—the Gallo brothers, Crazy Joe, Larry, and Kid Blast.

The Gallos had their own small gang and often served as troubleshooters for Profaci, handling delicate assignments that Profaci did not want to give to his own members, for one reason or another. Five Gallo gunmen went to the Park Sheraton. While two of them entered the barbershop, two others watched the front and side entrances in case Albert tried to escape. The fifth assassin drove the getaway car.

Sidney Slater, a businessman who hung out with the Gallos and later turned informer, met Crazy Joe and four of his men in a Manhattan bar a few nights after the murder. According to Slater, he asked Joey who killed Albert and Gallo replied: "From now on, Sidney, you can call the five of us the Barbershop Quintet."

Gambino now achieved his lifelong ambition—Mafia bosshood. The crime combine formerly headed by the Mangano brothers, Joe Adonis, and Albert Anastasia became the Gambino Family. And Carlo, who had friends in all the important mobs, also won a seat on the national Commission.

His appointment to the Syndicate's Supreme Court came at the historic Mafia powwow in Apalachin, N.Y., held only three weeks after Anastasia's murder.

The biggest underworld gathering since Little Caesar Maranzano's accession to the throne of "boss of bosses" was called by Vito Genovese for the threefold purpose of explaining why Anastasia was eliminated, approving Gambino as Big Al's successor, and dividing Anastasia's underworld estate. There also were several minor matters on the agenda, such as a motion to repeal the long-standing

Mafia rule against dope-trafficking by gang bosses—an unwritten law which the bosses generally ignored.

The crime conference was held November 14 at the hilltop mansion of Joseph Barbara, a millionaire mobster with top Mafia connections. Genovese had suggested meeting in Chicago where the non-interference of local authorities could be guaranteed. But the Buffalo don, Stefano Magaddino, didn't want to travel that far from home and proposed the woodsy, bucolic Barbara estate. There had been previous Mafia meets at Apalachin and none of them had attracted any attention.

So the date was set and more than 100 Mafia chiefs descended on the little town near Oswego, N.Y., a few miles north of Pennsylvania. Comprising a virtual Who's Who in American Crime, they came from as far away as Texas, California, Florida, and Puerto Rico.

They rented nearly all the motel rooms in the Apalachin area and clogged the roads with their Cadillacs, Lincoln Continentals, and Chrysler Imperials. Barbara's long, winding driveway looked like the world's most exclusive used car lot.

Gambino was the guest of honor. In the best of spirits, he drove upstate with four companions—cousin Paul Castellano, Salvatore (Charlie) Chiri, Frank Cucchiara, Carmine (The Doctor) Lombardozzi, and Joseph (Staten Island Joe) Riccobono.

Riccobono was Carlo's *consigliere*. A dress manufacturer who had belonged to the old Lepke-Gurrah extortion gang that terrorized New York's billion-dollar garment industry, he was 62 at the time of the Apalachin gathering and highly respected by the mobs. The same could not be said of

Lombardozzi, who was then a Gambino *caporegime*, as was Castellano. Charlie Chiri was a Gambino "button man."

Cucchiara (alias Frank Caruso, Frank Russo, and Frank the Spoon) was a Boston racketeer who imported Italian cheeses and was said to be very big in gambling and dope.

Lombardozzi later told investigators he was invited to Apalachin by Gambino when they met at a wake in a Brooklyn mortuary. He said Gambino told him he might have to undergo heart surgery and wanted to discuss it with Barbara, who had survived a similar operation. So Carlo decided to drive to Barbara's home and asked Lombardozzi to go with him.

Asked how come so many people made the trip with Gambino, Lombardozzi replied: "Carlo explained he was invited to bring all his friends."

In a sense this was true. *Amico nos* (our friends) is one of several terms used among Mafiosi to describe their organization and its members. But Lombardozzi didn't bother to point this out to his questioners.

He claimed the Apalachin reunion was nothing more than "a party, a barbecue." What it really amounted to, however, was a coronation for Genovese, a confirmation of family fatherhood for Gambino, and a court-marshal for Lombardozzi.

The Doctor, a handsome, curly-haired ex-convict, had been sentenced to death by Genovese for various infractions of underworld rules. Soon after the Gambino party arrived at Apalachin, Lombardozzi was told to wait in Barbara's four-car garage while a court of Mafia commissioners convened to decide his fate. Gambino pleaded for Carmine's life, pointing out that he was in charge of the family's Wall

St. operations and that his financial manipulations, including stock thefts and swindles, had made millions of dollars for the Mafia.

As a result of Gambino's argument that Lombardozzi was too valuable to execute, the commission commuted the death sentence to a $10,000 fine.

Then, turning to more important affairs, it gave its official approval to Genovese's actions against Costello, Scalise, and Anastasia. Don Vito presented his case so eloquently that the commission bestowed upon him the old title of "boss of bosses" of the five New York families, which meant that he automatically became chairman of the Syndicate's board of directors.

As a reward for handling the murder contract, Brooklyn boss Joe Profaci received a share of Anastasia's rackets. But the maverick Gallos, who carried out the contract, got nothing beyond their original fee. This slight to their lethal skill was one of the factors that later caused the Gallos to declare war on the Profaci mob.

Alerted by the sight of so many expensive cars with out-of-state license plates, state police raided the crime convention and grabbed 65 delegates. The rest escaped. Some of them ran into the woods around Barbara's home; others managed to drive off before the house was completely surrounded.

Among those caught in the Great Gang Roundup were the heads of four of the five New York families. Gambino, Genovese, Profaci, and Joseph Bonanno. The fifth boss, Thomas (Three Finger-Brown) Lucchese, either did not attend or slipped through the police net.

The Apalachin raid set off a flood of county, state, and

federal investigations that went on for years. Twenty delegates, including Castellano and Lombardozzi, were hit with federal jail sentences totaling 94 years and fines totaling $130,000 for refusing to tell what went on at the Barbara barbecue. But Don Carlo avoided the heat due to a heart ailment that saved him from embarrassing questions and punishment for not answering.

Immigration officials noticed his name on the Apalachin guest list (he was described in most newspaper accounts of the gang-bust as a "labor relations consultant") and recalled he had been arrested 17 years earlier as an illegal alien.

They dusted off his file and reopened the deportation proceedings begun in 1940, stalled by World War II, and then forgotten. After a further delay of almost a year, a deportation hearing finally was begun in October 1958. Called to the witness stand, Gambino collapsed and was carried out on a stretcher. And that was that.

For all practical purposes, the deportation campaign collapsed with him although the government kept on maintaining that it had not given up the fight to send him home to Sicily. Gambino used his heart condition as an excuse to duck further deportation hearings, grand jury quizzes, and the hearings of various government agencies probing organized crime.

But his failing health did not prevent him from running the rackets. Nor did it stop him from dining with other Mafia lords and keeping a strenuous schedule of appointments that took up several hours of his time almost every day.

To the undercover agents assigned to observe his numerous activities, Don Carlo appeared as active as he had ever been. Apparently, only his doctor could tell the difference.

CHAPTER 5

THE PLOT TO KILL DON CARLO

THOUGH THE MAFIA COMMISSION RULED that Albert Anastasia's demise was justifiable homicide, not all of Albert's associates accepted this finding. One who did not was John (Johnny Roberts) Robilotto, a mortician who got lots of business from Albert.

Robilotto was a former Genovese gunman who left Vito's army to become a captain in Anastasia's crew. He was the chief suspect in the 1951 murder of New Jersey mob boss Willie Moretti and had been indicted for this crime but was never brought to trial.

He was very close to Anastasia and he told several people that he intended to avenge the assassination, no matter what the Commission decided. Robilotto apparently was unaware that his old boss, Don Vito, had ordered the hit with the approval of his new boss, Don Carlo.

At 3:30 a.m. September 7, 1958, the vengeful Johnny Roberts was shot four times in the head on Utica Ave. near

Kings Highway in the East Flatbush section of Brooklyn. Whoever did it held the gun so close to his head that it left the powder burns on his face and skull. Police noted that the fastidious undertaker was wearing $35 shoes, a $200 suit, and a solid gold belt buckle. In keeping with his trade, the suit was a funereal black. It's pockets had been turned inside out, his wallet was missing, and the cops found only $3 on the corpse. But detectives weren't fooled by this over-obvious effort to make it appear Johnny was killed in the robbery.

Shortly thereafter, one of his henchmen, Armand (Tommy) Rava, disappeared forever. Another member of the Gambino gang had gone underground, so to speak.

The Senators who questioned Joe Valachi five years later inquired about the Anastasia rubout. Valachi told them: "I believe that Vito Genovese worked hand in hand with Gambino and Joe Banty (Carlo's underboss). In other words, they have the right to do something like this... being that Albert Anastasia was doing so much wrong and it was up to his own family to act."

After the Anastasia hit, Valachi made a special trip to Brooklyn to ask Johnny Roberts what, if anything, he planned to do about it. He asked Johnny if he intended to "make a comeback," a reprisal killing. Johnny said no, but several months later Valachi heard he had changed his mind and was hunting the killers.

"Well, he was killed not long after this," Valachi said.

"Now, after Johnny Roberts was killed, Paul Gambino came up in the Bronx (to Valachi's office). He wanted to have a talk with me. We walked up and down. He was curving me. He knew I liked Johnny. 'In other words (Gambino said), what I am trying to get out of you is, what should we do?' He says, 'I have a lot of respect for your opinion regardless of how other people feel.'

"This is Paolo Gambino now, the one Steve Rinelli shot in the 1930s. We were close friends.

"I said, 'Paul, there is no sense curving. Have you got an idea? Have you people any idea at all?

"He said, 'Yes.'

"I said, 'Well, then, act. What are you waiting for?'

"He said, 'You advise that?'

"I said, 'Go right ahead before they (Robilotto's men) pounce on you.'

"A week or two later they caught up with him (Tommy Rava) in some club in Brooklyn. They fired up about 18 shots. Some of them got away, some were caught. I don't remember just how it went, but some of them (the intended victims) made it. They jumped out of the window.

"I heard they had gotten Tommy Rava. Everything was peaceful then."

With Johnny Roberts and Rava gone, there was no more talk about avenging Anastasia. The remaining members of the old Anastasia gang accepted Gambino's leadership and he kept them all gainfully employed. He built a solid wall of legitimate businesses around his underworld labyrinth, making it almost impossible for investigators to find out what he was really doing.

Genovese's downfall came in 1959. Convicted of masterminding an international narcotics ring that had smuggled millions of dollars worth of heroin into the U.S., Don Vito was sent to federal prison and died there a decade later. Though he continued to run the rackets from behind bars until his death, his departure from the New York underworld meant that more and more of the decisions involving all five families were made by Don Carlo.

Genovese didn't mind this arrangement, for he trusted Gambino not to cheat him. But Joseph (Joe Bananas) Bonanno was jealous of Gambino's ever-increasing stature in the mob hierarchy. Though younger than Carlo, Joe had been a boss much longer.

Born in 1905 at Castellammare Del Golfo, Sicily, Bonanno entered the U.S. illegally at the age of 19 and joined the original Castellammarese gang of Little Caesar Maranzano. When the Castellammarese War ended, Maranzano rewarded his young lieutenants, Joe Bananas and Joe Profaci, by giving them their own Brooklyn gangs.

And so, at age 26, Bonanno became the youngest New York mob boss and the youngest member of the Mafia Commission. To avoid deportation, he left the U.S. in 1938 and made a legal re-entry from Canada. He became a naturalized citizen in 1945.

By then he was a millionaire and a mastermind of the underworld. Like Carlo Gambino, he combined his rackets with seemingly legitimate businesses. Then he became a partner in a dress factory employing non-union labor.

Then he bought a Brooklyn funeral parlor. Joe is credited with inventing double-decker coffins in which gangland murder victims were buried beneath the bodies of legitimate customers. Several other underworld morticians copied this innovation.

Bonanno also acquired an interest in the Grande Cheese Co. of Fond du Lac, Wisconsin; the Alliance Realty &

Insurance Co. of Tuscan, Arizona; and a score of other businesses scattered over the U.S., Canada, and the Caribbean.

His Canadian ventures conflicted with those of his cousin, Stefano Magaddino, a fellow mortician and fellow Mafia don who was then (and still is) rackets boss of the Buffalo-Niagara Falls area. Magaddino also came from Castellammare, but family ties didn't stop Joe from poaching on Cousin Steve's territory in Toronto and Montréal. He also trod on the well-shod toes of other important Mafiosi, but the shrewd, utterly ruthless Bonanno took care to remain on good terms with the equally crafty Joe Profaci.

Their cordial relationship was strengthened even more when Bonanno's oldest son and stout right arm, Salvatore, married Profaci's pretty niece, Rosalie Profaci. And when Joe Profaci died of natural causes in 1962, the biggest, most expensive floral tribute came from Joe Bonanno.

Until then, Bonanno had never interfered with the rackets of any other New York City family. He had expanded his operations far beyond the Metropolitan area, but he scrupulously observed the crime boundaries dividing the rackets within the city's five boroughs and the suburbs.

Now, with Joe Profaci dead and Vito Genovese in prison, Bonanno decided it was time to seize the underworld's greatest treasure. After all, he was New York's senior gang boss. Why shouldn't he be boss of bosses, supreme ruler of the New York City crime kingdom? Every time he looked in the mirror, he saw himself wearing a crown.

It was just like the TV commercials for a certain brand of margarine. Only Joe used the more expensive spread. He buttered up Profaci's brother-in-law and successor, the already well-larded Giuseppe Magliocco, known as Fat Joe or the Fat Man.

An indecisive, procrastinating type who preferred spaghetti dinners to Syndicate strategy sessions, the amiable Magliocco never really wanted to be boss. The decisions had always been made for him by Profaci, and now he gratefully accepted advice from the suave, smooth-talking Joe Bananas. The two Joes became bosom buddies. They shared rackets and business ventures; entertained each other at their homes; dined, golf, sailed, and fished together. Banana Joe even let Fat Joe in on a land development scheme he was working on in Arizona.

Then, one day in 1963, Bananas asked Fats to do him a small favor: Get rid of the other two New York mob bosses who were still around, Carlo Gambino and Tom Lucchese.

"Sure," said Magliocco. He gave the contract to a small, sad-faced, solidly-built gunman named Joe Colombo. As things turned out, he couldn't have made a worse choice.

Magliocco either didn't know or had forgotten that Colombo was deeply indebted to Carlo Gambino. A former Brooklyn longshoreman, Colombo had left the docks to become a salesman for Pride Meat Co., controlled by Paul Gambino and Peter Castellano. During his six years with Pride, he became acquainted with Don Carlo, who took a fatherly interest in him.

Gambino eventually found a good spot for Colombo in the Brooklyn underworld. Through the years, he had made it a practice to place promising young men in the ranks of other crime families, where they might someday be useful to him. He spoke to Joe Profaci about Colombo and the muscular meat salesman was appointed a Profaci-soldier.

He proved his worth during the Gallo uprising of the late 1950s and early 1960s. The streets of Brooklyn were littered with the corpses of Gallo and Profaci troops, and Joe Colombo emerged from the fray with the rank of captain.

It may have been his war record that earned Colombo the awesome assignment of killing Gambino and Lucchese. In any event, he promptly notified the intended victims. And they, in turn, notified other members of the Mafia commission.

This grand council then included Gambino, Lucchese, Bonanno, Genovese, Stefano Magaddino, Salvatore (Sam Mooney) Giancana of Chicago, Angelo Bruno of Philadelphia, John T. Scalish of Cleveland, John La Rocco of Pittsburgh, Joe Zerilli of Detroit and Raymond Patriarca, Mafia chief of New England.

As Genovese was in prison, he was represented on the commission by one of his underbosses. The seat vacated by Profaci's death had not been filled. And Bonanno was removed from the commission pending the disposition of charges that he conspired to murder other members.

The remaining nine commissioners ordered Bonanno and Magliocco to appear for trial. Fat Joe showed up, trembling like 300 pounds of Jello, and made a full confession. He was fined $50,000, relieved of his mob command and banished from the brotherhood. But Joe Bananas, who instigated the murder plot, was not present to share the blame. He ducked the trial and skipped to California.

At Gambino's suggestion, Magliocco's place at the head of the old Profaci family was given to Joe Colombo. Later, Colombo got the Commission seat which Bonanno had occupied for 32 years.

Disgraced and deserted by Bonanno, Magliocco retired to his high-walled, dog-patrolled Long Island mansion and died there, of an apparent heart attack, in December 1963. Joe Bananas didn't attend the Fat Man's funeral, but he was already making plans for a comeback.

After several months on the West Coast, Bonanno slipped over the border to Canada and conferred with his associates there about further incursions of Magaddino-controlled rackets. Don Stefano soon heard what his cousin was up to. Furious, he called a Commission conference and filed a fresh complaint against the slippery Bananas.

"This guy's planting flags all over the world," Magaddino roared at the meeting, held September 18, 1964, at the home of Genovese underboss Thomas (Tommy Ryan) Eboli in Englewood Cliffs, N.J.

Bonanno had been told to be there, but again he failed to show. Consequently, Magaddino demanded that he be sentenced to death *in absentia*. The Chicago commissioner, stumpy Sam Giancana, seconded this motion.

"Hit him!" Sam growled through a blue haze of cigar smoke. "Hit him!"

The Commission accepted this judicial advice and instructed Magaddino to handle the arrangements. Magaddino returned to Buffalo, summoned his captains and told them what to do.

Around 12:15 a.m. on October 21, 1964, Bonanno and his lawyer, William Power Maloney, left a Manhattan steakhouse, hailed a cab and road to Maloney's apartment house on Park Ave. near 35th St. They were discussing what Joe would say when he went before a grand jury later that day and they didn't notice the car following them.

As soon as the taxi deposited them in front of the apartment building, the car pulled up and two large men got out. Each of them was well over 6 feet tall and weighed more than 250 pounds. They wore dark hats and raincoats and they brandished revolvers.

One of them grabbed Bonanno and said, "Come on, Joe. My boss wants to see you." The other goon pointed his gun at Maloney, ordered him to "get out" and fired a warning shot to prove they meant business. Maloney hurried inside the apartment building to call police. The gorillas shoved Bonanno into their car and drove off. Next day, newspaper reports of the kidnaping speculated that the bumptious Bonanno either had been bumped off or had deliberately dropped out of sight to avoid the scheduled grand jury appearance.

And Maloney's hazy description of the kidnapers didn't do much to dispel the suspicions of skeptical cops and reporters.

"I only saw the men for 20 seconds," the lawyer said. "It was a dark rainy night and there was a gun in my face. How can you recognize a man under those circumstances?"

But the kidnaping was genuine. Bonanno was taken to a mob hideaway in the Catskill Mountains and held there for several weeks. Though he had been sentenced to death, he persuaded the commissioners to let him live. His murder, he argued, would set off a national gang war and cause the Mafia to suffer heavy revenue losses. If his life was spared, he promised to give up his international crime empire and let the Commission dispose of his gang and rackets.

Placing greed above vengeance, the commissioners

commuted the death sentenced to banishment. Joe was ordered to leave the country and remain in exile until his underworld enterprises had been divided. He was turned loose in December 1964.

Around this time, Sam DeCavalcante was planning a Christmas party to be held "just for the *borgata*" at Ange and Min's Restaurant in Kenilworth, N.J. And Carlo Gambino would play Santa Claus, even though he couldn't be there in person.

"I'm gonna have all the kids that are proposed (for mob membership) all down, too," Sam the Plumber told a henchman while the FBI listened in on his pipeline. "Carl (Gambino) gave me two thousand dollars for that score we made over there in New York, so I'm gonna give everybody in the outfit fifty dollars. A Christmas present from us, which I think will be a nice thing."

Sam disclosed he had tried to act as a mediator between Bonanno and the Commission, but the negotiations collapsed when Bonanno refused to attend the Commission parlay at Englewood Cliffs, and the kidnaping followed. Now, in the closing days of 1964, Sam wasn't sure what would happen next.

On Dec. 23, he received a visit from Joseph (Bayonne Joe) Zicarelli, a Bonanno lieutenant who was also very close to DeCavalcante.

"Friday night I saw Joe (Bonanno) and I was trying to reach you since," Zicarelli said. "If I could have got you over the weekend, he would have come and saw you, today he said he might go to the grand jury because they threatened to pick his kid (Salvatore) up. His kid went before the grand jury a couple of times. They want to pick the kid up and prove the kid is perjuring himself and use that as a threat to make him (Bonanno) come in.

"But a couple of things he wanted to talk to you about, he brought me up to date a little bit. He told me to tell you the old man has resigned (an apparent reference to Giovanni Bonventre, Bonanno's uncle and underboss, who attended the Apalachin conference with Bonanno and Profaci). And the rest (of Bonanno's underbosses and capos) are resigning.

"But most of all (Bonanno wants to know) if you are in any position to find out who the Commission favors to make the boss."

Sam replied: "The Commission just selected three people that they are going to look to or be in contact with. Gasparino, Caruso, and Alfano."

Zicarelli said Bonanno was in touch with all three, "and he's been negotiating to make certain moves before they (the commissioners) put the thing together. Negotiating for some sort of conditions before they all resign. Being that the old man stepped down, the other two (capos) tentatively stepped down and they're out with the old man, they're looking for some sort of conditions."

Sam said: "The only way the Commission will accept the other two in is as soldiers."

Zicarelli then expressed the opinion that the new boss would be Gasparino— "and if it's Gasparino, they're afraid of reprisals. This is my own opinion. I sounded people out."

"Joe, I like the way you talk," Sam replied. "I'd like to bring you in front of Carlo Gambino, in front of the Commission."

JOE: "In front of Carlo?"

SAM: "Yeah, in front of Carlo or in front of Jerry (Catena, Genovese underboss). You see, the Commission knows this but they like to hear it from a person like you. Joe, I'd like to see you become something."

JOE: "I'm nothing. I don't want to become nothing."

SAM: "Joe, you deserve a position. You make more sense to me than the whole bunch of your friends (the Bonanno gang) put together. Cause you're sincere, Joe. I'd like these people (the Commission) to meet you themselves."

JOE: Carlo I know. Carlo knows me since I was a kid."

SAM: "He said he knows you."

JOE: "We did business with him since he was a boot-legger, when I was a little kid with Gypsy Joe (Pritchard). And I've done business with his brothers. I know Paul, I know Joe and I know Carlo. Jerry (Catena) I know for a long time. I would be only too glad to see them, but I don't know enough about the situation."

Sam the Plumber and Bayonne Joe interrupted their chat to listen to a newscast reporting that Joe Bonanno had failed to keep a scheduled appointment with his lawyer that day.

SAM: "Do you think he is going to show up?"

JOE: "Yeah."

SAM: "You think so?"

JOE: "I thought he was."

SAM: "Joe, between you and I, I don't think he's going to show up anyplace anymore."

But the top Banana was still around. He was the subject of another crime conference that took place on a cold January night in 1965 at the Villa Capri, the Catering establishment in Cedarhurst, Long Island, a few miles east of the New York city line.

Five commission members attended—Gambino, Lucchese, Colombo, Magaddino, and Angelo Bruno of Philadelphia. The Genovese Group was represented by underbosses Eboli and Catena and counselor Mike Miranda. Several other high-ranking racketeers were there, including Sam the Plumber. And undercover agents of the law were watching and listening.

Magaddino started the ball rolling by nominating an obscure Brooklyn clothing manufacturer, Gaspare DiGregorio, to take over the Bonanno mob. DiGregorio, whose friends called him Gasparino, was related to Magaddino by marriage. He was not well known in the Mafia and he was virtually unknown to the law enforcement agencies who keep track of Mafia goings-on.

He had been best man at Joe Bonanno's wedding and was godfather to Joe's firstborn, Salvatore.

He had once been charged with murder, but had never been convicted of any crime. He was the same age as Bonanno (then 59) and came from Castellammare Trapani, four miles from Bonanno's home town. He lived with his family in a comfortable but unspectacular home in West Babylon, Long Island.

Magaddino assured his fellow commissioners that his unassuming relation could handle the Bananas bunch. His appointment was approved unanimously, though few mob leaders had ever heard of DiGregorio before. So the load wouldn't be too heavy for an inexperienced boss to bear, the commissioners lightened it by a few hundred mobsters and several ripe rackets.

Sam the Plumber later told two of his lieutenants, Louis Larasso and Frank Majuri, what went on at the Villa Capri.

"Jerry (Catena), Tommy (Eboli) and me went in together. We transferred maybe four cars that night (to avoid being followed). But even so, I told Tommy, 'Jesus Christ, every time a waiter comes in, they're looking at us.'

"... The waiters were around, and everybody was speaking. They made it look like we were having a buffet there. There was over two hundred dollars worth of food on the table and nobody tasted anything. It would have been better if they had put the food in bags and took it out and dumped it someplace."

Sam said that Salvatore (Sam Mooney) Giancana of Chicago had decided not to attend the meeting. "Mooney got disgusted. He said, 'This Commission! Sometimes I don't know how they run it. To hell with him (Bonanno). As far as I'm concerned, do what you want to do.' "

According to Sam the plumber, the Commission had become "a three-man thing," run by Carlo Gambino, Tom Lucchese, and Stefano Magaddino.

He said Lucchese was authorized to vote for Chicago's Giancana and Detroit's Joe Zerilli. "Ange (Bruno) will do whatever Don Stefano tells him. And Joe Colombo is like an echo for Carlo. It's a three-man thing, understand what I mean?"

The Commission now had 11 members, including the imprisoned Genovese (Catena voted for him at the Villa Capri). And the Gambino-Lucchese-Magaddino triumvirate controlled seven votes.

"You know," Sam the Plumber once observed, "I've heard all of these guys talking. My father makes more sense than all of them... Us, we're not even a little crumb in the basket."

What he heard at the Villa Capri convinced him that

"the thing (the Bonanno furor) has calmed down now.... You could see the big to-do that Tom and Carl are making so that nobody can destroy them. Now Stefano is going to be strong...

"Stefano's got about a hundred guys (Bonanno soldiers) out of this. See now, between Tommy and Carl they got this Joe Colombo. Bonanno's outfit, they're breaking it up.

"Only the guys in New York still belong to it. Canada— this stays here (in other words, this information isn't to be repeated)—will go to Don Stefano. Arizona to Frank DeSimone (California boss whose territory Bonanno tried to invade).

"They (the commissioners) made me mad. They asked me, 'What's your opinion?' As if it counted."

Sam added he had heard that Joe Notaro was the only *caporegime* who stuck with Joe Bonanno "and that Gasparino was going to kill him."

Because FBI agents had infiltrated the Villa Capri and word of the meeting had leaked to the press, the owner was in deep trouble.

"Well, this poor guy, they're gonna destroy him," Louis Larasso predicted. "The guy that owns that restaurant. They're gonna drive him crazy."

Gang goons reportedly beat up the caterer and broke both his legs.

Soon after the Capri sitdown, DeCavalcante had lunch with Gambino at a small restaurant in Manhattan's Little Italy. During the meal, Gambino talked about his children and other things that had nothing to do with his other family. Then he excused himself and went to the men's room. Sam waited a few seconds, then followed him.

Locking the toilet door behind them, Gambino went to the sink and turned on both faucets full force. Then he flushed the urinals and the sitdown toilet. Sure that the rushing water would drown out any electronic eavesdropping devices that that might have been installed, he placed his mouth to the Plumber's ear and whispered Mafia secrets.

But Sam was about as leakproof as a sieve. He hurried home to Kenilworth, N.J., and blabbed about everything to his underboss, Joe La Selva. Joe asked him about Joe Notaro, the loyal Bonanno *capo*.

"Well, I straightened him out a couple of weeks ago," Sam Replied, "but there seems to be a little hard feelings. He stuck with Bonanno. In fact, we were supposed to hit some people (kill some Bonanno members) over there, but we straightened that out. Carlo and I straightened it out.

"We're going to take them in (Bonanno's lieutenants) and everybody comes under the rules. The men are all supposed to forget the old scores."

JOE: "How about the kid, Sally (Salvatore Bonanno), the son?"

SAM: "We don't trust him."

JOE: "He's got two sons. What about the other kid?"

SAM: Well, Joey—he's nothing. He'll be all right. They haven't decided yet what to do with the father. This guy (Bonanno) robbed his own mother. We figure we'll take him to Florida. The guy ruined himself. See, Gasparino looks like the favorite to be the boss. He's got the Commission behind him...

"He (Bonanno) put Magliocco up to a lot of things—like to kill Carl. He put him up to hit Carl and Tommy Brown... Now they feel that he poisoned Magliocco.

"Magliocco didn't die a natural death. Because the only one who could accuse him (Bonanno, of plotting against Gambino and Lucchese) was Magliocco. Joe, Magliocco confessed to it. But this Joe (Bonanno) didn't know how far he went. Understand? So they suspected he (Bonanno) used a pill on him (Magliocco). That he's noted for."

(As a result of this conversation, picked up by the electronic bug in DeCavalcante's office, Magliocco's body was exhumed from its grave in Suffolk County, Long Island. Complicated chemical tests were conducted, but medical examiners found no trace of poison. They concluded he died of a heart attack, as his doctor originally reported.)

Sam also told his underboss that Bonanno once "tried to take California over. He sent the kid (Salvatore) out there with 40 guys. The Commission stopped him. That's where the trouble started."

And it was not yet over, by any means. Unhappy with their new boss, Bonanno soldiers began deserting in droves. Many of them signed up with Joe Colombo. And DiGregorio turned out to be tougher than anyone, including the other bosses, expected. He had agreed to give away Bonanno interests in Arizona and Canada. Now he wanted them back.

Bayonne Joe Zicarelli asked Sam the Plumber about the possibility of getting a transfer from DiGregorio's group to the DeCavalcante *borgata*.

"Well, they ain't gonna do nothing to you (for asking)," Sam replied. "See, I was talking to Carlo yesterday. And he was telling me what has taken place (in the former Bonanno mob). He had the list of all the *caporegimes*. So I said, 'The only person I'm interested in is Joe (Zicarelli).'

"He said, 'Just now, don't do nothing.'

"He said, 'You know, they were gonna give the (Bonanno) guys in Canada away to Buffalo (Magaddino). They were gonna give the guys in Arizona to Simone (Frank DeSimone). Now Gaspare doesn't want to give nothing away.

"He (Gambino) said, 'Now this guy is changing his tune.'"

Sam said he asked Gambino to intercede with DiGregorio about a transfer for Zicarelli, and Gambino replied: "Sam, Gaspare told me he's gonna keep Joe. He'll probably want Joe close to him. You know, Joe's a producer."

A few months after he became boss, DiGregorio suffered a heart attack. He appointed Sereno Tartamella, an official of the independent Beauty Culturists Union, and Nicholas (Eye Glasses) Marangello, Joe Bonanno's former chauffeur, to run the mob for him. But neither of these men could control the already rebellious troops.

Several soldiers signed up with Salvatore Bonanno, who had begun a recruiting drive with the eventual aim of recovering some of his father's old territory. On Friday night January 28, 1966, he went to the home of a relative on Troutman St. in the Ridgewood section of Brooklyn to confer with the men who had rejoined the Bonanno camp.

Someone tipped off DiGregorio. And when the meeting broke up, Gaspare's gunmen were waiting. Three carloads of pistoleros roared along Troutman St., firing at anything that moved. Bonanno's boys blazed away from doorways, fire escapes, and behind parked cars. An estimated 100 shots went off like strings of firecrackers, but apparently no one was hit. Salvatore reportedly burst into a ground-floor apartment on the block, crashed through a rear window and vanished over a backyard fence.

Now that the shooting had started again, Carlo Gambino tried to prevent an all-out war. He urged DiGregorio to retire. Reasoning that his poor health would not be improved by a dose of lead poisoning, Gaspare was only too happy to step down. Gambino then huddled with Stefano Magaddino and proposed DiGregorio's brainy underboss, Paul Sciacca, as the new family head.

The Commission's "three-man thing" was now a two-man show, run by Don Carlo and Don Stefano. Carlo's lifelong friend, Tom Lucchese, had entered Manhattan's Columbia-Presbyterian Medical Center the proceeding August for treatment of a brain tumor and a heart ailment.

He was still there and, for all practical purposes, his long crime career was over. Carlo Gambino now handled the affairs of the Lucchese crime family and voted for Three-Finger Brown on Commission matters. Joe Colombo invariably voted the same way. On most occasions Carlo also had the proxy votes of the Chicago and Detroit commissioners.

With five votes in his pocket, Gambino was now the most powerful commissioner, the first among equals, even though Vito Genovese still outranked him as "boss of bosses."

And the Commission confirmed his candidate to replace DiGregorio. Like the publicity-shunning Gasparino, Paul Sciacca was a Brooklyn clothing manufacturer who was almost unknown to most mobsters and their investigators. His name did not appear on any of the charts of underworld leaders prepared by the FBI and the Senate

Investigation Subcommittee on the basis of Joe Valachi's revelations. Valachi had never heard of him.

An apparently respectable pillar in his suburban community on Long Island's South Shore, he was a former director of the Hackensack Bank & Trust Co. in Hackensack, N.J. His clothing firms, Sands Fashion and S&S Garments, held Government contracts to make military uniforms.

Sciacca lived at 31 Lake Court, Massapequa, not far from the $100,000 home where Don Carlo spent his summers. He had been arrested only once, long ago, on a burglary charge, but the charge was dismissed. With no experience in Mafia warfare, he seemed a poor choice to command an army that was preparing for its biggest battle. But he turned out to be a capable general. And he had the invaluable advice and resources of two seasoned specialists in survival, Carlo Gambino and Stefano Magaddino.

The bloodless shoot out on Troutman St. was followed by more skirmishes, in one of which a former Bonanno lieutenant who had switched to the DiGregorio camp was wounded by machine-gun fire.

Joe Bananas returned from his long exile in May 1966, holed up at Salvatore's modest but well-guarded home in East Meadow, L.I., and repudiated his promise to stay out of New York gangland. From then on, the bodies began dropping with almost monotonous regularity.

Although many former defectors now returned to the Bananas bunch, still more remained loyal to their new bosses, Paul Sciacca and Joe Colombo, who loaned some of his best gunfighters to Sciacca. In a desperate effort to reduce the odds against him, Bonanno imported a top Mafia executioner, Gaspare Magaddino.

Magaddino, a cousin of both Bonanno and Stefano Magaddino, had personally killed more than 50 men in Italy, North Africa, Cuba, and the Americas. He handled at least 10 murder contracts in the New York City area alone. Though built like a beer barrel, he struck with the speed and force of lightning. On the night of November 10, 1967, he entered Cypress Gardens Restaurant in Queens near the Brooklyn border and mowed down three diners with a submachine gun he carried under his black raincoat. Two of the three dead men were Sciacca aides.

But not even a one-man execution squad like Gaspare Magaddino could turn the tide of battle in favor of Bonanno. Finally, after about 20 killings, most of them scored by the Sciacca side, Joe Bananas gave up his comeback try and retired to sunny Tuscan, Arizona, where he had lived off and on for 20 years.

The Bonanno War was never a serious threat to Don Carlo, but Joe's surrender removed even the possibility that Gambino might get hit with a stray bullet or face eventual competition from the only mob boss who had ever wanted to kill him.

Joe's departure to Arizona brought peace to the New York underworld. Still, Don Carlo could not relax. He sensed danger from a source that was both unknown and unpredictable—a maverick mob that made the Mafia tremble.

CHAPTER 6

KIDNAP, INC.

GEORGE FERACCO WAS BORN AND raised in East Harlem and the longest he was ever away from the neighborhood was the six years he spent in Atlanta, Ga., as a resident of the Federal Penitentiary there.

Starting at age 17, he was arrested many times for armed robbery, burglary, grand larceny, counterfeiting, and other things. Then he saw the light and became a traveling salesman. He traveled to Montreal, Canada to buy heroin and to Detroit, Cleveland, Chicago, and other places to sell it.

He served two federal prison terms for federal narcotics violations and when he left Atlanta in 1959 he returned home to East Harlem and went right back into the junk business.

Around 10 o'clock on the night of May 31, 1962, Feracco left his comfortable apartment at 341 Pleasant Ave. to buy a newspaper at the stand on the corner of Pleasant and 116th St. The short, swarthy, 40-year-old racketeer was unarmed. As a two-time loser, he couldn't afford to be caught carrying a gun. Besides, he felt perfectly safe.

He wouldn't dare walk alone after dark on the nearby streets of Harlem, but Pleasant Ave. was a white atoll in a dark sea. And it took care of its own. Only nine blocks long, it sheltered more resident Mafiosi than any other street in America.

George was half a block from the newsstand when a blue Buick sedan stopped alongside him and two neatly-dressed men hopped out. One of them flashed a police shield. The other pointed a revolver at George's bulging belly and told him to get in the car. Thinking he was under arrest again, George went along peaceably.

He had been carried off by contract killers, hired by a Cosa Nostra chieftain who complained he had paid George for five kilograms of pure heroin, but the powder he received was diluted. George was taken into a Bronx apartment and questioned by a tiny man who appeared to be the abductors' boss.

"We got a contract on you, George," he explained, his beady eyes blinking myopically behind oversize horn-rimmed glasses. "But maybe we can make a deal. Your life for information."

Under the circumstances, the offer was good enough to make George break the Mafia code of *omerta* (silence). The little guy wanted the names of drug dealers, bookmakers, card and dice game operators and others who, by the nature of their work, kept large amounts of cash on hand.

George named just about everybody he had ever seen flashing a fat bankroll. The tiny thug wrote it all down. And when George was all talked out, the executioners fulfilled their contract. They shot him in the head, stuffed his suety body into a 50-gallon oil drum, and buried him on an upstate farm.

The Mafia dons didn't miss George Feracco, but his last words were to haunt them for seven terror-filled years. With the information he supplied, a new gang was formed: Kidnap, Inc.

The men on his list began vanishing from the streets of New York. Some were killed, but most were held for ransom and released when it was paid. None of the victims reported what had happened to them, so police and the Mafia bosses were at first unaware of what was going on. The gang grabbed a dozen dope dealers without a word of the operations leaking out.

Emboldened by repeated success, the kidnapers decided to go after bigger game. They started stocking and grabbing Mafia capos, a sport as dangerous as it was lucrative. And not as difficult as it might seem. The captains paid cash for their freedom and kept their mouths shut for fear their bosses or the law would find out how much money they had lying around. All of the kidnaped Mafia captains were in narcotics, another fact that they didn't want publicized.

The Mafia caste system and the lack of intermob communications worked in favor of Kidnap, Inc. Family bosses confer frequently with each other and underbosses and even capos. But there's almost no communication between the generals and their troops. And the soldiers of one family have little contact with the rank-and-file of other outfits.

Even the capos and underbosses don't always tell the boss what's going on, especially in matters concerning their own personal rackets and profits. Such as the dope game.

The boss gets a share but seldom knows how much the actual importers and distributors are making.

So the kidnap gang didn't have to worry about victims calling the cops or blabbing to their bosses. The kidnaped capos sought vengeance, of course, but they tried to handle it themselves and they didn't have the slightest idea who was responsible for their humiliation.

Kidnap, Inc. was New York's first completely integrated underworld gang. It's members represented most of the city's minorities.

Most of them were stickup specialists who became acquainted in prison and eventually concluded there was much more profit in snatching Mafiosi than in heisting candy stores.

To keep their identities secret, they used their ethnic mix to best advantage. For example, black and Spanish-speaking gunman would grab Mafia members while whites bagged Negro and Puerto Rican racketeers.

One of their targets was a rich racketeer called Pizza Jake. He ran a string of pizza parlors in Manhattan and the Bronx as a legitimate front for his heroin business. The outwardly-respectable Jake lived with his wife and small son in a $75,000 home in the fashionable Pelham Gardens section of the Bronx.

Two men in dark business suits called at the house on a mild spring evening in 1966. They flashed badges and Jake quickly admitted them, not wanting the neighbors to notice that he had received a visit from the cops.

Once inside, they produced pistols, tied up the family and searched the house from cellar to attic. They found more than $20,000 worth of jewelry and furs, but they wanted cash. Jake had only a few hundred dollars on him and his wife's purse contained nothing worthwhile.

Then one of the gunmen found a steel spike and a small sledgehammer in the garage. Bringing them up to the bedroom where the family was being held, he put the spike against the frightened boy's forehead.

"We want fifty grand," the hood said. "Get it now or I'll drive this spike right through the kid's skull."

Jake didn't have $50,000—or even $500—in the house, but he said he could get it from a business associate. He made a phone call. One of the gunmen then drove him to a rendezvous with his associate while the other thug stayed with Jake's wife and child. The full $50,000 was paid without any argument and Pizza Jake's family was left unharmed.

Jake kept quiet about this unusual caper. He didn't want anyone to know how easily he could raise $50,000.

Frank Angelo, 36, known to police and the mob as Whitey Marsh, also was in the food and junk businesses. He was a silent partner in a Bronx restaurant and he looked as if he spent a lot of time consuming the output of its kitchen. His other partnership was in a wholesale heroin operation that sold drugs to dealers in New York, New Jersey, and New England.

Two men with badges picked him up on Pleasant Ave. on the night of June 11, 1966. He entered their car just three blocks from the spot where his old pal, George Feracco, began his one-way ride four years earlier. And, like George, he thought the men were detectives or federal narcotics agents. They took him to a Bronx tenement where they locked him in the basement room, pistol-whipped him, and demanded $60,000.

Whitey was permitted to phone his partner, Rudy DeLuca, who promised to raise as much of the ransom as possible. But all he could come up with was $30,000. The pickup was made outside a dress shop on Gun Hill Rd. in the Bronx.

Rudy handed a paper bag full of cash to a Kidnap, Inc. courier. Weighing the bag in his hand, the courier asked, "How much is in here?"

"Half of it," Rudy replied. "Thirty thou. It's the best I can do."

"It's not good enough," the pickup man said. "We'll tell Whitey you said so long."

A week later, the handless, headless corpse of Whitey Marsh was fished from the Hudson River in the Riverdale section of the Bronx. Divers searched the river bottom for the missing parts but failed to find them. The gang figured Whitey could not be identified without his face and fingerprints, but the Police Department's crime laboratory compared body hair from the corpse with hair found in some laundry the missing Whitey had left in his East Harlem apartment. The hairs matched perfectly.

By this time, detectives and mob bosses had begun to hear rumors that several big dope dealers had been kidnaped and some of them had been killed. According to one underworld report, Kidnap, Inc. had collected more than $500,000 in ransoms. The cops and dons became convinced the rumors were true, but they still didn't know who the kidnapers were.

In the spring of 1967, investigators got their first solid evidence to substantiate the rumors. Detectives learned that the gang had attempted to abduct Joseph (JoJo) Manfredi, a

Gambino lieutenant who was very big in the Harlem dope and gambling rackets.

Somehow, JoJo escaped. The hoodnapers then settled for one of his henchmen, Mike Luongo, 46, operator of an East Harlem gas station that was known to police as a mob hangout. The cops listed Luongo as a soldier in the Gambino mob.

Luongo left home on the night of April 24, 1967, and drove seven blocks to his social club on Pleasant Ave. near 116th St. There he played cards, drank wine, and discussed business with his friends, having a thoroughly enjoyable evening. He left the club around midnight and was walking to his car when the kidnapers got him. Witnesses saw the snatch and one of them took the unprecedented action of notifying police. Unprecedented, at least, for Pleasant Ave.

Lt. Thomas Cavanaugh of the E. 104th St. police station got the original tip and assigned detectives to keep tabs on Luongo's relatives, associates, and fellow Gambino mobsters. Through court-authorized wiretaps and informers, the cops found out that the kidnapers had contacted Luongo's nephew, Anthony, a Bronx hoodlum, and demanded $50,000 ransom. Tony was told to bring the money to a Queens bowling alley at 6 p.m. April 26.

Mike's boss, JoJo Manfredi, helped raise the ransom and accompanied Tony to the Woodhaven Bowling Lanes. Tony carried an airline bag full of cash. Several other Gambino gangsters, all of them armed, were in and around the bowling alley.

Anticipating just such a turnout, the kidnap gang also turned out in force. More than 20 detectives and federal agents added to the traffic congestion. The regular bowlers were surprised to find so many tough looking strangers there.

"The place was crawling with bowlers and hoods," one of the detectives said later. "There were about fifteen Gambino mobsters and at least 20 other hard guys, most of whom probably belonged to the kidnap gang."

"We had hoped to make an arrest, but our superiors called it off. There was nothing we could do but watch. If we had moved in, there would have been a shootout. Innocent people might have been killed."

As soon as they walked through the door, JoJo and Tony recognized some familiar police faces, so they decided to split up. JoJo mingled with some of the bowlers. He was jostled by a husky, sport-shirted man who mumbled "excuse me" and then showed him a badge.

"Give me the bag," the man said. "We'll handle the payoff. We've got the place surrounded."

Thinking the man was a cop, Tony handed him the bag. A detective who was watching Tony thought the pickup man was a federal agent. By the time anyone figured out what had happened, the man and the ransom were gone. And a few hours later Mike Luongo was back on Pleasant Ave., none the worse for his adventure.

At least six Mafiosi—all of them from the Gambino and Lucchese families—had been abducted and ransomed in the utmost secrecy. But the furor of the Luongo snatch shattered the shield of silence that had protected Kidnap, Inc. The Mafia bosses were now thoroughly alarmed. And cops and gunmen were in a deadly race to see who would catch the kidnapers first.

Gambino held an emergency conference with Tom

Eboli, the Genovese underboss. Then they offered a $50,000 reward for the identity of any one of the kidnapers.

"One is all we need," A Gambino *capo* said. "If we get one, we'll get the names of the others out of him."

Gambino's concern was understandable. He had learned that some of his most valuable officers were among the kidnap victims. But Eboli's interest was a much more puzzling matter. As far as investigators knew, no members of the Genovese clan had been snared by Kidnap, Inc.

While trying to determine how Eboli fit into the puzzle, detectives picked up the interesting rumor that Eboli himself had provided the gang's biggest score.

According to this report, two gunmen posing as cops bagged the infamous Tommy Ryan as he strolled along a Greenwich Village Street without his bodyguards. He was hustled into a car, driven uptown and held prisoner, with tape over his eyes, for about 36 hours. He was released unharmed after a whopping $100,000 dollars ransom was paid by his brother Pasquale (Patsy Ryan) Eboli.

Unwilling to turn to any of the Mafia brothers for help, because he didn't want them to know what had happened to Tommy, Patsy borrowed part of the ransom bundle from a friend who owned a large printing business and could be trusted to keep quiet.

If Eboli actually was a Kidnap, Inc. victim—and detectives who worked on the case are convinced he was—this would explain his willingness to split a $50,000 reward with Carlo Gambino.

Investigators also heard that the Tommy Ryan caper has made the kidnapers so confident that they now planned to grab Don Carlo and swap him for $1 million.

The Luongo abduction gave Eboli the excuse he needed to launch a hunt for the kidnapers. Although he was supposed to be working with Gambino, he reportedly planned to dispose of the snatch pack before the Gambino crew would get them and learn of Eboli's embarrassment.

Eboli sent one of his top guns John (Buster) Ardito, to the Bronx for a strategy session with Rocco Mazzie, a Gambino *caporegime*. Ardito and Mazzie had a lot in common. Both were convicted dope dealers and we're still active in the narco trade.

Mazzie then had nine arrests to his credit and five convictions, including a 12-year sentence for his part in the international dope-smuggling syndicate run by Vito Genovese.

By this time, Ardito and Mazzie had heard all the rumors about Kidnap, Inc. They knew most of the victims were fellow junk merchants and they planned to question those who were still around, hoping to find some clues that might lead them to the elusive gang.

At their meeting, in the back room of a small restaurant, they talked about catching and killing the kidnapers. Ardito said his men were ready "as soon as we get the okay from the Commission."

"We already got it," Mazzie replied. "It came from downtown."

Gambino, now running the Commission, had authorized the search-and-destroy mission. But finding the hoodnapers proved a difficult chore for both the law and the lawless.

Nearly a year after Mike Luongo was kidnaped, he was summoned before a New York County Grand Jury and questioned about his experience. Assistant District Attorney Nicholas Scoppetta asked him:

"Mr. Luongo, were you told by those people who kidnaped you that you were kidnaped because of your connection with Joseph Manfredi and the fact that they knew you and Manfredi could raise that kind of money because of Manfredi's gambling and narcotics operations?"

Mike refused to answer.

He was asked if he knew "that the same persons who kidnaped you attempted to kidnap Joseph Manfredi before they kidnaped you."

Mike refused to answer. He also declined to answer 20 other questions about the case. His nephew, Tony, Manfredi and Mazzie also refused to talk on grounds of possible self-incrimination. But Mazzie conceded that he discussed the kidnapings of Mike Luongo and another mobster with Buster Ardito.

Ask if he hadn't suggested sending out Mafia execution squads to track down and liquidate the kidnapers, Mazzie squirmed uneasily in the witness chair and mumbled: "I might have said that people who do those things ought to be killed."

Eventually, some of them were. The first to exit were ex-cons Clarence Eugene Christian and Walter Allen (Butch) Hooker. The two blacks had served time for assault and robbery, and they had been sharing an apartment in the Bronx.

Their bodies were found December 23, 1968 inside a Ford station wagon parked on a quiet residential section of Westchester County just north of the New York City border. Both men had been shot through the head.

Solving the double bumpoff wasn't the official problem

of Westchester authorities, but the case was of more than routine interest to Bronx detectives investigating Kidnap, Inc. They learned that Christian and Hooker had been flashing thick bankrolls and had boasted of "grabbing Mafia guys."

"We got the Mafia running scared," Christian reportedly told a friend. "We tell the Italians 'Pay or die.' They understand that kind of talk."

Convinced that the two ex-cons were part of the kidnap gang and that the Mafia had caught up with them, the cops waited for more bodies to turn up. But no related murders took place in the next few days, so the detectives concluded Christian and Hooker were killed by their own gang because they had become too talkative.

Four months later, the kidnapers made what proved to be a fatal mistake. They grabbed the wrong man. His name, Richard Lawrence, was on the original kidnap list, but since it was made up he had served a prison term and had stopped selling heroin.

Lawrence was walking along E. 169th St. in the Bronx one April evening in 1969 when a miniskirted young woman beckoned to him from a doorway. Rising to this obvious bait, he followed the girl into a dark tenement hallway where he found two men waiting. They used the same old snatch trick—guns and badges—and whisked him away in a 1968 Oldsmobile. He was taken to a Bronx apartment, tied to a chair, and told he'd be dead within 24 hours unless he raised $50,000.

"Are you kidding?" Lawrence demanded. "I couldn't even raise five-hundred dollars as I'm not in the rackets anymore. Ask anyone in my neighborhood. They'll tell you I'm straight now."

One of the kidnapers, a small, dapper white man, made a few phone calls and found Lawrence was telling the truth. The second hood, a muscular young Negro, then pressed the muzzle of a .38 revolver against Lawrence's right ear.

"If he hasn't got any bread," the gunman said, "there's no use wasting our time. I'll hit him now."

"No, Jimmy," his boss replied. "Let him live. He could be worth a lot of money to us."

In exchange for his life, Lawrence supplied the names of several affluent dope dealers and agreed to find other victims for the gang. He was warned that he'd be killed if he failed to keep his part of the bargain.

Lawrence decided the only way out of this mess was to tell police what had happened. He contacted Bronx detectives who were investigating the mob kidnapings and agreed to help them set a trap.

Then he notified the kidnapers that a big-time racketeer from the West Coast was coming to New York to sell heroin to local distributors. "I'll let you know as soon as he arrives," Lawrence promised.

Detective Lt. Pasquale (Pat) Intrieri and Detective Delmar (Scotty) Watson, posing as the racketeer and his bodyguard, checked into the Bronx-Whitestone Motel, overlooking the Whitestone Bridge across the East River, on the morning of May 13. Both men wore expensive clothes and did their best to act like movie mobsters. Intrieri sported a pinky ring that looked like a four-carat diamond but was actually a dimestore sparkler. Husky, red-haired Watson had a revolver conspicuously stuck in his waistband.

Even more conspicuous was their curvaceous companion, a blond lady cop 5 feet 9 inches tall and 38-24-36 around. In the motel bar that night, the statuesque sexpot and her tough-looking free-spending escorts were the center of attention. Intrieri tossed a $100 bill at the bartender and ordered 12-year-old Chivas Regal for himself and his friends.

Two men entered the bar around 9 p.m., looked around a bit too casually and found stools near Intrieri. They were close enough to hear him and Watson discuss the "really big deal" they supposedly had completed that day.

Without mentioning narcotics, Intrieri bragged that he had sold something for a lot of money. He and Watson dropped names of underworld figures in the dope trade and they appeared to be getting drunk.

At 9:30, Intrieri got up unsteadily and told Watson to come with him to their suite "to see if we got any more customers." The blonde remained at the bar. The two eavesdroppers left a few minutes later.

Intrieri and Watson waited in their suite with the door unlocked and slightly ajar. A dozen other detectives, wearing bulletproof vests and armed with shotguns and rifles, were in the rooms on either side of the two-bedroom suite and across the hall. When no one showed up within 15 minutes, Intrieri decided to go out to the rear parking lot—a perfect spot for an ambush.

"We're going in back," he whispered into a hidden microphone. "Start the roadblocks."

As soon as Intrieri and Watson stepped through a back door leading to the parking lot, they were seized by three men who poked pistols against their backs. One of the men reached inside Watson's coat and yanked the revolver from his waistband, but a quick frisk failed to disclose the guns the cops were wearing inside their pants.

Intrieri and Watson were shoved into the back of a Chevrolet sedan parked a few feet from the motel exit. One of the gunmen got in with them and the other two sat in front.

The detectives were relieved to see that the man in the back seat with them was Dick Lawrence. But they couldn't be certain that Lawrence, who had already doublecrossed Kidnap, Inc., might not doublecross them, too.

The gunmen in the front seat were Stanley Emmett Tuttle, 40, a stickup specialist with a long record of arrests and convictions, and Frank Rivetti, 39, who had served time for assault and robbery. Tuttle drove while Rivetti kept his pistol trained on Intrieri and Watson. As they pulled out of the parking lot, a 1968 Oldsmobile followed the Chevy.

The two cars rolled along a road that curves under the Whitestone Bridge. The Chevrolet started around the curve. Suddenly, the darkness ahead changed into a wall of blinding light. Headlights were switched on in six police cars that were blocking the road and facing the kidnaped car.

"Christ, look at this," Tuttle shouted. Rivetti swung around to see what was happening. As soon as Rivetti's attention was diverted from the back seat, Lawrence handed Watson the revolver taken from the detective's waistband. Intrieri pulled a concealed gun from his trousers.

"It's a trap!" Tuttle screamed. "Kill them! Kill them!"

He tramped on the gas pedal and roared straight at the roadblock. Rivetti turned towards the back seat and started shooting. The detectives shot him twice in the head, killing him instantly. Tuttle was hit three times, in the head, shoulder and leg; but he survived. Police at the roadblock shot out the Chevy's front tires and it skidded, spun around and stopped just short of the barricade.

The Oldsmobile stopped about 100 feet behind the Chevy. And it was Anthony (The Shrimp) LaSorsa, a tiny thug with a Napoleon complex. He was the founder and boss of Kidnap, Inc. And when the headlights went on, he thought he had driven into a Mafia ambush.

LaSorsa swung the Olds off the road and down a grassy embankment to a river front parking area used primarily as a rendezvous for lovers. And a lot of them were there that night.

Several policemen raced after LaSorsa, firing as they drove. The lovers suddenly found themselves in the midst of a shooting gallery. LaSorsa zigzagged around several parked cars, his brakes screaming. Then he stopped the Olds, jumped out with a pistol in his small fist and dived headfirst into the open rear window of a car whose front seat was amorously occupied.

"The mob's after me!" he yelled at the startled couple. "Get me out of here!"

The driver and his companion left the river retreat with LaSorsa squatting on the car floor to avoid detection. They drove him over the Whitestone Bridge to Queens, then back over the East River via the Triboro Bridge to Manhattan, where they dropped him off at 125th St. and Lexington Ave.

Still shaking from their ordeal the couple told police what had happened. They were asked to look at police photos of criminals who matched the gang leader's description and *modus operandi*. After studying scores of mugshots, the couple identified a picture of LaSorsa. Lawrence confirmed this identification.

When they gave the story to the press, police officials

announced they were looking for LaSorsa. And as soon as the papers hit the newsstands, Gambino gunmen also started looking for him.

Realizing there was no place he could hide now that he was known to the Mafia, the maverick mobster phoned Lt. Intrieri and said he wanted to surrender. Intrieri and Detective Watson picked him up at a Bronx cemetery. Whether he knew it or not, the surrender spot chosen by the boss of Kidnap, Inc. was the place where the ransom money was paid in the historic Lindbergh kidnap case 37 years earlier.

LaSorsa, 5 feet 2 and 120 pounds, had never belonged to any of the city's crime families although he had performed several jobs for Mafia members. He hated the gangsters who made fun of his size and tossed him a few crumbs from the Cosa Nostra table. After a stretch in prison, he formed his own gang and made the Mafia pay. And pay. And pay.

Sentenced to a long prison term for abducting the cops, he was placed in a maximum security cell to protect him from gangland wrath.

"Kidnap, Inc. was the only gang that Carlo Gambino feared," a detective who worked on the case said recently. "Now it's Tony LaSorsa's turn to be terrified. He knows the mob is determined to get him—in or out of prison."

All of the original Kidnap, Inc. members wound up dead or in jail but their *modus operandi* was so successful that it was bound to be imitated by other daring schemers.

Three years after the law put LaSorsa and Co. out of business, another kidnap gang was formed for the specific purpose of abducting relatives of top Mafiosi and holding them for ransom. The new gang considered several likely prospects, including the son of a wealthy dope distributor, and finally chose Emanuel (Manny) Gambino, 29-year-old nephew of Don Carlo and the black sheep of the clan.

Manny, son of Carlo's kid brother Joe, was not the don's favorite nephew. He had done several things to irritate the old man.

He reportedly pocketed more than his share of the profits from the family's Blue Star meat market, in which he was a junior partner. He also had mismanaged gambling and loansharking rackets which had been placed under his supervision. According to the underworld grapevine, he had loaned out nearly $1 million in family funds to tough customers who either couldn't or wouldn't repay the loans.

The last straw, so far as Don Carlo was concerned, came when Manny announced that he wanted to divorce his wife and marry his latest girl friend, a curvy blonde model. The Don was aghast. Although keeping a mistress was standard mob practice, it was unthinkable for a Mafioso, even a minor one like Manny, to expose his family to the spotlight of divorce proceedings.

"No divorce," Don Carlo ruled.

Soon after this setback to his plans, Manny disappeared.

He phoned his girl friend's apartment on May 18, 1972. She wasn't home so he left a message with her mother, saying he was going to New Jersey to meet a man named Bob. Then he left his house in the Flushing section of Queens and drove off in his Cadillac.

Next day, his wife received a phone call from a man who said Manny had been kidnaped and would be killed unless $350,000 ransom was paid. Don Carlo authorized payment, but the instructions for delivery of the money were misunderstood.

The caller told the family to leave the ransom at the Molly Pitcher service center on the New Jersey Turnpike near Hightstown. Instead, Manny's father brought the bundle to the Molly Pitcher Inn in Red Bank, N.J.

Several elderly ladies were sitting in the lobby of the inn when Joe Gambino and two sinister-looking companions entered and took over the phones, expecting a call from the kidnapers. They carried suitcases containing $350,000 and two religious pictures—a mob message that the kidnapers wouldn't live to spend the money.

Joe and his companions waited more than an hour, but the call never came so they took the money home. The ransom negotiations were resumed a few days later. Manny's wife, Diane, received a letter which said in part: "If you want him back alive this is your last chance. If he dies, the killer will be you for not paying."

Also in the envelope was a photo of Diane which Manny always carried in his wallet. Diane notified Don Carlo of the letter and he told her to report the kidnaping to the FBI. This was done on May 24. Meanwhile, after considerable haggling and telephone negotiations with the kidnapers, the family had succeeded in reducing the ransom to $40,000.

The money was placed in a sack. At 1 a.m. May 25, Manny's brother, Tom, threw the sack from his car near a gas station on New Jersey's Palisades Parkway. As soon as he drove away, three men in a rented van picked up the bag. On their way home to the pickup site, they had been stopped by a parkway patrolman because the van had a defective rear light.

FBI agents watched the pickup but did not try to

apprehend the kidnapers for fear that premature arrests would endanger Manny's life.

When Manny failed to materialize after the ransom was paid, the search was intensified by both G-men and Gambino gunmen. The FBI picked up a rumor that Manny staged his own kidnaping in order to raise money for a getaway with his girl friend. But she was still around and she told investigators: "If Manny ran off, it certainly wasn't with me."

Manny's Cadillac was left in a parking lot at Newark Airport on May 30 by a person unknown. A parking attendant glanced into the car three days later and saw what appeared to be bloodstains on the front and rear seats. He called police.

Laboratory tests proved the stains were indeed human blood. But there was no record of Manny's blood type, so it could not be determined whether the blood was his.

Seven months after he disappeared, the FBI accused four men of kidnaping him. The suspects were identified as Henry Robert Sentner, a businessman and a compulsive gambler; William Joseph Solin, a Harvard graduate and former CIA agent; John Edmond Kilcullen, a nightclub bouncer; and John Peter Harrington, a nightclub maître d'.

Sentner, of Sea Girt, N.J., was described as the mastermind of the kidnap plot. He ran a mail-order business and had a contract for the manufacture, distribution and sale of National Football League pennants, dolls and other souvenirs. He made a lot of money and blew it all betting on horses and sporting events. To pay his bookies, he borrowed from sharks and at one point was $780,000 in debt to various racketeers.

FBI agents said Sentner rented the van used to pick up the $40,000 ransom and also left a fingerprint in Manny's abandoned car. Papers filed by the FBI in Federal Court said Sentner took about $23,000 of the ransom money and promptly squandered it. He reportedly gave $5,000 to Kilcullen, $2,500 to Solin and $1,000 dollars to Harrington. What happened to the rest of the money was not explained.

The court papers said Sentner admitted that he "devised a scheme to make a sum of money by kidnaping someone prominent in the underworld, with the idea that organized crime figures would be forced to pay a ransom and not go to authorities for help."

The kidnapers never dreamed Carlo would seek assistance from his old foe, the FBI.

Eight months after Manny disappeared, the FBI received a tip that his body was buried in a garbage dump near the Pearl Ammunition Depot in Colts Neck Township, N.J. Several G-men went there on Jan. 26, 1973, and started digging. At 2:35 p.m., they found a partially decomposed body buried four feet down in a sitting position.

The corpse was later identified as Manny Gambino. He had been shot once in the head. As this is written, it has not been determined whether the murder will be punished by the law or Manny's family. But it is a safe prediction that someone will pay.

The rough-and-scrabble village of Caccamo. This is the province in Palermo, Sicily where Carlo Gambino was born.

Vito Cascio Ferro, circa early-1900s. Cascio Ferro was mob chieftain of Sicily during Carlo Gambino's childhood. Gambino idolized Cascio Ferro and joined the latter's Mafia family while still in his early-teens.

Giuseppe "Joe the Boss" Masseria (left) and Salvatore Maranzano (right), the leading Mafia bosses in New York City during Prohibition. Both men wanted to be capo di tutti capi (boss of bosses), and fought each other in the "Castellammarese War," a bloody skirmish for control over New York City's bourgeoning liquor trade.

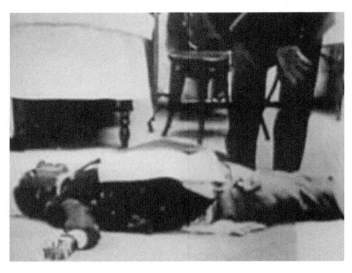

Joe "the Boss" Masseria lies dead on the ground at Scar-
pato's Restaurant, in Coney Island, N.Y., after being
set up by his underboss, Charlie "Lucky" Luciano.
Luciano conspired with Masseria's arch rival, Salva-
tore Maranzano, and agreed to lead Masseria into an
ambush from which Masseria did not emerge alive.

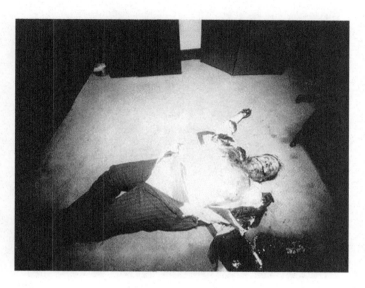

Salvatore Maranzano is murdered in his office on orders of Charlie "Lucky" Luciano, just five months after Luciano killed Maranzano's predecessor, Joe "the Boss" Masseria. The deaths of Masseria and Maranzano propelled Luciano to the number one spot in La Cosa Nostra's hierarchy.

Charlie "Lucky" Luciano, circa 1930s. After eliminating Mafia chiefs Giuseppe "Joe the Boss" Masseria and Salvatore Maranzano, Luciano did away with the title of capo di tutti capi (boss of bosses) and replaced it, instead, with a national crime syndicate called "The Commission." The Commission consisted of a board of directors made up of the heads of the nation's top Mafia families. Luciano presided as chairman of the board, and as a result of this more "corporate" and "democratic" structure, violence in the underworld was contained, while profits were maximized.

Vincent Mangano, circa 1920s. Vincent Mangano was the boss of the Mangano Family (today known as the Gambino Crime Family). Originally appointed by Lucky Luciano, Mangano was killed by his underboss, Albert Anastasia, in 1951, as Anastasia vied for control of the family's top spot.

Albert Anastasia leaving court, circa early 1950s (top), and Anastasia lying dead on the floor of the Park Sheraton Hotel Barbershop, circa 1957 (bottom). What comes around goes around. Just as Anastasia killed his boss, Vincent Mangano, to take over the Mangano Family, Anastasia himself was ultimately murdered by his own underling, Carlo Gambino. Gambino assumed, and maintained, control of the family's affairs until his death from natural causes in 1976.

A young Carlo Gambino, circa 1930s. Gambino first made a name for himself in the underworld as an unprecedented earner. Following the repeal of prohibition, Gambino obtained a monopoly on the untaxed liquor market in the northeast. Soon after, Gambino cornered the ration stamp business by acquiring and selling government-issued ration stamps on the black market. From these scores he made millions of dollars, money which he reinvested in legitimate operations, such as pizza parlors and other restaurants; nightclubs; meat market producers; trucking conglomerates; waste management companies; labor consulting firms; Wall Street brokerages; real estate development concerns; and clothes manufacturing warehouses, to name a few.

Carlo Gambino's most disarming weapon—both in his youth (top, circa 1930s) and in his old age (bottom, circa 1970s)—was a fawning grin. Unlike many of his mob contemporaries, Gambino rarely used violence to settle underworld disputes. He preferred using courtesy and diplomacy. "He doesn't look or act like a gangster," people often observed. But he thought like one. Behind Gambino's warm and charming exterior lay a dark pit of guile, an utterly ruthless personality that would do anything (or, do away with anyone) to expand his power and wealth.

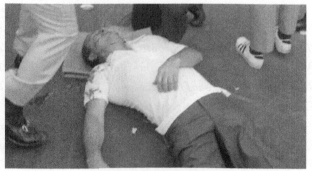

Two prominent underworld figures who incurred Gambino's wrath were Joseph Colombo, boss of the Colombo Family (top row, circa 1970s), and Colombo's underling, Joseph "Crazy Joe" Gallo (bottom row, circa 1970s). With Machiavellian brilliance, Gambino pitted the mob soldier, Gallo, against his own boss, Colombo. As chairman of The Commission, Gambino gave Gallo permission to whack the publicity-seeking Colombo during the Italian-American Civil Rights League rally of June 1971. Once the deed was done, Gambino then had the volatile and unpredictable Joe Gallo murdered, following the latter's birthday celebration at Umberto's Clam House in Little Italy, in April of 1972. Thus, with a mere smile and a nod, Gambino was able to rid La Cosa Nostra of two unruly members whose deliberate actions threatened to ruin the borgata as a whole.

Carlo Gambino attending his wife, Katherine Gambino's, funeral circa 1971 (left), and Gambino's mausoleum at St. John's Cemetery, in Queens, N.Y. (right). Gambino's health decelerated quickly after his wife's passing. He died a mere five years later, in 1976, of natural causes. But his legacy lives on. The Sicilian Horatio Alger, Gambino came to America penniless and powerless, and rose to a position of dominance in his chosen field, while accumulating immense wealth and influence along the way. A classic rags-to-riches tale, Gambino's story embodies the unencumbered, ruthless pursuit of the American Dream. Perhaps that is why his memory—and his progeny, The Gambino Family—still endures today.

CHAPTER 7

THE DOPE DEALERS

DOPE IS A FOUR-LETTER WORD that Mafia dons seldom use. In the Cosa Nostra caste system, drug pushers are the Untouchables, lowest of the low. No Brahmin Mafioso would dirty his carefully manicured hands on them. Still, the dope dealers are very much part of the mob structure. The Untouchables sell what the Brahmins import.

The narcotics racket is the Syndicates No. 2 moneymaker, exceeded only by gambling revenues.

The thought that pushers might attempt to prey on his grandchildren and godchildren is as abhorrent to Carlo Gambino as it would be to any other concerned senior citizen. Though some of his best friends have been deeply involved in the drug traffic that has wrecked the lives of millions of Americans, Gambino has seemed as shocked as his neighbors when the problem hit close to home.

One story often told in New York's Italian communities concerns an unhappy woman whose teenage son had become hooked on heroin. She found out that he purchased the stuff at a candy store on Myrtle Ave. in the Fort Greene section of Brooklyn. The woman complained to the local precinct and the store supposedly was placed under surveillance, but the owner was not arrested.

Neighborhood junkies continued to congregate there. Finally, in desperation, the woman contacted a relative who was a soldier in the Gambino organization. He arranged an appointment with Don Carlo.

After listening carefully to the woman's complaint, the don smiled a comforting, compassionate smile and told her: "Don't worry. Everything will be alright."

Next day, when the hopheads gathered for their after-school fix, they found the candy store closed. The owner never returned. No one in the neighborhood knew for sure what had happened to him, but they had some interesting theories.

The law also holds some interesting theories about Carlo Gambino and the narcotics racket. One investigative report, dated January 31, 1958, has this to say:

"The Gambino brothers (Carlo and Paul) were reported to exercise control over the narcotics smuggling activities between Mafia elements in Palermo and the United States, on behalf of Salvatore Lucania (Lucky Luciano). During 1948 both Gambino brothers met with Lucania at the home of their relatives in Palermo.

"Investigation conducted by the Bureau of Narcotics, after some 30 odd Sicilian aliens had been smuggled into the United States aboard the S/S *Pamormus* at the Port of Philadelphia in May 1948, disclosed that Carlo Gambino was involved in the smuggling of these aliens and that some of the aliens, in turn, had been smuggling substantial quantities of heroin into the United States as payment for being brought in the country."

Testimony before the Senate Investigations Subcommittee disclosed that all five New York crime families were in the dope business, especially the gang headed by Gambino's pal, Three-Finger Brown. Commissioner Henry L. Giordano of the U.S. Bureau of Narcotics told the committee in 1964 that the bureau had obtained narcotics convictions against 40 percent of Lucchese's members and 20 percent of Gambino's men.

John F. Shanley, then chief of the New York City Police Department's Central Investigations Bureau, gave the Senate crime committee his rundown on the Gambino crew:

"There are (an average of) six arrests for each man. There is one arrest out of every five men for homicide, on an average. Three out of every four have been arrested at least once for dangerous weapons. One out of every three has been arrested at least once for narcotics. Two out of five have been arrested for felonious assault."

Carlo's long-time underboss, Joseph (Joe Banty) Biondo, who retired in 1965, was in charge of the family's drug division. He was one of the biggest heroin importers in the United States and dealt directly with the heads of the international narcotics trade.

During the 1920s and early 1930s, narcotics traffic in the U.S. was controlled mainly by Jewish criminal organizations like the Bugs & Meyer mob. The Mafia moved in when Prohibition ended and the bootlegging routes became part of a nationwide dope-distribution network.

Nicole Gentile, a high-ranking Mafioso, traveled from

New York to Cleveland, Detroit, Chicago, Kansas City, New Orleans, Miami and other cities "in pursuit of a scheme involving a large-scale distribution of heroin throughout the United States."

Before this plan could be fully activated, Gentile was arrested in New York. He jumped bail and fled to Italy in 1938. Then World War II stopped the flow of heroin to the U.S. from Europe. When the war ended, Gentile resumed his business dealings with the opium suppliers of the Middle East and the heroin factories of Italy and Marseilles, France.

Several other major dope dealers were departed to Italy after the war, including Lucky Luciano, Frank (Chick 99) Callace and Dominick (Dom the Gap) Petrillo. According to a U.S. Senate report titled "Organized Crime and Illicit Traffic in Narcotics," this is what happened:

"During the early post-war period, this group impressed upon Mafia elements in Sicily and in Italy the fact that they had ready outlets for heroin in the United States and that considerable profits were available to those engaging in this traffic.

"It was not long before, through the influence of Salvatore Lucania (Lucky Luciano), there were formed agreements between these traffickers and certain corrupt officials of a number of Italian pharmaceutical firms in northern Italy. These firms had been formed by the Italian government to manufacture heroin for medicinal purposes."

Assured of a steady supply of heroin from the government-sponsored drug factories, Luciano envisioned an American dope market even bigger than the Prohibition booze boom. And he invited his old friend, Carlo Gambino, to get in on the ground floor.

The alchemistic urge to turn flowers into gold was strong enough to bring Carlo home to Sicily, even though he knew he would be barred from returning to the U.S. if American immigration authorities learned of the trip. Accompanied by brother Paul and carrying a forged passport, he drove to Canada and boarded a freighter bound for Palermo. There, he conferred with Lucky and Gentile about reactivating the old plan for a cross-country chain of drug outlets.

Carlo's secret visit to Sicily in 1948 was his first and last trip outside the U.S. since he jumped ship at Norfolk as a youth. He returned to New York the same way he departed.

He later sent his right-hand man, Joe Banty, to Italy for further discussions on the new business venture. Biondo always carried a suitcase full of cash to pay Lucky his share of the profits from completed transactions and to purchase fresh supplies.

On one such trip, in 1951, American narcotics agents tailed Banty around Italy. They observed him dinning with Lucky in Naples, sipping espresso with Gentile at a sidewalk café in Palermo and touring Roman night spots with deported dope dealers Chick 99 Callace, Dom the Gap Petrillo, and Giuseppe Pici.

Soon after Biondo returned to New York, Italian police seized Callace at the Rome International Airport as he was about to board a flight to New York with three kilos of heroin in his suitcase. He was murdered in New York three years later.

In the directorate of the Gambino crime organization, Biondo was the vice president in charge of narcotics importation and distribution. Among the executives who worked directly under him and supervised operations of the drug division were Rocco Mazzie, Frank Scalise, Michele Giacomo Scarpulla, Vincent Squillante and Steve Armone, all listed by the Justice Department as Gambino captains.

Soldiers Joseph (JoJo) Manfredi, Andy Alberti and Joseph Armone (Steve's brother) also were big dope dealers. Federal reports have this to say about the men in charge of the drug division:

BIONDO: "An international drug trafficker who is up among the highest echelon members of the Mafia in New York City."

STEVE ARMONE (deceased): "Engaged in large-scale narcotics smuggling and wholesale distribution for many years."

SCARPULLA: "High-ranking Mafioso, key member of the large-scale narcotics smuggling ring formerly headed by his brother-in-law, the late Francesco Scalici," also known as Frank Scalise or Don Cheech.

MAZZIE: "A wholesale dealer in narcotics who has supplied many important traffickers throughout the United States."

SQUILLANTE (deceased): "Top racketeer who financed narcotics smuggling ventures."

ALBERTI: "Makes trips to Italy in connection with narcotics smuggling operations and constitutes a major source of supply for wholesale dealers in New York."

JOE ARMONE: "A dangerous hoodlum, he took over the narcotics smuggling organization formally headed by his brother Steve."

MANFREDI: "A major importer and distributer of narcotics."

Rocco Mazzie was sentenced to 12 years in federal prison on April 3, 1959, as a member of a multi-million-dollar dope ring with branches in Europe, Cuba, Puerto Rico, Mexico and all over the United States. This ring supposedly was headed by Vito Genovese, but all five families shared the proceeds.

A few minutes after 6 p.m. on Sunday, October 2, 1969, a dignified little man stepped off a jetliner that had just arrived at New York International Airport from Paris. He was Dr. Mauricio Rosal Broz, Guatemalan Ambassador to the Netherlands, Belgium and Luxembourg. Because he was a diplomat, his six heavy leather suitcases were whisked through Customs without inspection.

Federal agents were expecting him. They trailed him to a swank hotel on the East Side of Manhattan and they were watching next day when he received a visitor, Etienne Tarditi, a Paris electronics dealer and exporter of narcotics. Tarditi conferred with him a few minutes, then left.

Rosal checked out of the hotel room around noon, October 3. His bags were placed in the trunk of a taxi that took him to 76th St. between 3rd and Lexington Aves. There he met Tarditi and two other men, Charles Bourbonnais and Nicholas Calamaras.

Calamaras was a pickup man for the Gambino drug division. Bourbonnais, an airline purser, was a courier who was to deliver the money to the dope suppliers in France.

As they started to transfer Rosal's suitcases from the taxi to Calamaras station wagon, narcotics and customs agents swarmed from a panel truck parked nearby and arrested them at gunpoint. The suitcases contained 115 pounds of pure heroin, worth nearly $20 million when cut and peddled to addicts. Largest heroin haul ever made in this country to that date, it was five times more than the previous record seizure.

Rosal and Calamaras each were sentenced to 15 in prison (the ambassador claimed diplomatic immunity, but didn't get it because he wasn't accredited in the U.S.); Bourbonnais and Tarditi drew 9-year terms.

Although Gambino was not mentioned in this case, investigators said his narcotics executives were the intended recipients of the shipment. A federal report states: "Calamaras had succeeded one Joseph Cahill as pickup man for New York City racketeers. Investigation has developed that both Cahill and Calamaras are closely associated with Joseph Armone, who has taken over the criminal activities of his brother, Steve Armone, since the latter's death on June 20, 1960.

"The criminal activities of the Armone group are headed by Joseph Biondo. Also associated with Armone and working under Biondo in the distribution of heroin is Andrew Alberti, an important (dope) trafficker."

On December 28, 1960 Cahill was arrested at his home in Franklin Sq., L.I. in connection with another large heroin shipment from France. Investigators learned that the Cahill house on Daffodil St. was actually owned by Biondo.

Armone, Cahill and 10 other racketeers later were indicted by a federal grand jury as members of an international dope ring that's smuggled a ton of heroin worth around $400 million on the addict market, into the U.S. during a five-year period.

Five years later, the French connection was cut again. Two Corsican gangsters from Marseille flew to New York to discuss a big dope deal with Miami mobsters Frank (Frankie Dio) Dioguardi, brother of notorious labor racketeer Johnny Dio, and Anthony Sutera.

The Corsicans checked into Manhattan's Americana Hotel. Narcotics agents rented the next room and used an electronic eavesdropping device to listen to the dope dealers' conversations.

A week later, the narcs raided a trailer park at Columbus, Ga. In the trailer home of a U.S. Army warrant officer, his wife and two children, they found six suitcases stuffed with plastic bags containing 209 pounds of pure heroin.

The dope had been shipped from France in the lining of a freezer that was among the soldier's household belongings when he was transferred from Europe to Georgia. Dio, Sutera, the French Corsicans and a retired U.S. Army major who arranged the freezer shipment were sentenced to long prison terms.

This investigation blocked the main-line route from Miami, where the drugs were to be delivered, to New York, the intended ultimate destination. Subsequent raids by police and feds smashed heroin distribution centers in New Orleans, New York and other cities along the Eastern seaboard. Millions of dollars worth of drugs were removed from the addict market. A global smuggling operation, stretching from Asia, Turkey and North Africa to Italy and France and then to North and South America, was seriously damaged.

As Tom Lucchese lay near death from a brain tumor, his narcotics network was falling apart. It was up to Carlo Gambino to salvage as much as possible. Then another urgent matter arose.

Early in September 1966, Louisiana state troopers and U.S. Treasury agents joined forces for an unexpected and unprecedented assault on the rackets bastion of Carlos Marcello. They raided a dozen gambling joints in St. John the Baptists Parish, north of New Orleans, and confiscated 50 slot machines and other gambling paraphernalia.

Several Marcello henchmen were arrested but Sheriff Percy Hebert refused to admit them to the local lockup. He turned them loose. The troopers rounded them up again next day, with a court order for their arrests.

Marcello demanded their immediate release. The judge who signed the arrest order turned down his imperious request. So Carlos called up an important Louisiana politician, who informed him: "I'm afraid there's not much I can do. This is a federal matter."

Carlos knew all about federal harassment. Like Gambino, he was an illegal alien who had proved impossible to deport. The Immigration Service was so frustrated in its efforts to oust him that it finally picked him up, put him on a plane and deposited him in Guatemala. But he sneaked back to Louisiana aboard a shrimp boat a few weeks later and since then had been unbudgeable.

The Mighty Mouse of Dixie, he ran all the rackets in Louisiana and adjoining stretches of Mississippi and Texas. And he had given orders to two generations of Louisiana office-holders, from senators and governors on down.

The raid on his gambling dens was a minor thing, but to Carlos it had major implications. He figured it was part of a federal campaign against the Mafia and it's dope and gambling rackets.

So Marcello made a phone call to New York and the

man who received his message related it to Gambino, who represented the Southern families as well as his own on the Mafia commission.

A few days later, Marcello flew to New York with three companions and Santo Trafficante, Mafia boss of Florida, flew in from Tampa. They all got together on the afternoon of September 22 in a private basement room at La Stella Restaurant in the Borough of Queens. 13 nattily-attired Mafiosi attended the meeting.

Waiters shoved four tables together and loaded them with Italian delicacies and bottles of vintage wine bearing the black rooster symbol of excellent quality. The diners included: Carlo Gambino, his new underboss, Aniello Dellacroce, and his *capo* in charge of gambling enterprises, Joseph N. Gallo (no relation to the wild Gallo Brothers of Brooklyn);

Joe Colombo, boss of the old Profaci mob;

Tom Eboli, underboss and heir apparent to Vito Genovese; his counselor, Mike Miranda, and family soldiers Dominick (Cokey Dom) Alongi and Anthony (Tony the Sheik) Corillo;

Santo Trafficante, Carlos Marcello, his brother, Joe Marcello, and New Orleans gangsters Frank Gagliano and Anthony Carollo.

They were deep in clam sauce and conversation when detectives broke up the banquet. The well-heeled hoods, none of whom had less than $600 cash on him were arrested on charges of consorting with known criminals—each other. After a night in civil jail, they were released on bail totaling $1.3 million.

Queens district Attorney Nat Hentel called the

luncheon meeting "bigger than Apalachin." And though this was untrue, it was obvious that the mobsters had more on their minds than the seizure of Marcello's slot machines.

Marcello believed the raids on his gambling dens were connected to narcotics crackdowns in New Orleans, Atlanta, Tampa and Miami. He felt the Treasury and Justice Department had picked the South as the target for a concerted drive on gambling and dope-dealing. If this campaign succeeded, other parts of the U.S. would be similarly slammed.

Trafficante thought this analysis was correct. A suspect in a string of Florida murderers, Trafficante had long been active in gambling and narcotics operations in the Sunshine State. He had run Havana gambling casinos until Fidel Castro shut them down. His partners in Cuban gambling included Carlos Marcello, Aniello Dellacroce, and Mike Miranda.

There were four mob bosses (Gambino, Colombo, Marcello and Trafficante) at the La Stella sitdown, two underbosses and a consigliere. All the others were gambling and narcotics specialists.

The fathers of Marcello lieutenants Anthony Carollo and Frank Gagliano both were deported to Italy for narcotics offenses and their sons literally grew up in the dope trade.

Besides discussing the federal moves against gambling and drugs, the rackets rulers considered what to do about the narcotics industry founded and still owned by the dying Lucchese. He was Don Carlo's oldest and closest friend. But business was business.

"They were there to divide and reorganize Lucchese's empire, not to name his successor," a police intelligence officer said. "Lucchese was the genius of the dope traffic. He set up the routes and the courier systems."

The organizational wizard known as Three-Finger Brown finally died in July 1967 at his palatial seaside home in Lido Beach, L.I. No details of the funeral were made public, but detectives and FBI men showed up to take pictures of the mourners.

Gambino continued to run the Lucchese Family along with his own, taking care to put Lucchese lieutenants in key posts to ensure their loyalty. And when Vito Genovese's hard heart gave out 19 months later in the Federal prison hospital at Springfield, Mo., Don Carlo inherited the title to match the power he already held.

Capo di tutti capi.

The title was unofficial, but understood by all the mobs. As Joe Valachi once explained: "They eliminated the boss of bosses, but Vito Genovese is a boss of all bosses under the table." And now it was Gambino's thing.

He exercised direct control over two of the five New York families—his own and Lucchese's—and indirect control over two others, headed by Gambino-appointed bosses Joe Colombo and Paul Sciacca.

His underboss, Aniello Dellacroce, had considerable influence with the Genovese clan, as did Gambino himself.

The two Genovese underbosses, Jerry Catena and Tom Eboli, were so busy watching each other that they had neither the time nor the inclination to buck Don Carlo. When Gambino made a suggestion, they went along.

There was no one left with enough muscle seriously to challenge Don Carlo. His friends were everywhere, in executive positions in all the mobs. He was surrounded by his palace guard of faithful old retainers and relatives, the family within the family.

"Most of his life is spent dealing with other people's concerns," says a man who has known him casually for several years. "The little people as well as the big guys come to him for help. He's like a cardinal of the church."

He commands and receives the respect due the honorable head of the Honored Society. Even the cops and prosecutors and FBI men treat him with deference. But his family is still in the dope business.

And that's one reason why the Manfredi cousins, Phillip J. and Philip D., aren't around anymore.

The two Phils were nephews of JoJo Manfredi, Gambino lieutenant and drug racketeer who had figured in the police probe of Kidnap, Inc. Both in their early 20s, they were muscular, wavy-haired bachelors who liked fast cars, curvy girls, and easy living. They hoped to make it big like Uncle JoJo.

Phil J. lived in Astoria, Queens, and Phil D. lived in New Jersey, but they got together often to pursue their mutual interests. Detectives believe both of them were involved in a gigantic narcotics ring masterminded by their uncle.

JoJo, Phil J. and several other suspected members of the dope ring were arrested April 30, 1972. Phil J. was charged with trafficking in cocaine and released without bail pending his trial, which was set for August 16.

On the evening of August 9, a week before the trial was to start, the cousins drove to the home of their aunt and uncle, Mary and Frank LaCosa, in suburban Rockland County, N.Y. The two Phils were wearing similar blue shirt and dark blue slacks. They were in good spirits and they laughed and joked at the supper table. They left early, around 7 p.m., and drove off toward the city in a 1971 Oldsmobile.

Shortly after midnight, a policeman saw the Olds with its headlights burning in a dark vacant lot in the Bronx. He looked inside the car and found Phil D. sprawled on the front seat, three bullet holes in his head.

The Body of Phil J., shot twice in the back and once in the hand, lay in the lot about 25 feet from the car. Detectives said the killer sat in the backseat of the Olds and plugged Phil D. through the skull in the classic style of an underworld hit man. Phil J. was gunned down when he tried to run away.

The detectives theorized that the double murder had something to do with narcotics. Perhaps it was a reprisal for the recent rubout of several black and Puerto Rican hoods who were moving into dope territory long held by Mafiosi.

Less than two weeks after the cousins were slain, Uncle JoJo and eight members of his wholesale narcotics ring went on trial in Federal Court. They were all convicted and sentenced to prison terms ranging from six to 30 years.

Evidence gathered in this case proved that the Gambino organization still was using its French connection and its Southern smuggling route. Federal agents learned that a large shipment of heroin seized in New Orleans in 1971 had originated in Marseille and was en route to the Manfredi wholesale house in New York.

Agents posing as drug racketeers penetrated the ring and bought more than $100,000 worth of pure heroin, "just off the boat," as the bootleggers used to say of their fresh merchandise. The investigators found that Manfredi was selling more than 10 kilograms (22 pounds) of top-grade heroin a week—enough for some 500,000 shots. At $5 to $10 per shot, this would mean a weekly business of $2.5 million to $5 million on the addict market.

The trial prosecutor, Assistant U.S. Attorney John M. Walker Jr., said the ring had poured "several million dollars worth of heroin into ghetto areas of the city." He called Manfredi "an incorrigible menace to society."

Federal Judge Harold Tyler zapped JoJo with a 30-year prison term and $25,000 fine. His nephew and partner, Joseph LaCosa—who dined with cousins Phil J. and Phil D. Manfredi at his parents' home on the last evening of their lives—got 30 years plus a whopping $100,000 fine.

The prosecution described LaCosa as a major heroin wholesaler with more than 15 regular customers, "just one of whom alone supplied 1,500 addicts with daily doses of heroin."

Judge Tyler called the Manfredi operations "shocking... vicious... frightening." But the Gambino family considers it a business too valuable to disband.

When the prison gates slammed shut on JoJo and his men, narcotics agents said their departure had left a large hole in the dope bag. The family lost no time filling it, for the junkies were going crazy and would pay anything to relieve their agony. So you lose a lieutenant and a few soldiers, but you make a few more bucks.

CHAPTER 8

BEAUTIES AND THE BEASTS; LETTERS FROM THE GRAVE

WALTER WINCHELL CALLED IT CAFÉ Society. And then it became the Jet Set and now it's seldom called anything because nobody much gives a damn.

But it is still there, still blaring and blazing away, still full of Beautiful People caroming from thrill to thrill, sampling the delights of every carnal smorgasbord. The Stork Club, El Morocco, the Peppermint Lounge, and other saloon society shrines are long gone. The durable Copacabana remains, and the swinging discotheques where the upper crust and the underworld meet.

Hippopotamus, Shepheard's, Le Club, Show Club. And their imitators. The places change frequently; the patrons grow bored and drift on to some unexplored oasis where they can see the same old faces. Whatever the "in" inn, the gorgeous girls are there—Madison Avenue secretaries, Park

Avenue debutants, aspiring actresses, $100-a-piece hookers, all kinds of models from porn to *Vogue*. And the idle rich are there, throwing their nights away like Kleenex tissues and their dollars like confetti.

Some of the sleazier go-go joints deal discreetly in drugs and flesh. You can rent a broad or get a fix as easily as you can order a drink, unless you look like fuzz.

New York After Dark. The glamour is going, going, but not quite gone. Among the go-go freaks are obvious crooks and hustlers, pushers, heisters, stock swindlers, flashy pimps with bankrolls as thick as the mattresses where the money was made. What once was Café Society is now a gilded sewer, but some still find it romantic.

The lure is tarnished yet still bright enough to attract lovely girls from all over. Girls like Nancy Sue Shelton and Patricia Parks, of whom a former acquaintance remarked sadly: "They were good girls as gang girls go, and as gang girls go, they went."

Not that they started out with any notions of playing their own private versions of Bonnie and Clyde or Ruth Etting and The Gimp. Things just worked out that way.

Nancy Sue, a blue-eyed, superbly structured redhead, had come a long way from Missouri where she was born, in Kansas City, in 1939. Her family later moved to Southern California and she became part of the drum-majorette, cheerleader, and beauty pageant culture and then made the pilgrimage to Hollywood, meeting her share of directors and stars, and getting her share of bit parts.

Next stop was Las Vegas where she worked as a showgirl. There she met many affluent admirers, including a New York "business executive" named Vincent Pacelli. He was old enough to be her father, but he took a most unfatherly interest in Nancy Sue.

Eventually he brought her to New York and installed her in a luxurious East Side apartment tastefully furnished with Oriental rugs, silk drapes, and custom-made French Provincial Furniture. To keep herself occupied when Vince wasn't around, Nancy studied dramatics and obtained small parts in TV shows and off-Broadway plays. She also devoted several hours a week to ice-skating, at which she was very good, and wound up her busy days in nightclubs and go-go spots, usually with Pacelli at her side.

A generation ago, Nancy Sue might have referred to Pacelli as her Sugar Daddy. But the white powder that enabled him to live the sweet life was not powdered sugar. It was pure heroin from Marseilles.

Pacelli, a member of the Lucchese mob, was a partner of Gambino gangster Joe Armone in a huge dope-smuggling operation. The U.S. Government charged that Pacelli and Armone bossed an international narcotics ring that brought a ton of heroin into this country in five years.

On the night of January 3, 1965, Armone got into an argument with another dope racketeer who emptied a pistol into him in a bar at Second Ave. and 12th St., Manhattan, near Carlo Gambino's favorite barber shop. Though shot six times, Armone survived. While he was hospitalized, Pacelli ran the business.

Federal agents seized Pacelli as he and Nancy Sue got out of a taxi at Lexington Ave. and 73rd St. on the afternoon of September 23, 1964. Armone and four other members of the dope gang were picked up the same day. Nancy was handed a subpoena calling for her appearance before a Federal Grand

Jury. She was questioned by the jurors on September 24 and told to come back in a week for further testimony.

Mrs. Yolande Angolet, whose husband was serving 10 to 20 years for narcotics violations, called at Nancy's apartment on the afternoon of September 27. They chatted for about 30 minutes, then Nancy said she had to get ready for "an appointment."

She did not say with whom, Mrs. Angolet later told investigators. Mrs. Angolet was the last person known to have seen Nancy Sue alive.

When the shapely ex-showgirl failed to show up for her second grand jury session, police and federal agents started looking for her. The search eventually covered the entire United States, Canada, Mexico, the Caribbean, South America, and Europe. But she was never found.

Among the things she left behind in her apartment were ranch mink and leopard skin coats, closets full of expensive clothes from Paris and Seventh Ave., drawers full of jewelry, $1,836 cash and other valuables. She also left $28,296 on deposit in a Las Vegas bank.

Investigators believe she was killed to keep from telling what she knew about the dope ring. But her testimony wasn't needed. Convicted of narcotics violations, Pacelli was sentenced to 18 years in Atlanta Federal Prison and Armone to 15 years.

William M. Tendy, who was in charge of narcotics investigations for the U.S. Attorney's office in Manhattan when Pacelli and Armone were arrested, had this to say about Nancy Sue Shelton:

"I'm convinced she was murdered. And I'm convinced that Pacelli had nothing to do with her disappearance."

The inference was that Joe Armone, the Gambino dope importer, was responsible for her sudden exit.

At the start of their trial, another beauty entered the case. She was statuesque Patricia DeAlesandro, a former Playboy Club bunny.

Pat hopped into a Manhattan shoe store one day, bought a pair of white boots and a leotard, and impressed manager Kenneth Feldman with her anatomical opulence. She accepted Feldman's invitation to dinner and he soon found out that it wasn't his company she craved.

Feldman was on the dope trial jury. Pat told him she was a friend of Joe Armone and hinted that Feldman could have his own shoe store if he voted the right way. She also mentioned $5,000 and a trip to Europe.

Next day, Feldman reported the incident to the trial judge. He was relieved from jury duty and Pat was arrested for attempted bribery of a juror. She was convicted and sentenced to five years in prison. Pacelli's lady lawyer, Frances Kahn, and her ex-con law clerk also were jailed for conspiring to obstruct justice.

Narcotics rings are like worms that survive after they have been cut in half. Every time the French connection was cut, it grew bigger than before. And it continued growing when Armone and Pacelli went away.

Pacelli no longer had a girl friend, but he had a son, Vince Jr., to carry on the family business. Junior had inherited his father's extravagant tastes and his eye for beautiful women.

One of the dolls in his life was slim, sexotic Patricia Diane Parks. Vince Sr. would have approved of Junior dating her. Whatever her shortcomings, she had class.

Patsy Parks and Nancy Sue Shelton came from different worlds. While Nancy grew up in a comfortable, middle-class California community, Patsy had a Social Register background. Private schools, summers in Southampton or the French Riviera, winters in Palm Beach or the Swiss Alps. Horses and yachts and high-powered sports cars. Debutante balls and private parties on country estates.

Patsy was the daughter of wealthy executive F. Newton Parks, vice-president of the management consultant firm of Booz, Allen and Hamilton International and director of its European operations.

After graduating from Le Grand Verger, a finishing school for young ladies at Lausanne, Switzerland, Patsy moved to New York and enrolled in the Parsons School of Design, the country's foremost fashion institute. She had some notion of becoming a fashion designer, but she found New York's nightlife more fascinating than her studies. In her second year at Parsons she was asked to leave because of a poor attendance record and failing grades.

Soon after that, she married a young industrial designer, George Pino, and tried to settle down. But neither marriage nor motherhood could keep her away from the go-go joints. When Patsy and Pino obtained a legal separation in 1969, she got custody of their son. Pino later learned she was running around with gangsters and dope dealers. He filed a custody suit, claiming she was not taking proper care of the boy. The court took the eight-year-old child away from Patsy and gave him to Pino who sent him to live with his parents in Bogota, Columbia.

Patsy worked as a fashion model, a discotheque waitress and a salesgirl in a boutique. None of these jobs paid very much, but she didn't care. She never had to worry about money. It might be said that Nancy Sue Shelton, a dancer and actress, worked at playing; Patsy Parks played at working.

Park Avenue Patsy, as her friends called her, patronized all the fashionable Eastside and Greenwich Village nightspots and was as entranced by the hard guys who hung out there as they were by her elegant airs. Even when she was waiting on tables, her breeding could not be disguised.

One of the places where she worked at was the Tarot, a discotheque on the fringe of Greenwich Village. The owner, Maurice Safizadh, accidentally discovered that Patsy had high connections in the mob.

"We we're having some problems with the Mafia," he said later. "They were trying to push into the club. They were starting fights in the place and demanding a percentage of the business for protection.

"Some of my employees knew about it and Patsy heard from them. She came to me one day and said, 'You don't have to worry about it. It's been taken care of.' After that, I never saw or heard from these guys again."

Patsy tried to perform a similar service for another Village disco owner, Robert Wood, but this time the connections didn't help. Wood was a self-styled swinger who made a lot of money in the used-car business and invested it in a go-go joint called Salvation. For a time it was one of the most popular, most profitable fun spots in New York City. Patsy was a Salvation regular and became a good friend of Robert Wood.

His troubles began when the club was charged with liquor law violations. Its liquor license was surrendered to the State Liquor Authority. The Salvation continued to operate as an unlicensed after-hours bar, but it's jet set clientele moved elsewhere and was replaced by a motley assortment of hippies, homosexuals, drug addicts, and pushers.

Some of the city's biggest dope dealers met there. Large deals were made and drugs frequently changed hands in the club's washrooms. Patsy worked at the Salvation for a time and reportedly got hooked on cocaine. She also fell for a narcotics racketeer who introduced her to Vince Pacelli, Jr.

The story of the Salvation's ruin was written by Wood in two long letters which he gave to his lawyer with instructions to turn them over to the authorities "in case anything happens to me." Something did. He was shot five times in the head and chest and dumped in a deserted street in Queens early February 18, 1970. His letters told why he had expected to meet such an end.

The preceding October, he said, "I met a young man named John Riccobono," who he later learned was the son or nephew of Carlo Gambino's longtime *consigliere*, Staten Island Joe Riccobono. Wood hired John at $300 a week to manage his club and John then induced him to hire a friend, Andy B—, as doorman.

As time went on, John and Andy paid so little attention to their duties, Wood wrote, "that I finally had to hire other men to do their jobs while continuing to pay their salaries."

He finally tried to fire John and Andy, but they informed him "that I couldn't do that." A few days later, John and Andy entered the club with Staten Island Joe and several other Mafiosi.

"These men came... to sit in judgment on me," Wood

wrote. "They decided I should pay John $4,000 dollars, keep Andy on the payroll at $200 dollars per week and pay them an additional $400 dollars per week for protection. I, of course, refused, at which time they proclaimed that the continued existence of the club and my very life were in danger."

So Wood kept Andy on the payroll and "he started using the club to sell drugs and forced one of my trusted employes to steal $900 from my safe."

As a result of the Gambino gangs takeover, Wood said, "my business became so bad that in order to continue there was no possible way of losing less than $2,000 a week. This left me in a position where my net worth had been depleted by some $250,000. I closed the doors and began an intensive program to sell the club."

A police official said the letters from the grave described "a classic case of how organized crime moves in on bars and nightclubs, puts its members and associates on the payroll and eventually takes over.

"Several of the Mafia families are in the act," he added, "and they're spreading their infiltrations so fast and so far that sometimes they don't even know whose joint is whose."

Patsy Parks was shocked by Wood's murder but she didn't believe that any of her gangland pals were responsible, even though several of them were questioned by homicide detectives. She had a brief romance with Vince Pacelli, Jr. and when this cooled they remained friends. She attended his wedding to Beverly Jalaba in St. Patrick's Cathedral in June 1971. She was also on friendly terms with another dope dealer, Demetrios Papadakos, who lived with his girl friend in an Eastside apartment directly over Patsy's pad.

Soon after his marriage, Pacelli was arrested for narcotics violations. So was Papadakos. On the second day of the trial in Manhattan Federal Court, a detective informed the prosecutor that the witness he had planned to call that day had been found murdered.

That witness was Patsy Parks.

The dark-haired beauty who had been called to testify against Vince Pacelli, Jr. had gone the way of the red-haired beauty who had been called to testify against Vince Pacelli, Sr. in another dope case eight years before. Vince Jr. was sentenced to 20 years for selling narcotics, plus an additional 15 years in another drug case.

What happened to Patsy Parks was described by Nassau County homicide detectives at a pretrial hearing for the dope racketeer accused of her murder, Barry Glen Lipsky.

The cops said that Lipsky told them he and Pacelli picked up Patsy at an Eastside discotheque on the night of February 3, 1972, and drove her to Massapequa, Long Island. During the drive, Pacelli stabbed her several times in the chest with a hunting knife.

Lipsky said he heard her cry out, "Don't... I'm a mother... my baby." He also heard stabbing sounds. Then Pacelli told him, "She's dead."

According to Lipsky's statement, they dumped the body on a vacant lot in Massapequa and Pacelli poured the contents of a gasoline can over it. His gloves got soaked with gasoline so he told Lipsky to light a match and toss it on the body.

At 7:30 a.m., February 4, a truck driver saw smoke rising from the vacant lot. "I thought it was a log burning," he said later, "but there were three dogs pulling on it."

He chased the dogs away and called police when he saw it was the charred body of a young woman. She was naked except for the remains of a sweater on her chest and an unusual amount of jewelry—14 rings, four bracelets, a wristwatch, and six gold crucifixes.

"I am a Catholic," said an inscription on one of the crosses. "Call a priest."

But it was too late to save Patsy Parks, the poor little rich girl who thought gangsters weren't really bad.

CHAPTER 9

HARRY THE HAMMER AND IRON CLAW COLOZZO

COUNT DRACULA WAS A PIKER compared to Don Carlo.

Commerce is the life blood of New York City. The land, sea, and air lanes are the arteries through which it flows. Gambino can pinch these arteries shut or drain them dry anytime he wants. But such drastic action is unnecessary. It is much simpler and safer to tap the commercial bloodstream a few drops at a time, a process which ceases to be painful once the victims get used to it. Some even appear to enjoy being bled. It is seldom fatal unless the donor resists the vampirish bite.

When Albert Anastasia was blown away, Gambino inherited the Brooklyn waterfront rackets. And when Three-Finger Brown passed on, he inherited the airport rackets, particularly chose at sprawling, bustling John F. Kennedy International Airport.

Trucking rackets, mail thefts, hijacking, flagrant pilferage, loansharking, illegal gambling and other crimes are still flourishing at JFK, gangland's Open City, despite numerous crackdowns, security shakeups, and official inquiries.

The FBI, Customs, the Postal Service, the New York City Police Department, the Port Authority (which operates the airport), the New York State Investigation Commission, the U.S. Senate Investigations Subcommittee, the Joint Federal State Task Force on Organized Crime, the U.S. Attorney for the Eastern District of New York and several federal and local grand juries have probed the murky depths of the JFK underworld. But the world's largest, busiest international airport remains firmly in the grip of Carlo Gambino and his associates.

More than $10 billion worth of air cargo passes through JFK every year, so it is comparatively simple for the mob to lift a few million dollars worth of assorted merchandise off the cargo platforms and trucks.

Less than a third of the 48 domestic and foreign airlines that fly freight to and from JFK have adequate security safeguards, such as electronic cameras to spot thieves. Many of the cargo handlers and truckers are on the underworld payroll. The mob employs "spotters" to locate cargo shipments worth $100,000 dollars or more. Then professional burglars, safecrackers, or hijackers go in to grab it.

It doesn't matter what the shipment contains—Scotch, furs, diamonds, watches, machine parts, pharmaceuticals, clothes, human hair, chemicals—Carlo Gambino and his associates have a market for it.

Investigators contend the cargo thefts could not be accomplished so easily were it not for an alliance between two mob-controlled groups, Local 295 of the International Brotherhood of Teamsters and the National Association for Air Freight (NAAF). Local 295 is the airport's most powerful union, representing nearly 1,500 cargo handlers. NAAF represents trucking firms doing business at JFK.

In 1971, a Federal Grand Jury indicted the association, its executive director, 13 member firms and six trucking officials on antitrust charges. One of those indicted was Anthony (Hickey) DiLorenzo, a racketeer formerly employed as a $40,000-a-year "consultant" to NAAF.

The State Investigation Commission has described NAAF and Local 295 as being dominated by "ex-convicts and racketeers." An SIC report says: "With Control of the dominant union and the trucking association at JFK in the hands of criminal elements, it could reasonably have been anticipated that the air freight industry would soon find itself caught between the hammer and the anvil."

The hammer is swung by Harry Davidoff, secretary-treasurer of Local 295 and a longtime pal and a business associate of some of the city's top mobsters. His union controls the flow of all air cargo in and out of JFK. A word from Davidoff could shut down the huge cargo terminal and backup freight all around the globe.

A squat, balding plug-ugly, Harry has a long criminal record that dates back 40 years and includes convictions for burglary, extortion, and gambling. Early in his crime career, he was associated with members of Murder, Inc.

He was then known as Little Gangy. His older brother, Bill, was Big Gangy. Members of the old Brownsville gang that spawned several professional killers, Big and Little Gangy were wounded in a Brooklyn bar in 1943 by a rival hood who emptied his pistol at them. Another brother, a boxer known to fisticuff fans as Al (Bummy) Davis, was shot dead in 1945 when he tried to thwart a tavern holdup.

Harry also served a short stint in the prize ring and still uses his pugilistic expertise on occasion. He reportedly slugged a *Life* magazine photographer in 1971 and growled: "I could have you killed." His other public outbursts have included cursing a Senate investigator and spitting at a lawyer who tried to serve court papers on him at his baronial home in Roslyn, L.I.

Trucking firms that have triggered his ire have had truck tires slashed, sugar poured into gas tanks and office windows smashed. He has used these goon tactics to pressure trucking officials into joining the NAAF and signing contracts with Local 295.

In two prize-winning exposés that appeared in 1970 and 1971, the New York *Daily News* describes how Davidoff crippled freight lines with strikes, threats, and violence. A new flurry of investigations followed. But Davidoff is still doing mob business as usual, and as this is written police supposedly are investigating another industry complaint of Davidoff harassment.

The bookies and loansharks who prey on airport workers also served as recruiters for the mob. For example, a cargo handler blows his pay on the ponies and borrows from a shylock so his family won't go hungry. Then he makes a few more bad bets and finds he can't meet his loan payments. Now he is in serious trouble and the only way to get out with no bones broken is to rob a bank or become a cargo spotter. He invariably chooses the latter option.

From then on, he keeps an eye out for valuable

shipments arriving at the terminal where he works. He may even case other terminals. For each tip he gives the hoods, he receives $50, $100 dollars or more, depending on what the merchandise is worth and the effort required to obtain it.

Not infrequently, despite tightened security measures, the tips come right out of the pigeonholes in the U.S. Customs offices on the ground floor of building 80, a mile from the passenger terminals. About 40 cargo brokers have offices on the second floor of Building 80. They handle the paperwork on international air freight. Pickup orders, invoices, and other cargo papers are sent to Customs for clearance, pending which they are stuck in the pigeonholes.

The papers are carried back and forth by brokerage employees known as runners. Dishonest runners often find an opportunity to pluck a pick up order from a pigeonhole, copy it on a blank form, and pass it on to someone working for the mob. Then a truck driver simply presents the bogus pick up order to the cargo platform and drives off with whatever shipment is mentioned on the paper.

Air freight firms are the most frequent targets of cargo crooks, but the mob doesn't hesitate to rob the U.S. mails. A registered mail pouch, containing $70,500 in American Express travelers' checks plus bond and stock certificates worth between $20 million and $30 million, vanished somewhere between the JFK post office and the American airlines terminal.

A truck carrying 100 bags of mail from Europe was hijacked between a runway where a Swissair jet deposited the sacks and a hangar rented by the U.S. Post Office. Investigators never determined how much cash, negotiable securities and other valuables were in the air mail cargo, but estimates ran as high as $10 million.

Due to a tremendous increase in mail thefts at JFK, the Postal Service assigned armed guards to all mail trucks entering and leaving the airport. This reduced postal piracy, but no one rides shotgun on the ordinary cargo trucks that are still being stuck up by hijackers.

A police raid on a Manhattan warehouse turned up $7.5 million worth of hijacked goods. Investigators said at least half of this huge treasure trove came from JFK shipments. Similar raids in Manhattan, Brooklyn, and Queens recovered additional millions of dollars worth of stolen cargo.

All five crime families share in the JFK bonanza, but Carlo Gambino is the only mob boss to get a piece of all the action. His longtime lieutenant and sometime irritant, Carmine Lombardozzi, was a specialist in the fencing of stolen securities, including stocks and bonds lifted from airmail shipments. Lombardozzi, who accompanied Gambino to Apalachin and was the defendant in a Mafia trial there, was the family's man on Wall St. Among other things, he ran a chain of bucket shops that peddled the public $3 million worth of worthless stocks. More on the versatile Carmine later.

The JFK labor, trucking, and hijacking rackets were organized by Thomas Lucchese and supervised by two of his men, John (Johnny Dio) Dioguardi and Anthony (Tony Ducks) Corallo. After Lucchese died and Dio and Ducks went to prison, Gambino took over JFK with the approval of the Lucchese group.

The JFK takeover, like the airport rackets themselves, followed a pattern established earlier on the Brooklyn waterfront. This busy shoreline has been a beehive of market activity for at least half a century. Every crime committed at JFK has its counterpart on the docks. The only difference is that the pier pirates have been at it much longer.

Albert Anastasia ran the waterfront rackets and his brother, Anthony (Tough Tony) Anastasio (the brothers spelled their last name slightly differently), ran the Brooklyn docks. Tony headed the International Longshoreman's Association's 8,000-member Local 1814. And after Albert died, he was stuck with Carlo Gambino whether he liked it or not.

He did not like it, reliable sources claim, because he suspected Carlo helped set up his brother's barbershop sendoff. But there was nothing he could do about it. Tony bossed the country's biggest longshore local, but Gambino now bossed the Anastasia mob and all of its enterprises on or off the waterfront.

When Tough Tony died a natural death in 1963, his union post automatically went to his son-in-law, Anthony (Young Tony) Scotto, then 28. A brainy, articulate man who had worked as a longshoreman while attending Brooklyn College, Scotto was hailed by the press as one of the "new breed" of brilliant young labor leaders.

In addition to heading the giant Brooklyn local, he was appointed a vice-president of the 116,000-member ILA. At his first press conference after stepping into Tough Tony's shoes, the 6-foot-2, 200-pound Scotto was asked about persistent reports that crime was rampant on the docks.

"That's a myth that is perpetuated by a few sensational newspapers," Young Tony said. "Besides, with all the agencies that are supervising the waterfront these days, I don't feel that my primary responsibility is that of a policeman. My job is the welfare of our members.

"When these agencies talk about crime on the waterfront, they are condemning themselves. It's up to them to enforce the laws."

During the next few years, Scotto became a political power in New York City. He conferred with Mayor Lindsay at City Hall and Gracie Mansion, the mayor's official residence. He visited President Johnson at the White House. He lectured on labor relations at Harvard and other universities. It seemed he was changing the waterfront's soiled image.

Then, in 1969, the U.S. Justice Department prepared a crime chart titled: "La Cosa Nostra: The Commission." It listed Carlo Gambino as boss of the Mafia. Not merely head of a New York mob, but chairman of the board of the National Crime Syndicate. His family, the Justice Department noted, "exercises control in New York, New Jersey, Connecticut, Maryland and Florida."

The chart named Aniello Dellacroce as Gambino's underboss and Joe Riccobono as counselor. Then came the names of 27 alleged Gambino captains. On this list was Anthony Scotto and Joseph Colozzo, head of another ILA local in Brooklyn.

Scotto, who was then working for Lindsay's reelection (even though Tony was a registered Democrat, with close ties to several Democratic politicians, and the mayor was then a registered Republican) denied that he was a Cosa Nostra *caporegime*.

But the Waterfront Commission hastily assembled a

task force of 25 lawyers and investigators to find out how much of its domain Don Carlo actually controlled.

"Testimony given by FBI director Hoover (to the Senate Investigations Subcommittee) concerning Scotto's association with Gambino is presently the subject of investigation by the Commission," one of its members said.

Other sources maintained Colozzo ran the dock rackets for Gambino. These investigators said Scotto took orders from Colozzo, who had been listed as a Gambino *capo* on charts prepared by the Senate crime commission back in 1963.

"I know everything you could tell me about Colozzo," Scotto once told an interviewer. "He is supposed to be telling me what to do. No one tells me what to do."

One of the most interesting witnesses to appear before the Waterfront Commission was a dockworker named Salvatore Passalacqua. Testifying at commission hearings held in 1968, he said Tony Anastasio hired him as a foreman-cooper on Pier 1, Brooklyn, in 1959. He said he paid Anastasio $30 a week for the job, making the payments to Scotto and other union officials when Tough Tony wasn't around.

In July, 1965, Passalacqua said, he was approached by his pier superintendent, Gaspar Romano, who "told me that the next Sunday Mr. Joe Colozzo wanted to see me at the office of the union." Colozzo was then head of the ILA Local 1277. Passalacqua said he went to the union headquarters that Sunday morning and found about 15 men there with "all kinds of foods and drinks." Among them, he said, were Carlo Gambino, Colozzo, and Scotto. His testimony continued:

Q: "Now, who spoke to you when you first went into the room?"

A: "Joe Colozzo."

Q: "What did he say to you?"

A: "He told me that the reason for this meeting was to introduce me to the boss, Carlo Gambino, because if there was anyone who deserved to become a member of the honorable family, the Cosa Nostra, then he (Gambino) should know about it, so that we could, after following the tradition of the laws of Cosa Nostra, and if I was willing to accept an invitation, they were ready to take me into the family as one of their peers.

"I told them I was not ready to give an answer on the spot, because that was not the reason I had gone in the first place to the meeting. I asked for time to think it over… but Mr. Colozzo asked: 'Why do you need to think about it?' Why don't you answer me right now?' But I insisted I needed some time to think it over."

Q: "Did Mr. Anthony Scotto say anything to you at that time?"

A: "He asked me: 'Why don't you give me an answer? Why are you thinking so long about it?' "

Q: "Did Mr. Scotto participate, in any way, in the introductions… Would you please state what Mr. Scotto said?"

A: "He asked me: 'Why don't you accept his invitation? After all, we also belong to the same family.' "

Q: "Now, did Mr. Carlo Gambino say anything to you?"

A: "He said: 'Give him time so he can think about it.' "

Q: "Did Mr. Carlo Gambino say anything about any kind of conditions?"

A: "He told me: 'When you leave this room, don't say

anything to anybody, so that what we speak about here is between us.' "

Q: "Did Mr. Gambino say anything about Anthony Scotto and you?"

A: "Yes, he told me that if I accepted his conditions, then I would have to submit to his orders at the risk of my life."

Q: "Whose orders?"

A: "To Anthony Scotto's orders."

Q: "Did you have any conversation with Gaspar Romano at that meeting?"

A: "Yes, he told me: 'What are you waiting to accept? I am a member, too, of this family.' "

Passalacqua said Romano approached him about 10 days after the meeting and again attempted to persuade him to join the Mafia, but he stalled for more time. Later, he met Colozzo and told him he needed more coopers to work on the piers.

"I asked him if he could help me somehow," Passalacqua testified, "but he answered that he cannot do anything for me. He asked me: 'Did you give the answer that you are expected to give to Mr. Gambino?'

"I said no. Then he said: 'I don't have anything to do with you.' And then I left."

The witness said Romano fired him on September 23, 1965, about a month after the meeting, and he asked Scotto to get his job back. He said Scotto replied: "For you, Mr. Gambino will think about it," and told him to come back later.

Passalacqua said he went to Scotto again a few days later and Scotto told him he had seen Gambino and had gone "down on his left knee with his hands together in front of his face to pray" to Gambino to help Passalacqua.

"I told Mr. Scotto that Mr. Gambino was a scoundrel," Passalacqua continued, "and Scotto said, 'Don't let anyone hear about it'... that I was a scoundrel because I had insulted him."

Passalacqua later complained to the Mayor's Committee on Exploitation of Workers, charging that he had been dismissed from his job and "harassed" because he turned down the "criminal offer" to join the Gambino family.

Scotto insisted he never attended any such meeting. He was not called to testify at the commission hearings. Asked why, a commission spokesman said: "We assumed that because of the nature of the case, he would be a hostile witness, so we didn't call him."

New York State Joint Legislative Committee on Crime summoned Scotto to testify at a public hearing held February 5, 1970, six months after the disclosure that his name was on the Justice Department list of Mafia leaders. On the grounds of possible self-incrimination—the old Fifth Amendment dodge—he refused to say whether he was a Mafia member. He also declined to answer 28 other questions put to him by the committee.

One of the questions concerned the presence of Carlo Gambino and his wife at the Plaza Hotel reception following the wedding, on New Year's Day, 1957, of Scotto and Marion Anastasio.

Joe Colozzo (NYPD No. B-189380) was one of the original members of the old Albert Anastasia mob. Known on the docks as the Iron Claw, he was a master of bailing-hook and pistol diplomacy. He ran the waterfront rackets for Anastasia and continued running them for Gambino. He placed 20 of his "button men" in key positions on the Brooklyn piers, where they operated such lucrative concessions as policy, bookmaking, loansharking, cargo thefts from petty pilferage to entire truckloads, pay kickbacks from longshoremen and shakedowns of shippers.

Frank Nawrocki, then business agent of ILA local 808, told a Kings County Court judge in 1952 that Colozzo had tried to kill him during a wildcat longshoreman's strike that Nawrocki led the preceding year.

Nawrocki reportedly had been interfering with mob operations on the piers, so Albert Anastasia ordered Colozzo to kill him. Colozzo and two other ILA officials accosted Nawrocki in October 1951 as he sat in his car on a Brooklyn wharf that had just been a bloody battleground for strikers and nonstrikers.

Colozzo stuck a pistol through the car window, pressed it against Nawrocki's head and pulled the trigger twice, but the gun failed to fire, the witness testified. Nawrocki then filed a complaint charging Colozzo with assault, but withdrew it after a series of threats to murder his wife and children.

On the night after he signed the complaint, Nawrocki's wife answered the phone and a man's voice said: "We're ready to bomb your house. You better get the kids out."

The following night, she received another anonymous call: "You better not drive your car out of the driveway because you'll never reach the corner alive."

Colozzo, once described by the New York Times as "a mousey little man, wrapped in mystery," didn't look dangerous, but dock wallopers twice his size and half his age were terrified of him. He was a suspect in waterfront killings and beatings, though none of these violent crimes were ever pinned on him. Federal narcotics agents arrested the Iron Claw and three of his goons "on information that they were involved in the sale and delivery of a large quantity of heroin." They were later released due to insufficient evidence.

A Federal Grand Jury, investigating Mafia penetration of the waterfront, indicted Colozzo in February 1962 on charges of false union reports in violation of the Lanrum-Griffin Law. For four years, the Government tried to bring him to trial. But Colozzo obtained delay after delay because, like Carlo Gambino, he suffered a convenient heart ailment.

At a U.S. District Court hearing in March 1966, he sat hunched over at the defense table, an oxygen tank at his feet and a physician beside him, taking his pulse from time to time.

"The court's problem is this," said Judge George Rosling. "Had they (the two judges who presided over previous hearings) directed a prompt trial, it may be that the defendant might have withstood the strain. But if the court gambles on this now, and the wrong number comes up, the error is irreversible.

"I've no intention, unwittingly, of imposing the death penalty."

So Colozzo escaped trial and when he finally did die of a heart attack it was not behind bars but on vacation in Italy.

During his four-year fight with the Justice Department, he was an extremely active invalid. He held 11 union jobs, for which he was paid $22,500 a year. As a vice-president of the ILA's Atlantic Coast District, stretching from Canada to the Gulf of Mexico, he attended more than 100 negotiating meetings while he was under indictment.

He also drove his Cadillac all over the metropolitan area, made numerous air flights around the country, attended innumerable banquets and climbed the flight of 18 steps at his Brooklyn home every day. And he made frequent trips to the Massapequa, L.I. home of a fellow heart patient, Carlo Gambino.

On these journeys to Papa's place, Colozzo often was accompanied by Dominick Petito (NYPD No. B-92004), also known as Joe Pip and Joe Pitts. An ILA organizer, Petito was listed by the Senate crime committee as a Gambino soldier. He had been arrested 12 times, including two homicide raps and several assault and robbery charges. But he was only convicted once, for playing dice, and that sentence was suspended.

"When Petito speaks on the waterfront," a high-ranking police official once said, "the listener knows he is hearing the words of Carlo Gambino."

In 1963, the NYPD Central Intelligence Bureau and other mob-watching agencies received information that Gambino, Carmine Lombardozzi, Colozzo, and Petito were plotting to take over building trade unions on Long Island. They reportedly planned to seize control of the Nassau-Suffolk Buildings Trades Council for the purpose of extorting large sums from contractors in Nassau and Suffolk Counties.

While investigating this conspiracy, detectives from Nassau District Attorney's Office tailed Colozzo and Petito to Gambino's home on several locations. Other investigators observed Gambino and his brother Joe dining with the ILA officials in a Massapequa restaurant. A surveillance report on this luncheon meeting notes that Don Carlo had retained the common touch:

"Carlo Gambino before entering the premises shook hands and conversed with workmen on the premises."

Nassau DA William Cahn questioned Petito about his visits to Gambino's suburban fortress. Petito admitted driving Colozzo there in a Cadillac registered to the ILA, but he denied taking part in the discussion between Colozzo and Gambino, who presumably were comparing heart stimulants.

Colozzo also held many Brooklyn conferences with Joe and Paul Gambino and their first cousin, Thomas Masotto. A butcher and meat merchant all his adult life, Masotto has only been arrested twice (one of these was because he was having lunch with Cousin Carlo) and has never been convicted of anything. His name does not appear on the Cosa Nostra charts prepared by the FBI, NYPD and Senate crime probers. He is so little known to investigators that they sometimes spell his name two ways—Masotto and Massoto—in the same report. He doesn't even rate an underworld nickname.

Some mob observers dismiss him as Carlo's "gofor"— go for coffee, go for sandwiches, etc. But he is much more than an errand boy. He is Gambino's personal messenger, a man to be trusted and therefore respected by all the mobs. He carries instructions to supervisors of the various family enterprises and relays the replies to Cousin Carlo.

He drives a Cadillac through the main gate of Brooklyn Pier 1, parks in a spot reserved for ILA officers, makes himself comfortable in the ultramodern headquarters of the ILA and the pier superintendent. He goes here and there on family business, visiting meat markets, garment factories, restaurants, warehouses, garages and other places all over the metropolitan area.

One stop he had dropped from his daily itinerary is the Brooklyn Supreme Court Building where he formerly frequented the chambers of a well-known justice. On at least one occasion, the judge asked Tom to convey his warmest regards to Don Carlo. He added: "Tell Papa I'm working very hard."

Masotto and the hard-working justice dined together in a Brooklyn restaurant and drank together in the privacy of their homes, but their secret meetings weren't as secret as they believed. Finally, Masotto realized he was under surveillance and decided to stay away from court.

Several of the New York City judges have treated Gambino associates with unusual leniency. Mafiosi with long criminal records have been let off with small fines and suspended sentences while common criminals charged with similar offenses were hit with stiff prison terms. It is literally possible for a well-connected mobster to get away with murder. A survey conducted by the *New York Times* proved that New York justice treats Mafia mobsters much better than unaffiliated felons.

Masotto's first non-social visit to court occurred in November 1959 following his arrest for allegedly selling a stolen gun. Police said the transaction took place in Masotto's Independent Meat Market in Brooklyn.

The gun was one of 45 stolen from a weapons shipment on a Greenwich Village pier. One of the guns was used to kill Frank (Frankie Shots) Abbatemarco, the biggest policy racketeer in Brooklyn, outside of a Brooklyn bar on November 4, 1959.

Masotto was arrested nine days later and the *Daily News* called him "a key figure in the Brownsville Arsenal Gang which has been supplying guns to the underworld." Police officials were quoted as saying Masotto was the supplier who sold stolen guns two middlemen who peddled them to customers in need of firearms. One of the guns was purchased for $70 by an undercover cop who traced it back to Tom.

Despite all the unfavorable publicity—resulting mainly from police disclosures that Masotto was a cousin of Apalachin delegates Carlo Gambino and Paul Castellano—the worst thing that happened to Tom was the loss of his Police Department pistol license.

The charges of illegal possession and sale of a hot rod were dismissed.

On a scorching July day in 1968, Gambino decided to switch from his customary Italian dishes to some Chinese delicacies. Masotto's air-conditioned Cadillac called for Carlo at his Brooklyn home and drove him to the house of Chan in mid-Manhattan. There they met two other Mafia bosses, Joe Colombo of Brooklyn and Angelo Bruno of Philadelphia, who were accompanied by their prospective lieutenants, Vincent Aloi and John Scimone.

They were sampling some exotic specialties when detectives broke up the meal and charged them with loitering. The charges were dismissed by a Criminal Court judge a few hours later. And by this time, of course, they were all hungry again.

Investigators never learned why the luncheon meeting was called, but they believe it was the only top-level Mafia conference ever held in a Chinese restaurant.

For a more private gathering of the clan, at Gambino's Long Island home, Masotto ordered 100 pounds of lobsters from a Brooklyn fish market. The lobsters were delivered on a Saturday morning, in plenty of time for the feast.

When the fish store opened the following Monday, the owner received a phone call from Masotto. "Papa was very disappointed with the lobsters," Tom reported. "They were too big, too tough. He wanted a lot of little lobsters. The tender, juicy ones."

The fishing dealer apologized profusely and offered to make restitution, either in cash or in produce of the sea. As one merchant to another, he agreed with Masotto that the customer is always right. Especially when the customer is Carlo Gambino.

Born in Italy in 1907, Masotto emigrated to New York as a child, became a naturalized citizen, went to work in a meat store and later bought it. He acquired several other meat markets, often in partnership with Gambino and Castellano cousins.

A sister, Yolanda Stroncone, was stabbed to death on Foster Road in Highland, N.Y., on July 29, 1942. A brother, Constantino Masotto, was murdered in New Orleans the following year and buried in a shallow grave. So far as police know, they were the only Gambino kin to meet violent deaths although many members of Carlo's other family have been slain.

Still active in the meat and poultry business, Masotto has prospered along with his cousins. He has lived in Don

Carlo's shadow for 50 years. And he probably knows as much about the Gambino empire as anyone except the don himself.

CHAPTER 10

THE BOYS AT THE BIG S GARAGE

IN THE DARKEST HOUR BEFORE dawn on the cold, windy morning of March 22, 1963, two men in hooded jackets and work pants slipped up to the Big S Service Center at 446 Coney Island Ave., Brooklyn, and silently picked the front door lock.

When the door was open, they signaled to a panel truck parked in a nearby alley and then took up lookout positions where they could spot an approaching police car. Three other men entered the service station and planted an electronic bug about the size of a half-dollar in the office of the owner, Michael (Mike Scandi) Scandifia, a soldier in the Gambino crook corps.

After the tiny microphone had been concealed in the office ceiling, wires were run from the bug to the garage roof, then down to the ground and along the fence to a house on the street behind the garage.

The pre-dawn prowlers were detectives from the office of Manhattan District Attorney Frank S. Hogan. With the cooperation of a friendly citizen, they set up a listening post in the basement of the house in back of the Big S. The electronic surveillance was authorized by State Supreme Court Justice Mitchell D. Schweitzer for the specific purpose of obtaining information about the theft of $75,000 in diamonds from a Manhattan gem firm. Scandifia had been implicated in this caper and it was felt that the bug would provide enough evidence to clinch the case.

For four months, while J. Edgar Hoover's men were plugged into Sam the Plumber's pipeline in New Jersey, Hogan's heroes eavesdropped on Scandifia and his brother Mafiosi. They heard conversations dealing with all sorts of crimes, from hot cars and hijackings to murder.

One of the discussions concerned Carlo Gambino's plans for the 1,000-member Local 47 of the Mason Tenders Union. The State Investigation Commission later investigated this local and reported:

"Outwardly, Local 47 was the very model of a properly functioning labor union. Its officers seemed to be duly elected, its governing board seemed to exercise proper control over all union affairs, and its records and reports were duly filed with appropriate government agencies.

"However, the Commission established that Local 47 had become racketeer dominated."

A Gambino soldier, Accursio (Swifty) Marinelli, was a shop steward who "conducted the local's daily business under Gambino's instructions," SIC found.

Marinelli went to the Big S garage on May 10, 1963 for a chat with Scandifia and Gambino *caporegime* Peter

(Peter Pumps) Ferrara. They talked about how to implement orders issued the previous December by the ruling council of the Gambino family. These orders were to make certain that a union member named Thomas Cucciara became assistant business representative of Local 47.

Marinelli asked about the council meeting where the decision on Cucciara was made.

MARINELLI: "At that time, who was present?"

FERRARA: "Joe Riccobono (family counselor); Carlo (Gambino), Joe Banty, Carmine (Lombardozzi) and myself and Joe Zingaro."

SCANDIFIA: "In other words, this came from the Administration, right?

FERRARA: "That's right. They made it up, the Administration, that Tommy is the fellow to be the next delegate there."

MARINELLI: "Delegate or assistant (business agent)?"

FERRARA: "Both. He's the next guy to get in if the guy dies… He's the next fellow in line, assistant."

Investigators identified "the guy" whose demise was discussed as Frank Stratico, then business representative of Local 47.

At one point in the conversation, Scandifia asked Ferrara: "Now, Pete, who's Frank? Who's Frank belong to?"

Marinelli replied: "He belongs to me."

"He belongs to Swifty," Ferrara agreed.

The State Investigation Commission later concluded that "as Stratico was Marinelli's man, Marinelli in turn was Carlo Gambino's man." But Stratico denied he was Marinelli's man, and the Gambino gang planned to get rid of him when he refused to make Cucciara his assistant.

The hidden bug picked up a remark by Scandifia that Stratico was to be "hit" in the union hall if he again failed to obey Don Carlo's orders. On the night of the scheduled murder, the union hall was staked out by a small army of detectives. But Stratico didn't show and Gambino apparently granted him a reprieve.

Soon after this incident, the mike in Mike's garage revealed a much more startling murder plot.

On July 10, Scandifia received a call from a man whose voice was new to the listening sleuths. The visitor said he could supply "dum-dum" bullets to kill informers. As he left the garage and drove off, a detective noted his description and the license plate numbers.

He was quickly identified as Patrolman Leonard Grossman, 40, a member of the New York City Police Department for 13 years. Grossman returned to the garage July 23 for a second tape-recorded rap session with Scandifia. The cop's presence in the mob hangout was the subject of top level, top-secret discussions in the offices of the Manhattan and Brooklyn district attorneys.

Grossman was arrested at 12:15 a.m, July 25. Detectives found two stolen guns in his car. DA Hogan's chief assistant, Alfred Scotti, conceded that the hasty arrest had ended the effectiveness of the garage bug.

"Circumstances compelled us to take immediate action," he said. "We couldn't wait until we had a corpse on our hands."

As a matter of fact, they already had a corpse on their hands. Brooklyn florist Alfred Sanantonio had been shot dead among his fragrant blooms two weeks earlier. The underworld grapevine claimed he was killed because he had informed on his confederates in a plot to cash $1 million worth of stolen U.S. Treasury bonds. His partners in this scheme reportedly included some important members of the Gambino clan.

Conversations in the Big S garage indicated that one of the gunmen who blasted Sanantonio in his sweet-smelling shop, Flowers by Charm, was *Caporegime* Petey (Pumps) Ferrara. In June 1964, a Brooklyn grand jury charged Ferrara with first-degree murder. Also indicted on the same charge were Angelo Meli, a convicted dope dealer and suspect in a $45,000 American Airline holdup at JFK Airport, and New Jersey mobster Nick Russo.

In another indictment, the jury charged Patrolman Grossman, Ferrara, and Scandifia with conspiring to murder another federal informer. Ferrara went into hiding. He was finally located in a Staten Island hospital where he was a heart patient under an assumed name.

The murder and conspiracy charges eventually were thrown out by State Supreme Court Justice Nathan Sobel. He ruled that the tape-recorded evidence of a plot to murder informers could not be used in court because the eavesdropping was authorized only in connection with the jewel theft case. The Court of Appeals upheld this decision.

Meanwhile, Grossman had been suspended from the force for refusing to tell the Brooklyn grand jury what he knew about Sanantonio's murder. And a Manhattan grand jury indicted Scandifia and John Lombardozzi, Carmine's FBI-fighting brother, for stealing the diamonds.

When the Brooklyn indictments against Grossman and the Gambino gangsters were dismissed, the Police Department filed its own charges against the rogue cop. He was accused of violating NYPD regulations by conspiring to murder federal informers; stealing two revolvers from a Brooklyn house; failing to report the unregistered guns to his superiors and failure to turn them in to the police property clerk; and conspiring to supply guns and bullets to the Gambino mob. He also was charged with consorting with a known criminal, Scandifia.

Grossman's departmental trial began in September 1968, more than 5 ½ years after the investigation began. Tapes of his conversations with Scandifia were introduced as evidence. On one of them, the cop and mobster discussed using dum-dum bullets that would blow large holes in the victims as a lesson to other squealers.

At one point, Scandifia said: "Who gives a fuck, as long as it blows a hole in his head this big?"

He assured Grossman that the guns and bullets would be used only on federal informants. "Only stool pigeons," he said. "The cops like stool pigeons to go, especially federal stool pigeons. I said the cops, New York policemen, like it when a federal stool pigeon is hit."

Found guilty of conduct unbecoming a policeman, Grossman was dismissed from the force on November 11, 1968. A month later, his lawyer reported him missing. Attorney Harold Foner said the former cop "had been afraid all through his departmental trial that the underworld was planning to get him."

Scandifia, who shared these fears, disappeared around the same time. He left his expensive split-level home in Hillsdale, N.J., around 10 p.m., December 5, telling his wife he was going to an all-night pharmacy to get a prescription filled. He drove off in his 1968 Cadillac convertible and she never saw him again.

The car was found a week later, wiped clean of fingerprints and stripped of license plates, on a country road near Blooming Grove, N.Y., about 60 miles north of New York City. State troopers, sheriff's deputies and FBI men searched the woods and swamps near the car for his grave. Bloodhounds did a lot of sniffing and a little howling, but they couldn't find him. Neither could the lawmen, though they dug up a lot of country acreage in the attempt.

Grossman turned up in Israel with his attractive blonde wife, but Scandifia's fate remains a mystery. Wherever he went, it is safe to conclude that his talking days are over.

The bug in his garage resulted in 70 arrests for a wide variety of crimes, including extortion, grand larceny, armed robbery, hijacking, conspiracy to murder, and murder.

More than 60 of the defendants pleaded guilty to felony charges or were convicted after trials. About 50 received prison times. And as nearly all of them were Gambino troops, this caused a serious manpower shortage in the clan.

Carlo Gambino's name was mentioned many times in the discussion at the Big S garage. A lot of his illegal operations were described in minute detail. The bug picked up countless clues to large and small projects of the Gambino crime conglomerate. But the tape-recorded evidence that sent some 50 of his henchmen to jail apparently was not enough to get Don Carlo as much as a traffic ticket.

CHAPTER 11

IF YOU CAN'T GET THEM FOR MURDER, GET THEM FOR DOUBLE-PARKING

CLOTHES MAKE THE MAN AND man makes the clothes. Making clothes is New York City's biggest industry. The garment center in midtown Manhattan produces and sells $7 billion worth of apparel a year—70% of all the clothing sold in the U.S.—and employs hundreds of thousands of workers with a total annual payroll of more than $1.5 billion.

The garment center stretches from 34th to 41st St., between Sixth and Eighth Aves. An area only seven blocks long with Seventh Ave. as its main stem. Not large, but one of the busiest places on earth, thronged with trailer trucks, wheeled racks of dresses, suits, slacks, children's clothes, sport clothes, cloth and fur coats.

Greater fortunes are won and lost regularly on Seventh

Ave. than in Las Vegas. And the Mafia gets a percentage of all the action.

The garment center is a city within the city. And in recent years it has become known as the new Fashion Capital of the World. It is also a greenback jungle where the lions and hyenas stalk profitable prey, while the vultures watch in hungry anticipation.

James (Jimmy Doyle) Plumeri was one of the fattest lions. A captain in the old Lucchese mob and uncle of the racketeering Dioguardi brothers, he had been around Needle Alley almost long enough to qualify as a historic landmark. He was one of the original Mafia skull smashers who invaded the district in the early 1930s and drove out the Jewish gangs that had run the rackets there for years.

Always willing to lend large sums to fashion firms that needed extra cash in a hurry, Jimmy Doyle became a partner in several dress, suit, and coat companies that couldn't meet his interest levies. In the same way, he acquired garment-hauling truck lines. He also ran many of the garment trades extortion, gambling, and labor rackets, with the occasional help of his greatly-feared nephew, Johnny Dio.

Two of Jimmy's partners, Dominick Didato and Nat Nelson, wound up dead of bullet wounds. Jimmy Doyle was the chief beneficiary of these murders, 20 years apart, but the cops couldn't prove he was guilty of partnercide. He was charged with Didato's murder and the case was dismissed due to insufficient evidence.

Doyle lived with the wife in a plush pad on 59th St. and conducted his business transactions from an office in the New York Hotel and the bar of nearby Damon's in the heart of the garment center. Plump and jowly, with a fringe of white hair, he was growing old and suffered from emphysema and a heart ailment. But he still spent his evenings in nightclubs and dimly-lit lounges, still put away a fifth of whiskey a day. And when his boss, Three-Finger Brown died, he felt he was best qualified to assume control of the country's richest crime clan.

Carlo Gambino had other plans for his old friend's estate. And most of Lucchese's captains, including the imprisoned Johnny Dio, felt they would be better off with Gambino then with the unpredictable Jimmy Doyle.

Gambino's oldest son, Thomas, inherited some legitimate garment and trucking businesses from his father-in-law, Tom Lucchese. And Carlo himself had a foothold in the garment center. Now that Lucchese was gone, the Gambino organization rapidly expanded its interests in this lucrative field.

Around this time, the garment industry was hit by an unprecedented wave of truck hijackings. During 1969 and 1970, these robberies were running up to $50 million a year and the hijackers had become so brazen that they were grabbing trailer trucks in broad daylight on the fringes of the center itself.

Not surprisingly, none of the trucks owned by Gambino or his mob allies were bothered. But the hijack victims included some truck and garment firms in which Jimmy Doyle had interests and other firms which had been paying him for protection against just such incidents.

As the hijackings increased, so did insurance premiums. Several of the hardest-hit firms were warned that their insurance policies would be canceled if the robberies continued. Forced to the brink of bankruptcy, garment manufactures and truckers desperately turned to any source that might help—the police department, the FBI, the Mafia.

The word went out that businessmen would be much better off dealing with Gambino and his associates then with Plumeri. And Jimmy Doyle, sensing a threat to his long rule as rackets king of the dress district, retaliated by moving into two Gambino-dominated fields—garbage hauling and pizza parlor supplies.

Jimmy Doyle was sipping scotch in a lively bistro near Times Square on the night of September 16, 1971, when two younger men came in and joined him at the bar. He left with them about 20 minutes later. They climbed into a Cadillac, Jimmy sitting in front alongside the driver, and drove over the East River to Queens.

During the ride, Jimmy was garroted with his own silk necktie. The killers dumped his body on a quiet street near the Maspeth section of Queens and took his wallet, either to make it look like a robbery murder or to get a dividend on their contract. They ignored some loose bills in a pants pocket and the large diamond ring on his pinkie.

It was an unusual end for a mob chief and not without a twist of irony. The man who held a stranglehold on the garment center for four decades had in turn been strangled with one of its products. And it was not inconceivable that the little king of the fashion rackets was assassinated because, like so many little kings before him, he plotted against a much more powerful monarch.

Garment truck hijackings decreased sharply after Jimmy Doyle's death. Police were not sure whether this was the result of improved security methods or a decision by Gambino Inc. to take the heat off the needle industry.

In any event, Seventh Ave. soon returned to normal and the garment-makers who had done business with Jimmy Doyle had no trouble finding new partners.

Then a new problem arose. As more and more mobsters entered the garment scene, less and less curb space was available for the trucks of legitimate firms. Entire blocks were staked out by the mobs as their private parking preserves. Police Headquarters received many complaints from manufacturers and truckers who were having trouble getting shipments into and out of the clothing factories.

Before dawn on October 30, 1972, a small army of policemen invaded the garment center. Their weapons for this particular foray were ballpoint pens and books of summonses. The target was mob-run trucking firms whose vehicles were hogging precious curb space.

The cops slapped hundreds of summonses on illegally parked trucks owned by six firms allegedly connected to Gambino and his associates. Deputy Police Commissioner Richard Kellerman said these firms have been linked to Carlo Gambino, Sebastiano Aloi, Carmine Tramunti and Natale Evola—representing four of the five crime families.

Kellerman called the traffic-ticket blitz "the start of a major drive against organized crime." Other police sources said it resulted from Mayor Lindsay's order to Police Commissioner Patrick Murphy to "run the gangsters out of town."

No one seriously expected that traffic tickets could accomplish what countless investigations, indictments, convictions and prison terms have failed to achieve. But, if nothing else, the garment center crackdown revealed that the mob bosses were working in harmony for a change.

Gambino, Tramunti, and Evola we're still family heads, as was Sebastiano Aloi's son, Vinnie, who also had garment trucking interests.

One of the six firms identified by the Police Department as mob-connected was the Consolidated Carrier Corp., whose officers included Gambino's sons, Thomas, vice-president, and Joseph, secretary-treasurer. Consolidated denied the accusations and sued the city for $1 million, charging harassment.

Only a super boss like Don Carlo could bring the mobs together, double-parking side by side, rolling along the roads untroubled by hijackers, claiming curb space for a consolidated underworld. Only Gambino could put it all together and when he goes it may all come unglued.

This is his fear, his constant worry. That his carefully-constructed conglomerate with its labyrinth of illegal and legal enterprises could turn out to be a *papier-mâché* pyramid.

CHAPTER 12

EXIT LITTLE RABBIT AND CARMINE THE DOCTOR

THE COSA NOSTRA CHART PREPARED by the FBI in 1969 contained more than one surprise. To the New York press, the most newsworthy name on the list of Gambino captains was that of labor leader Anthony Scotto. But the omission of two veteran *Capi Mafiosi*—Joseph (Joe Banty) Biondo and Carmine (The Doctor) Lombardozzi—caused a much greater stir in the underworld than the headlines about Scotto.

Mob watchers were as stunned as baseball fans would be by the sudden dismissal of the manager and star pitcher of a team that had just won the World Series.

Only five years before, the Senate crime committee had listed Joe Banty as Carlo's underboss and Lombardozzi as one of his captains. And now, inexplicably, they were out of the lineup.

Unless the FBI chart was wrong (which it wasn't), two almost unprecedented demotions had taken place. No one could recall the previous case in which a Mafia chief was removed from his post without bloodshed—his own or someone else's. When a Syndicate executive is fired, the firing is done with a gun.

When Vito Genovese became displeased with underboss Anthony (Tony Bender) Strollo, for example, the fact that Don Vito was in prison did not prevent Strollo's swift departure from this world. The only way a boss steps down is into a grave. And yet Joe Banty and Carmine had not yet tumbled into the obituary columns. By the grace of God and Don Carlo, they were still around because Gambino believes that even Mafia justice may on occasion be tempered with mercy.

Joe Banty was a wrinkled relic of the bad old shoot-em-up days. His nickname derived from his bantam stature—5 feet 4, 130 pounds—and cockiness. Among the characteristics he shared with that fearless fowl was an insatiable appetite for barnyard romance. He was also called *Cunniglieddu*—Little Rabbit.

A native of Barcelona, Sicily, he had been a prohibition bootlegger and then had entered the labor field in an effort to organize New York cab drivers into a mob-run union. He set off a violent taxi strike and cab fleet owners who refused to pay his price for peace had their taxis bombed, battered, and burned.

Little Rabbit hopped from racket to racket, gathering lots of lettuce on the way and a record of arrests (NYPD No. B-50466, FBI No. 62666) for such things as homicide, extortion, gun-toting, and narcotics violations. Federal

Narcotics Bureau files listed him as "an important international drug trafficker."

He made frequent trips to Italy to confer with Lucky Luciano and other key figures in the global dope trade. At one of these conferences, in 1951, a nationwide network of dope routes was set up to facilitate the distribution of heroin throughout the United States. For further details, see the chapter on narcotics.

Joe Banty (sometimes spelled Bandi or Bondi on investigative reports) and Carlo Gambino came up through the ranks together under the Mangano brothers and Albert Anastasia. And when Carlo succeeded the murdered Anastasia as boss, Joe succeeded the murdered Frank Scalise as underboss. Joe retained his own personal rackets while helping Carlo supervise the overall operations of the entire family.

At this time there were a dozen captains, each in command of about 50 men. Paul Gambino, Paul Castellano, Aniello Dellacroce, Carmine Lombardozzi, and Ettore Zappi dealt directly with the boss. The others took their orders from Biondo.

Carlo and Joe ran a smooth, profitable corporation, with no noticeable friction between them, for several years. Then Carlo began to suspect that his underboss was holding out on him—making deals behind his back and pocketing the proceeds. Other bosses, such as Sam the Plumber, complained that Biondo was acting too big for his banty britches.

Specifically, Sam said Joe Banty had cut himself in on a lucrative garbage-hauling deal in which Sam's own family was interested. Sam added that he didn't mind splitting the profits with Carlo, but he didn't want to give Joe the lion's share unless Carlo had authorized Biondo's action.

This was news to Gambino. He promised to look into the matter and assigned his own kinsman to find out what Biondo was up to. They quickly determined that Sam's gripe was justified. And they also learned something about the personal life of the underboss that Carlo considered smellier than the garbage scheme.

At the age of 66, Joe had left his wife and was living with a prostitute young enough to be his daughter. Or perhaps his granddaughter. Don Carlo, a moral man in an immoral world, was genuinely shocked.

Whatever his sins, adultery was not among them. While other mobsters supported mistresses and casual sleeping companions, Gambino had always been a faithful husband, devoted to his wife and children. He could forgive the carnal conduct of his captains and soldiers, but he expected better behavior from his underboss. By his rank, Joe Banty was "a man of respect." But how could the bosses and men respect that dirty old man who was living—not just playing around but actually living—with a common whore?

On a sunny April morning in 1965, Joe Banty was awakened by the telephone. He picked up the receiver and heard the gruff voice of a *caporegime* who was very close to Gambino.

"Carl wants to see you," the *capo* said.

"I'll be there in an hour," Joe replied.

His hand trembled as he hung up and he suddenly felt the full weight of his years. The strutting, crowing bantam at last realized he was no longer cock o' the walk. A day or two earlier he had heard a disconcerting rumor that one of his partners in the garbage deal, Joey Surprise Feola, was missing and presumed dead.

It struck him, with the impact of an icy shower, that this was what the Don wanted to see him about. Somewhere in the back of his mind, Biondo could hear the roar of a garbage shredder.

So he failed to keep his appointment with Don Carlo. He sent word that he would not meet Gambino alone, at family headquarters, but would be happy to meet him in some public place.

This response catapulted Gambino into a rare rage. None of his followers had ever seen him lose his temper before. He turned white and fired a volley of Sicilian curses that he had never previously uttered in all his long career.

No one who heard Don Carlo that day expected Joe Banty to live much longer. What he had done was inexcusable, unforgivable. It was the underworld equivalent of General MacArthur's refusal to obey orders from President Truman. Only MacArthur didn't have to worry about facing a firing squad.

No *Capo Mafioso*, especially one of Biondo's rank, had ever dared ignore a direct command from their chief. Furthermore, Joe's insubordination and obvious lack of trust was compounded by ingratitude.

Over the past six years, Gambino had given Banty more than $200,000. And this was how his generosity was repaid.

There is little doubt that Banty's actions would have been suicidal in any other crime family. Gambino, however, has never been known to waste anything of potential value, including his underlings.

"Don Carlo never has anyone killed without a reason," a member of his group once observed.

In Biondo's case, he had ample reason. But he did not demand the supreme penalty. After the explosion of anger, his customary calm returned and he considered what course to take. Perhaps his decision to let Joe live was based in part on sentiment—they had worked together, off and on, for 35 years. Or perhaps it was based on more practical considerations. Joe Banty had powerful friends in the mobs, particularly in the Syndicate's narcotics branches. At least two of the Gambino captains, both convicted dope dealers, were loyal to Joe and might resent his execution enough to start a revolt. One gangland killing invariably led to another.

And so, instead of signing a death sentence, Carlo took the remarkable step of appointing a committee of seven mobsters to meet with Banty and discuss the situation. According to an FBI report, the committee was instructed to "approach Banty and evaluate his attitude."

The committee conferred with Joe and reported back to Gambino. He considered the committee's recommendations, then dismissed Biondo from his post. The other Mafia commissioners concurred.

On June 9, 1965, Gambino had lunch with Sam DeCavalcante and informed him that Biondo's retirement was now official. In Carlo's words, the old bantam had been "put on the shelf."

He also disclosed that he was considering "making my cousin," Paul Castellano, the new underboss and anticipated some criticism if he showed such favoritism. Sam was noncommittal. He later told his own captains that it wouldn't make much difference who succeeded Biondo since Gambino made the big decision anyway. The post eventually went to Aniello Dellacroce.

Carmine Lombardozzi, long a Gambino favorite and the family star, was out of the running when the underboss opening occurred. And he had no one to blame but himself.

Carmine's fall from grace was a much more complicated matter then the Biondo banishment. The Lombardozzi demotion resulted from the classic combination of wine, women, and song. His fondness for the former two was well known in the mob, but his singing was something else. All the underworld loves a lover and hates a singer.

The dapper Doctor was the family "money mover." In other words, he invested the profits from gambling, loansharking, narcotics and other rackets more or less in legitimate ventures.

As Gambino's man on Wall St., he bought and sold millions of dollars worth of stolen securities and peddled the public about $3 million worth of mining stock that wasn't worth the paper it was printed on. Some of the brokerage houses whose securities wound up in his hands were not even aware of the thefts.

He ran what the Securities and Exchange Commission described as "a typical boiler operation"—large rooms furnished with tables, chairs and a battery of telephones manned by high-pressure stock salesmen. Most of the salesmen were bookmakers and loansharks, soldiers in Carmine's *borgata*.

A few, like Irving singer, were the victims of those bookies and loansharks. Singer borrowed $1,400 dollars from Carmine's chief moneylender and enforcer, Arthur

(Artie Todd) Torterello. Due to the high rate of "vigorish" (interest), he wound up owing nearly $6,000 dollars.

"After four or five payments (of $200 a week in interest alone), I could no longer pay," Singer later told the State Investigation Commission. So Torterello suggested that he "work it off" as a salesman in one of Lombardozzi's boiler rooms, which is how Singer got out of hock to the mob.

A former sports broadcaster, whose voice was familiar to millions of fans throughout the U.S. and Canada, ran up a $100,000 tab with the Lombardozzi loan company. He paid off by steering some of his millionaire pals to a crooked dice game.

A well-known Manhattan hairdresser squared himself with his shylock by letting Lombardozzi lieutenants take a peek at his appointment book. While some of his wealthy customers were under the dryer, burglars looted their apartments.

One thing invariably led to another. When the head of a ship-repair firm hired Lombardozzi to "keep labor peace" on the waterfront, Lombardozzi offered to rent him a generator. Over the next four years, the ship repairman paid Lombardozzi $40,000 in rental fees, then purchased the generator for $15,000. It originally costs Lombardozzi $13,000 dollars, so he made a $50,0000 profit—and no one could prove the deal wasn't perfectly legal.

One of his biggest scores involved the theft of $1,370,475 in blue-chip stocks from the vaults of Bache & Co. Investigators said a $120-a-week clerk in the brokerage firm's vault department simply stuffed the stocks into his attaché case and turned them over to the mob.

A subsequent hunt for the securities lead New York

police and G-men to California, Florida, and other states. Then an FBI man posing as an out-of-town buyer spread the word around Wall St. that he had a market for the Bache loot. A Lombardozzi emissary contacted him and set up a meeting.

The trap was sprung at the Robert Treat Hotel in Newark on July 21, 1962. Carmine's brother, John Lombardozzi, and an accomplice, Joseph Martinelli, arrived at the hotel in a gleaming white Cadillac with Florida license plates. On the dashboard was the gold shield of a deputy inspector in the New York City Police Department.

FBI agents pounced on the suspects and recovered securities worth nearly $200,000. 16 men were indicted on federal charges stemming from the gigantic stock robbery, but Carmine Lombardozzi, believed to have masterminded it, was not among them.

A onetime waterfront loanshark and strongarm goon, Carmine has been arrested about 25 times and has a dozen convictions. As adept at breaking hearts as he was at busting skulls, he was the glamour boy of the Gambino clan. His rugged, slightly sinister appearance was enhanced by a dazzling, gold-capped smile, thick black brows, graying curls and a coppertone complexion that made him look as if he had just returned from Miami.

He joined the Mafia in 1951 and, through hard work and moneymaking ability, was appointed a *caporegime* within a few years. Gambino's senior captain, Joe Franco, died in October 1957 and it was a tossup who would succeed him, Lombardozzi or Corrao.

Gambino considered the choice carefully, then summoned one of his soldiers, Accursio Marinelli, and told him to instruct Corrao to come to headquarters immediately. Instead, Marinelli tipped off Lombardozzi. Carmine assured him there was no rush about locating Corrao. And when Corrao failed to show up, Gambino gave the job to Carmine, who just happened to be there at the right time.

A month later, Carmine accompanied Gambino to Apalachin and waited nervously in Joe Barbara's garage while the Mafia commission debated whether he should be put to death for trying to grab some jukebox concessions owned by the Genovese gang. After Apalachin, Lombardozzi owed not only his rank but his life to Don Carlo.

Gambino trusted him enough to give him up to $1 million cash at a time to invest for the family. And Carmine never kept a penny more than his share of the profits. He split everything with Carlo, even when no split was required. He spent his own money, not the mob's, at his favorite hangouts—race tracks, nightclubs, gourmet restaurants and suburban motels where he was a regular overnight customer.

Gambino didn't care if his underlings had girl friends, so long as they kept their liaisons quiet. But the wives and daughters of other members were off-limits, even to Lothario Lombardozzi.

Sabato (Sammy Mintz) Muro, a Gambino soldier, approached the Don in the summer of 1964 and demanded satisfaction in "a matter of honor." Muro charged that his captain, Lombardozzi, had seduced his nubile daughter, Arlene.

"If Carmine doesn't do the right thing by my daughter," Muro said, "I'll handle this my own way."

Although Carmine was the organization's top

moneymaker and very close to the don, Gambino didn't hesitate to court-martial a captain on the strength of a soldier's complaint. He ordered Lombardozzi to divorce Mary, his wife of 20 years, and marry Miss Muro.

"It's the only honorable thing to do," Gambino explained. "Mary will understand."

He also decreed that Carmine would have to continue providing for Mary and the children in the manner to which they had become accustomed. Lombardozzi, then 51, got a Mexican divorce and married Arlene, then 24, September 3, 1964, at a secret ceremony performed by a Yonkers justice of the peace. And what Papa has joined, let no man put asunder.

With two families to support and a pretty bride half his age, Carmine might have been expected to spend most of his nights at home from then on. But soon he was off and running again. His next bosomy buddy was Mary Napolitano, an extremely attractive brunette about the same age as his new wife.

The night of August 27, 1965, was uncomfortably warm so detectives Alan Rich and William Bett decided to cool off in the air-conditioned cocktail lounge of the Golden State Motor Inn, a swank motel in the Sheepshead Bay section of Brooklyn. They found Lombardozzi sitting at the bar with Marie and his chauffeur-bodyguard, Phil Arcuri.

The detectives weren't exactly surprised for they were investigating complaints that Carmine and his associates were trying to muscle into the area's lucrative nightclub-restaurant-motel-cabana industry. In fact, they we're looking for Lombardozzi.

"We walked up to Carmine and told him he was under arrest," Detective Rich said later. "He went into a rage. He kept shaking his head and saying, 'I won't go with you guys. Nobody is going to take me in. Why don't you go out and lock up some criminals?'

"I tried to calm him down, but he cursed us. I finally told him to come along. He came off the stool swinging with both hands."

Rich grabbed Carmine by his curly locks. Then Marie jumped on the detective's back and clawed, punched, and kicked him, Rich said. Just as the two detectives brought Carmine and his girlfriend under control, Arcuri got into the act. The detectives finally subdued the trio and charged them with felonious assault.

The publicity given this incident distressed Don Carlo, but not nearly as much as a previous fracas in which members of Lombardozzi's family tangled with the FBI.

G-men and gangsters traded punches at the funeral of Carmine's father, Carmello Lombardozzi, on April 3, 1963. Armed with the candid camera, FBI agent John Foley was taking pictures of the mourners outside Brooklyn's Immaculate Heart of Mary Catholic Church just before the Solemn Requiem Mass was to begin. Suddenly, several burly, black-suited men pounced on him.

They smashed his camera, fractured his skull with a gun butt, knocked him down and kicked and stomped him as he lay on the ground. Other agents and cops rushed to Foley's aide and arrested Carmine's brother, John Joseph Lombardozzi. A large force of G-men later showed up at the burial in Calvary Cemetery, Queens, and grabbed three nephews of the deceased.

On this occasion, Carmine sided with the law for perhaps the first time in his life. He and a few other men restrained screaming women mourners who tried to attack the arresting officers.

Gambino felt that Carmine, as a Mafia captain, should have been able to control his relatives and prevent the attack on Foley—which was sure to have widespread repercussions. The second brawl, three years later, proved that Carmine couldn't even control himself.

Just as Gambino had feared, both brawls were followed by federal, state, and local investigations of Mafia operations. This may have been coincidental, but the don blamed Lombardozzi and stripped him of his captain's rank.

Then Lombardozzi was indicted on a state charge of perjury and federal charges of conspiracy to cash checks stolen from a Wall St. brokerage firm and conspiracy to cheat the government of tax revenues on winning tickets at Roosevelt Raceway.

He had already served several prison terms and he had spent 14 months—from August 14, 1958 to October 19, 1959—in New York City Civil Jail for refusing, despite being granted immunity from prosecution, to answer the State Investigation Commission's questions about the Apalachin gathering.

In 1969 he was sentenced to one year in jail for lying to a Brooklyn grand jury about mob infiltration of legitimate businesses. While appealing this rap, he underwent surgery for kidney cancer. The operation prolonged his life but the doctors could not restore his good health. Then, in 1970, he was convicted of the check-cashing conspiracy and sentenced to the federal prison and hospital complex in Springfield, Mo.

Carmine decided he would rather travel to Springfield by himself then with a federal marshal at his side. He arrived there on Friday evening and took a taxi to the prison to begin serving his term. But prison officials refused to admit him because he wasn't due until the next day. So he had to spend the night in a Springfield motel, at his own expense, before checking into the Hoosegow Hilton.

As this was written, Lombardozzi was still in Springfield and Joe Banty had retired to Florida. And though they were both on the shelf, they were both better off than two other breakers of gangland rules—Joe Colombo and Crazy Joe Gallo.

CHAPTER 13

THE BALLAD OF CRAZY JOE

"I DON'T UNDERSTAND HOW A guy like that belongs on the Commission," Sam the Plumber said of Joe Colombo soon after Colombo was appointed to the Mafia high command.

"How come they made him?" inquired Sam's under-boss, Frank Majuri.

"He was made because there was Carl (Gambino)," Sam replied. In other words, Gambino wanted Colombo on the Commission, so Joe's nomination was promptly approved.

Sam felt that he himself was much better qualified.

"Sometimes, Frank, the more things you see, the more disillusioned you become... You know—honesty, honorability, all those things."

"Yeah," Frank agreed. "If you're a real honest guy you wind up hunchback and with headaches."

In a further discussion of Colombo, Sam said: "This

guy, he sold out his outfit. He played position. You could look at it that way, too...

"He sits like a baby next to Carl all the time. He'd do anything Carl wants him to do. So who the hell you gonna trust?"

Other Mafia old-timers shared Sam's low opinion of Colombo. Outside of the Brooklyn gangs, he was virtually unknown. As a mob boss, he was considered little more than a dummy whose thoughts, words and actions were controlled by Gambino.

But the underworld Charlie McCarthy eventually developed a voice of his own and in time it became the loudest of any Mafia chieftain in history.

By following Gambino's instructions, Colombo grew rich and as respectable as a man in his profession can ever hope to be. His rackets prospered and he invested the profits in legitimate businesses. His loansharking operations alone were so successful that he reportedly had more than $5 million cash out "on the streets" bringing in interest. As for his other racquets, a federal gangbuster reported: "He's in everything."

He continued to live modestly with his family in a peaceful, middle-class Brooklyn neighborhood and to work as a real estate salesman. His employee, Anthony Cantalupo, told the Joint Legislative Committee on Crime that Colombo was "a real gentleman."

"He has the sincerest group of clients," Cantalupo added. "They don't cheat him out of his commissions."

These commissions earned Joe about $35,000 a year. He also was a part-owner of a funeral home and a garment-cutting firm. Comfortably established behind legitimate fronts, he let his capable captains run the rackets reaching from Brooklyn to Manhattan, Queens, and Long Island.

In the mob hierarchy, he was the Invisible Man. Then he suddenly became the world's most visible, most voluble Mafioso.

On April 30, 1970, Joe Colombo staged his own version of the Sicilian Vespers uprising. He led a march on the oppressor's stronghold, 201 E. 69th St., the New York City headquarters of the FBI. Reporters, press photographers, and TV camera crews were on hand to record the historic event.

Colombo complained that the FBI had "framed" his son, Joe, Jr., who was indicted (and later acquitted) on charges of conspiring to melt down coins for their silver.

"I was willing to suffer through the attacks made by authorities," Colombo said, his sad eyes attesting that he had indeed suffered much. "I accepted it as part of my life. Unfair, but a part of life. But when they framed my boy Joey, then I decided I had to do something. That's why I'm picketing the FBI."

When he heard what was happening, J. Edgar Hoover reacted as if the ghost of Scarface Al Capone had appeared in his office, a spectral tommy gun under his arm. Colombo's gangland peers were as surprised as the G-men.

Joe had not informed Don Carlo that he planned to declare war on the FBI. The dummy had broken the strings at last and jumped off the ventriloquist's lap. And, whatever his subsequent successes, he would never be able to climb back up on the old man's knee.

Through the spring and summer, Colombo's men paraded outside FBI headquarters, carrying placards and shouting anti-FBI slogans so lustily that residents of the block complained to police.

Colombo formed the Italian-American Anti-Defamation League to carry on the fight. When the long-established Anti-Defamation League of B'nai B'rith accused him of name-grabbing, he changed the title of his group to Italian-American Civil Rights League. Money and membership applications poured in from Italian communities in every part of the country.

The league's first major rally drew 100,000 persons to New York's Columbus Circle, which on that day was certainly Colombo Circle. Five Congressmen and a dozen other conservative, liberal, and middle-road politicians addressed the cheering, flag-waving throng while FBI agents and detectives watched through binoculars and telescopic cameras.

Tony Scotto, the ILA leader, shut down the Brooklyn waterfront for the day and was up on the speaker's platform with the other publicity-minded dignitaries. The city's normally bustling Italian neighborhoods were almost deserted, the stores closed so that employees and customers could go to the rally.

When the stumpy, sport-shirted Colombo appeared on the podium, flanked by his sons and bodyguards, the crowd's roar could be heard for blocks around. The vocal explosion actually made him wince, as if he had been slugged by an unseen fist. He assured his almost hysterical audience that his one ambition was "to help all people of Italian American heritage."

Nicholas Pileggi, a freelance writer and crime expert, later reported in *New York* magazine: "On June 29, 1970 in midtown Manhattan, Joseph Colombo had performed a feat of traditional 17th-century Sicilian sleight of hand. He managed to convince enough men and women that whoever defames the Honored Society also defames them. He made allies of his own victims."

He did even better than that. He convinced millions of Americans that the 700-year-old society had never existed. And he virtually erased the word Mafia from contemporary American history.

Soon after the rally, Attorney General John Mitchell ordered the FBI and all other Justice Department branches to stop referring to "Mafia" and "Cosa Nostra" in their reports. They were told to substitute some ethnically neutral term like "organized crime."

U.S. attorneys and local prosecutors all over the land immediately dropped Mafia from their press releases and legal briefs. The governors of Alaska, Connecticut, New York, Texas and South Dakota instructed all state agencies not to knock the Mafia anymore.

The *New York Times* stopped mentioning Mafia and Cosa Nostra after League members, led by Joe Colombo's son Anthony, picketed the newspaper's West Side plant. That night's editions carried only one story about a Mafia member, who was referred to as "a reputed organized crime leader."

Another picket line appeared outside the plant of the *Staten Island Advance*, which refused to stop using the naughty words. Four goons in a car forced an *Advanced* delivery truck, loaded with 10,000 newspapers, off the road and set it afire. The driver and a district circulation manager were dragged from the truck and beaten with tire irons.

Instead of supporting the *Advance* with editorial screams of outrage, the other New York dailies downplayed the Staten Island incident and continued to treat Colombo as a new folk hero. The terms Mafia and Cosa Nostra virtually vanished from the nation's newspapers, news magazines, and news broadcasts.

The FBI and other TV crime shows also deleted the offending terms from their scripts and gave their gangsters Anglo-Saxon, Irish, or Middle European names. Colombo even succeeded in killing TV commercials in which actors spoke with Italian accents ("Mama mia, datsa somma spicy meatball!").

And the producer of *The Godfather* agreed not to mention the Honored Society in the movie. He also consented to hire League members as consultants and extras during filming and to donate proceeds of the movie's premiere to the League (a concession that was quickly countermanded by the owners of Paramount Pictures).

Joe was interviewed on TV talk shows and by syndicated columnists. He called press conferences. He spoke at banquets and meetings of civil rights groups. His lieutenants were photographed with Governor Rockefeller and Mayor Lindsay.

Colombo boasted that the league had 150,000 members, a figure which many observers believe was extremely conservative. Frank Sinatra and other showbiz stars performed at a Madison Square Garden benefit that raised nearly $500,000 for the League.

In the spring of 1971, some 1,500 Colombo fans paid $125 each for the privilege of dining with Joe at a posh Long Island restaurant and hearing him proclaimed Man of the Year. The league gave him a solid gold plaque, honoring him for "restoring dignity, pride and recognition to every Italian." Joe, in turn, had some kind words for his civil rights group.

"It is under God's eyes," he said, "and those who try to stop it will feel its sting."

Around this time, two small dark clouds appeared in the otherwise sunny sky of Joe Colombo. One was a perjury conviction for making false statements on his application for a real estate broker's license. The other was the return to Brooklyn of Crazy Joe Gallo after nine years in prison.

Neither of these events worried Colombo very much at first. But it soon became clear that the government was determined to put him in jail and Gallo was equally determined to take back the rackets he had lost to the Colombo gang.

Crazy Joe acquired his apt nickname when a psychiatrist described him in court as a dangerous psychopath with homicidal tendencies. Gallo considered the doctor's diagnosis a complement. As a boy, he was fascinated by actor Richard Widmark's portrayal of a sadistic gangster, Tommy Udo, who laughed maniacally as he shoved an old lady in a wheelchair down a steep flight of stairs.

Joe saw this movie several times and in future years he would ask people he met at cocktail parties and nightclubs: "Do you think I look like Tommy Udo?" To make sure he did, he wore black silk shirts, white silk ties, and striped suits that were straight out of the MGM gangster wardrobe. But he wasn't just acting tough.

He kept a young lion in the basement of his President St. headquarters and often made his nightly rounds with his pet walking beside him on a leash. The lion was about the size of a Great Dane and people often mistook it for a large dog until they took a second look and then quickly got out of the way. On occasion, Joey would bring home a borrower who had fallen behind on his payments to Gallo shylocks. Joey would take a steak from the refrigerator, open the basement door and fling the steak downstairs. The lion would roar its appreciation, and the petrified debtor would get the message.

Joey never threw any humans to the lion, but no one would have been surprised if he had. He led the outnumbered Gallo troops in the bloody Gallo-Profaci War, which ended in 1962 when Crazy was sent to prison for extortion and Profaci died of cancer. Larry Gallo, the oldest brother and brains of the gang, also died of cancer in 1968 while Joey was still in the slammer.

Joey was smitten with brotherly love during his long sojourn in upstate Attica and Auburn prisons. He became friendly with several black convicts and threatened to beat up a prison barber who refused to trim a black's hair. Some of the white cons called him a "nigger lover." Three of them entered his cell one night while he was sleeping and tried to strangle him.

On November 4, 1970, he single-handedly prevented a race riot between black and white cons and he rescued a guard who had been beaten unconscious by militant blacks.

A few months later, Auburn Superintendent Harry Fritz wrote a letter to the State Parole Board describing Joey's good works. He said Joey walked into the central yard where hundreds of blacks had gathered, and took the injured guard away from them. After taking the guard to the prison hospital, he returned to the yard, walked into the no-man's land between the black and white cons and urged them to cool it, which they did.

The parole board was so impressed that it rewarded Gallo's integration efforts with a parole. He hurried home to South Brooklyn in March 1971 and announced, at a "coming out" party the gang threw for him, that he planned to recruit blacks for his underworld ventures. Some of his members opposed this plan, but Joey convinced them they would need all the help they could get when they invaded Colombo territory.

Some former Gallo gangsters who had joined the Colombo camp while Joey was away returned to the fold. Gallo also signed up some of his former pen pals who were now out of prison. Within weeks after his release, he had put a fighting force together.

At peak strength, his gang was outnumbered at least 5 to 1 by the Colombos. But they didn't call him Crazy Joe for nothing. He muscled into Colombo-controlled policy, loanshark and jukebox rackets for starters. And the underworld heard he had received the green light for this go-ahead from Carlo Gambino.

Gambino did not want a renewal of the Gallo-Profaci War. On the other hand, he was fed up with the antics of Colombo and the Italian-American Civil Rights League. He had never approved of Colombo's loud-mouth crusade and his worst fears had been realized.

Some of Colombo's own captains complained to Don Carlo that their boss was spending so much time on TV shows and picket lines that he was neglecting family business.

They said he had refused to use League funds to appeal a

prison sentence for Sonny Franzese, chief of the mob's hijacking and bank robbery division, but had spent whatever was needed for his own son's defense in the coin-melting case.

They also beefed about Colombo's camaraderie with a fellow civil rights leader, Rabbi Meir Kahane, founder and head of the militant Jewish Defense League. The rabbi and racketeer had appeared side by side on speakers' platforms, before TV cameras and at various demonstrations. Their troops had marched together to protest the treatment of Jews in the Soviet Union.

"What the hell have Russian Jews got to do with Cosa Nostra?" an irate Colombo captain asked Gambino. And for once, the don had no ready answer.

Don Carlo had his own list of grievances against Colombo. His picketing of the FBI had removed the name Mafia from public view, but it also had set off a new wave of investigations, indictments, arrests and trials. Under the intense heat generated by federal, state, and local probes, some of the most lucrative rackets broke down. And some of the most capable mob administrators either went into hiding or were yanked out of action by the law.

Although the League had collected more than $2 million, this was only a drop in the rackets bucket overturned by the probers. Gambino had known from past experience what would happen when Colombo took on the FBI. He could have warned his protégé, but Colombo no longer asked his advice.

Not only had Colombo broken the rule against deliberately antagonizing the authorities but he ignored another gangland precaution: Never get caught with anything that could be useful to the other side.

On the afternoon of December 16, 1970, a gold Buick station wagon passed through Manhattan's Foley Square, a downtown complex of federal, state, and municipal courts and office buildings. It entered a parking lot for court officials just north of the State Supreme Court Building and stopped in a Supreme Court Justice's parking place.

In the wagon were Joe Colombo and his lookalike, dressalike, walkalike, talkalike bodyguard, Rocco Miraglia. The roly-poly pair were known to detectives assigned to keep an eye on them as Tweedle Dum and Tweedle Dee.

FBI agents we're looking for Miraglia to arrest him on a perjury indictment accusing him of lying to a federal grand jury investigating the M——. Two G-men saw the gold wagon roll into the parking lot. They rushed there and grabbed Miraglia as soon as the Tweedles emerged from the Buick. They also grabbed a black attaché case Miraglia was carrying.

"That's mine!" Colombo yelled. "That's mine!"

He tried to take the case away from the agents and a shoving-and-shouting match ensued. The commotion attracted a traffic cop who slapped a $25 ticket on the wagon's windshield for illegal parking in the judicial parking spot.

Colombo kept insisting that the case was his. The agents were equally insistent that it must belong to Miraglia because he was carrying it. And because he was under indictment in a federal case, they had a legal right to search it.

Accompanied by the loudly protesting Tweedle Dum and the arrested Tweedle Dee, they took it to the FBI offices, opened it and found, among other things, lists of names and numerals indicating large amounts of cash. Among the names were "Tony the Gawk," "Frankie the Beast," "John the Wop," and plain ungarnished "Carl."

The amounts listed opposite the names ran as high as five figures. Colombo was told he would have to testify before a grand jury if he wanted his attaché case and its mysterious contents back.

In response to the jury's queries, he identified "Tony the Gawk" as Tony Angello and "Frankie the Beast" as Frank Falanga, both members of the Colombo crime family. And "Carl" turned out to be Carlo Gambino.

Asked about the $30,000 figure that appeared after Carl's name, Colombo explained this was the amount Gambino had raised by selling tickets to a League-sponsored civil rights rally.

No one seriously believed that Don Carlo had been out peddling tickets to a League affair. The FBI held a more logical theory—that the $30,000 was a kickback to the boss of bosses. But if Colombo thought he could buy his way back to Gambino's good graces, he was wrong.

In the spring of 1971, the League completed plans for a mammoth Unity Day Rally. Posters announcing the big event appeared in store windows in every Italian neighborhood from the tip of Coney Island to the top of the Bronx.

Crazy Joe sent out his men to remove the placards from South Brooklyn and he personally chased a Colombo *capo* off President St. Furthermore, he warned the merchants in his bailiwick not to contribute to the League and not to shut their shops for the rally.

Gallo's reaction had been anticipated. But the Colombo group was not prepared for what happened next. Gambino himself told Brooklyn storekeepers to take the League posters out of their windows. His captains made similar demands in all Italian sections of the city except Colombo's home base.

Like an old Mack Sennette comedy, hoods ran all over New York, putting up and tearing down placards. Then Anthony Scotto announced that his Brooklyn longshoreman, who had walked off the waterfront to attend the 1970 rally, would stay on the piers this Unity Day. Several politicians got the word and asked that their names be stricken from the rally speakers' list.

Undaunted, Colombo predicted that the second IACRL Unity Day would be an even more colossal spectacle then the first. And when he arrived at Columbus Circle around 11:30 a.m. on June 28, he was gratified to find several thousand of his fans waiting for the rally to begin.

Festive red-white-green banners fluttered in the warm sunshine. Buttons proclaiming "Italian Power" and "We're No. 1" decorated almost every chest. Well-wishers cheered and surged towards Colombo as soon as he stepped into the Circle. His wooden face cracking into an almost friendly smile, he pumped hands and posed for photographs.

A young black man with League press credentials and a 16mm Bolex movie camera took several pictures of him and the wildly enthusiastic crowd. Then he walked behind Colombo, dropped the camera, whipped out a 7.65-millimeter automatic and, from a distance of less than three feet, fired three bullets into the gang chief's head.

Critically wounded, Colombo flopped to the ground. One of his bodyguards (police never learned which one) pulled a .38-caliber Smith & Wesson revolver from a black attaché case and shot the assassin dead.

The first name mentioned in the subsequent investigation was Crazy Joe Gallo. He and Colombo were old and bitter foes. Gallo had made friends in the black crime community and had recruited blacks for his gang. The gunman who shot Colombo was black. Therefore, press and police suggested, he must have been sent by Crazy Joe.

Colombo's sons and many of his associates were certain this theory was correct. But none of the many detectives and FBI men who investigated the shooting were able to link Gallo to the dead assassin, Jerome A. Johnson.

The only gangsters Johnson knew, so far as investigators could determine, were members of the Gambino family.

Police officials later said the execution attempt was not the random act of an insane gunman but a carefully-concocted underworld plot. Johnson, 25, reportedly was promised $200,000 to kill Colombo and had made plans to leave the country immediately after the murder.

"Several people were involved in the plot," Detective Chief Albert Seedman disclosed. "The conspirators met just prior to the shooting to work out last-minute details."

Deputy Police Commissioner Robert Daly said Colombo's intended murder was carefully planned and organized and was "approved only days before" the shooting. He declined to say who approved it, but he said Johnson was hired by "rivals of Colombo in the Italian underworld community."

"Johnson associated with people known to be connected to the Gambino family," Seedman said. "Johnson hung out in a club that was controlled by Paul DiBella, who is reputed to be a soldier in the Gambino family."

The club was Christopher's End, an after-hours joint on the ground floor of the Christopher Hotel, 180 Christopher St. in Greenwich Village. Police knew the club as a homosexual hangout, although Johnson apparently was not gay.

"Johnson frequented the Christopher's End in the

weeks immediately preceding the shooting," Chief Seedman said, "and he was associated with Michael Umbers, the front man and operator of the bar. "Johnson was known to have been an intimate of Umbers."

Other police sources described Umbers as a Gambino "button man" and one of the city's biggest pornography peddlers. He had served time in several New York State prisons—Sing Sing, Auburn, Clinton, Greenhaven—and was wanted in Massachusetts as a fugitive from justice.

Besides Christopher's End, he owned a frankfurter emporium on the same street, "Gay Dogs." He promoted it as "the world's first gay hot dog stand" and called its best-selling item "Queen of the Hot Dogs."

Because of his gay clientele and gang connections, detectives sometimes referred to him as "the fairy godfather."

He also printed and published homosexual books which were prominently displayed in his porno book store, Studio Bookshop. He was arrested on pornography charges in 1969 and again in 1972.

Detectives questioned Umbers after the Colombo shooting. He said he was only slightly acquainted with Johnson and new nothing at all about the most public execution attempt in gangland history.

"We reached out and found him," Seedman said of Umbers. "Found him physically but it was hard to reach him mentally. He wasn't very communicative."

The chief added that Umbers and Johnson shared an interest in "weirdo sex." Johnson was "interested in making pornographic movies and interested in procuring women. What he was trying to do was make a score. He went to numerous females and tried to establish himself as a pimp. He wasn't too successful."

Johnson was unemployed, a drifter who sometimes slept in a vacant store in Little Italy. He spent much of his time trying to pick up girls in Washington Square Park in the Village and in the East Village hippieland. He had no visible means of support but someone gave him enough money to buy flashy clothes and make trips out of town and rent an expensive movie camera. Someone gave him a gun, a box of bullets, and a New Jersey police press card identifying him as a news photographer.

Umbers' police record lists 15 arrests, one of them in Cambridge, Mass., in 1969 on obscenity and procuring charges. He was convicted on this rap and sentenced to six years, but the conviction was overturned on a legal technicality. Reindicted for the same crimes, he never showed up for trial. A Massachusetts warrant for his arrest was issued around the time he met Johnson.

Soon after he became acquainted with Umbers, Johnson began making frequent trips to Cambridge, although he had never been there before. On his last visit to Cambridge, the weekend before he shot Colombo, he rented the Bolex movie camera. He returned to New York on Sunday, the day before the League rally. He phoned a friend that evening and said he was going to "make a big score" the next day and would then leave immediately "for the islands."

Although detectives considered Umbers the link between Johnson and the Gambino family, they were unable to connect the busy purveyor of hot dogs, after-hours booze and pornography to the Colombo shooting.

Some investigators were convinced Gambino ordered

the hit. Others said he merely approved it. One police source said Gallo asked the don's permission to liquidate Colombo, and Gambino replied: "As long as you don't bother me, I don't care what you do."

Colombo's son, Anthony, called the police theories "ridiculous."

"Mr. Gambino is a very dear and very close friend of my father's," Tony said. "And he is a real gentleman. He is the godfather of my six-year-old sister, Catherine. I don't have to say any more than that."

Among Don Carlo's many other godchildren was Vincent Aloi, son of Sebastiano (Buster) Aloi, an old-time Brooklyn mobster who was in the gambling and shylock rackets. Carlo and Buster had been friends for many years. When Buster retired in 1963, he turned his underworld operations over to Vincent. And when Colombo took over the old Profaci gang, Gambino suggested that he elevate Buster's boy to the rank of *caporegime*.

Colombo agreed that Vinnie was just the type of junior executive the mob needed to build a new image. Born September 22, 1933, he is 6 feet 2, 200 pounds, smooth-spoken, intelligent, and hard-working. With his modish but not too mod clothes, oversize gold-rimmed glasses and neatly barbered, moderately long black hair, he looks like a young lawyer or businessman.

He lives with his wife and three children at suburban Ramapo, N.Y., about 30 miles from the city, and commutes to his job at Cameo Weeding Time, a Queens firm that handles all the arrangements for elegant, old-fashioned weddings. Among other things, Vinnie supplies leads to young couples who might need Cameo's services. Vinnie is also part-owner of a trucking firm in Manhattan's garment district.

After Colombo was shot and it became apparent that he was no longer able to handle the family's affairs, the newspapers began speculating about who would succeed him. Several names were mentioned. Vinnie's was not, but a word from Don Carlo was all it took to get him the post of acting head of the Colombo crew. And this put the family right back in Carlo's pocket.

The papers also were wrong in their predictions that the Colombo troops would quickly massacre Crazy Joe and his men. Gallo stayed out of sight for a few weeks, then became even more of a public figure than before. He traveled around the city unarmed and without a bodyguard, which would have been suicidal if the Colombos were gunning for him. He claimed he was going straight and made new friends in the theatrical and literary sets.

He didn't act in any way like a man who expects to be murdered. And if a contract had been put out on him, he would surely have known about it.

He married a beautiful brunette divorcee, Sina Essary, on March 18, 1972, at the Manhattan apartment of actor Jerry Orbach and his wife Marta, with whom Gallo was collaborating on a book about how he gave up his wicked ways. Crazy Joe certainly seemed to have turned over a new leaf, but detectives said it had the same old script written on it.

During the week of his wedding, the supposed start of his new life, Gallo and two of his goons, Frank (Punchie) Illiano and John Cutrone, invaded a Long Island nightclub in which a Colombo *capo* was a secret partner. Joey informed the manager that he wanted a share of the business. The frightened manager notified the Colombo group and the incident was reported to Vincent Aloi and his godfather.

Then, on the night of Easter Sunday, April 2, something much more serious occurred. Safecrackers hit Ferrara's, a famous 80-year-old pastry shop and café in the heart of Manhattan's little Italy. The robbers got at least $55,000.

Ferrara's is a legitimate, multi-million-dollar business. Its goodies attract every type of sweet-toothed citizen, from school kids and housewives to mob bosses. Don Carlo had held court there many times over the years. Vinnie Aloi and his father are regular patrons.

Though gangsters meet and eat there, Ferrara's could not be described as a mob hangout. Its very respectability is a lure almost as strong as its aromas of cappuccino and fresh-baked pastries. Mafiosi feel as secure in this Little Italy landmark as they do in church. And there is an understanding that the rackets flourishing elsewhere in the neighborhood shall not disturb the tranquility of Ferrara's.

It was even more crowded than usual on Easter Sunday. Families in their best clothes flocked in after mass in Old St. Patrick's Cathedral two blocks away. Other families drove down to Ferrara's from uptown, the Bronx, Brooklyn, Queens, and the suburbs. People waiting for tables and takeout orders lined up on the sidewalk.

The staff was so busy that nobody noticed that a man who ducked into a washroom shortly before 6 p.m. was still there when the café closed at six. After the managers and employees left, he unlocked the back door and admitted an accomplice. They entered the red-carpeted, wood-paneled office at the rear of the restaurant and inserted a telegraph-type key in the electric alarm box on the side of the large steel safe standing against the far wall.

Using the code signal assigned to Ferrara's, they signaled Holmes Protection, Inc. that the safe was going to be opened. Holmes signaled back that the message had been received. So the protection service was not alarmed when a light went on, indicating that Ferrara's safe was open.

The burglars used an acetylene torch with a white-hot magnesium bar to cut through the safe's outer and inner doors. As they worked, they accidentally started a fire which they doused with water from the kitchen.

At 10:30 p.m., Holmes' headquarters noticed Ferrara's alarm light was still on. Holmes signaled the café and the signal was answered, indicating all was well. About 45 minutes later, Holmes again signaled Ferrara's, but this time there was no reply. Holmes guards and police arrived at the café a few minutes later, but the robbers were gone with the weekend receipts.

Don Carlo was shocked when he heard about the robbery Monday morning from one of his captains. He ordered an investigation to determine if the safecrackers were Mafia members or outsiders. Whoever did it obviously knew all about Ferrara's, its security setup, and the fact that Easter weekend receipts were in the safe.

Tuesday, Vincent Aloi and seven other gangsters held an emergency conference at the upstate farm of Carmine (The Snake) Persico, a senior Colombo *capo* who was serving time in Atlanta Federal Prison. Carmine had led Profaci forces in the Profaci-Gallo War. He had once tried to garrote Gallo and had sworn to kill Crazy Joe.

Wednesday, Carmine's brother, Alphonse Persico,

and his bodyguard flew to Atlanta to see Carmine. They returned to New York that night and a 36-year-old safe-cracker named Richard Grossman suddenly vanished from his Brooklyn haunts.

Thursday, Brooklyn restaurateur Gennaro Ciprio was seen talking to Gallo outside his President St. headquarters. Detectives who observed them together said Ciprio seemed excited. The detectives were there because they had just received a report that the long-rumored contract on Joey had finally been issued.

Why Ciprio was there was even more intriguing. A former Joe Colombo bodyguard, he went berserk when his boss was shot. Howling hysterically, he jumped off the bandstand and assaulted every black man within slugging distance before police restrained him. But he also did business with Crazy Joe. And with the missing Grossman.

Ciprio was well known at Ferrara's and had been there several times within the past two weeks. He frequently conversed with the owners, cooks, bakers, and waiters. It sometimes seemed that he took as much interest in the café's operation as he did his own place, which made sausages and other Italian specialties sold every year in Little Italy's colorful Feast of San Gennaro.

Thursday, April 6, was Crazy Joe's 43rd birthday. But Ciprio didn't drive over to President St. just to wish him happy birthday. A few hours after that chat, Gallo got into his Cadillac with his bride; her 10-year-old daughter by a previous marriage; Joe's sister, Mrs. Carmella Fiorello; his bodyguard, Peter (Pete the Greek) Diapoulas, and Pete's date, Edith Russo. They went to Manhattan to celebrate the occasion with a champagne supper at the Copacabana nightclub.

They left the Copa around 3:30 a.m. Friday and drove downtown to Little Italy for a late snack. As his black Caddy cruised along Mulberry St., Joey noticed the neon sign outside Umberto's Clam House, a new place he had never tried. He told Pete to stop the car.

Mulberry St. is usually busy even at 4 a.m., but now a cold drizzle was falling and the street was almost deserted. Pete parked the Caddy around the corner on Hester St. and they all hurried into Umberto's. Two men were at a table near the front door and as soon as Joey's party was settled at two butcher block tables at the rear of the small, sparsely-furnished restaurant, one of the men got up and left.

Gallo and his companions were enjoying seafood and hot sauce, washed down with soft drinks, when the back door opened and two or three gunmen came in. Gallo and Pete had their backs to the door and they didn't realize anything was wrong until women started screaming and clam-lovers began diving under tables.

One of the gunman walked up to Joey, firing steadily. Pete the Greek was shot in the left hip as he reached for his .32-caliber revolver. A customer at the counter also pulled a pistol and fired at the assassins.

Hit in the left buttock and left elbow, the unarmed Gallo made a dash for the door and took a third bullet in the back. He stumbled outside and fell dead in the middle of Hester St., a few feet from his Cadillac. His passing was in the best James Cagney tradition, befitting a man who modeled his life after Hollywood hoods.

As she knelt in the wet street beside the body, his sister sobbed: "He changed his image. That's why this happened."

Monday, April 10, was a particularly busy day in

mob-land. At 2:45 a.m., Gennaro Ciprio left his restaurant, Gennaro's Feast Specialties, in the Bath Beach section of Brooklyn where Al Capone got his start. As soon as Ciprio came out the door, two men emerged from the shadows. Ciprio grabbed his gun but a hail of bullets struck him before he could fire. When the cops got there he was dead on the sidewalk, a loaded .38 beside him and $1,300 cash in his pocket.

Later that day, Joey Gallo was buried in his wedding suit and a $5,000 casket with a gold nameplate. Still later, Pete Diapoulas limped into Manhattan Criminal Court to answer a charge of unlawful gun possession. And that night police found the missing Richard Grossman. His body, badly beaten and shot through both eyes, was discovered in the trunk of a car that had been abandoned in the Sheepshead Bay section of Brooklyn, a favorite mob dumping ground. Medical examiners estimated he had been killed the previous Wednesday.

The Gallo, Ciprio, and Grossman hits appeared unrelated at first. But the word on Mulberry St. was that Ferrara's safe was cracked by Ciprio and Grossman, who had worked together before, and that Joey Gallo had authorized them to open the pastry box. If so, it was a typical act of Gallo bravado and a final nose-thumb at Mafia authority.

Several more murders followed, with Colombo and Gallo associates the main casualties. Then police got an unexpected break in the Gallo murder case.

Early in May, a hefty hoodlum named Joseph Luparelli surrendered to the FBI in California and confessed that he set up the Gallo kill. Luparelli had been a chauffeur–bodyguard to the Colombo *consiglieri* Joseph (Joe Yak) Yacovelli.

He said he was sitting in Umberto's when the Gallo group entered. Knowing about the contract on Joey, Luparelli hurried to a mob rendez-vous down the street where he found four Colombo members—Carmine (Sonny Pinto) DiBiase, Phil Gambino (no relation to Carlo), and two brothers known to Luparelli as Cisco and Benny.

The mobsters phoned Yacovelli, told him Gallo was in the clam house and received authorization to strike. Then they drove to Umberto's in two cars, one of them driven by Luparelli, and parked near the back door on Hester St. While the drivers waited, DiBiase and two other gunmen went inside and started shooting. They fled in the getaway cars after Gallo was slain.

Luparelli said he later became convinced that the gang planned to kill him next so he couldn't talk about the clam-house shootout. He fled to California and then sought protection from the FBI. New York police and federal agents picked up Phil Gambino, but Sonny Pinto was gone from Mulberry St.

Dodging the law was an old game for DiBiase. He had once gone underground for seven years while sought for the 1951 murder of his best friend at a Mulberry St. club. During this period, he made the "most wanted" list of the FBI and NYPD. When he was finally caught, he was convicted of first-degree murder and sentenced to die in the electric chair, but he won a second trial and acquittal.

One other interesting fact about DiBiase: He was Gennaro Ciprio's godfather.

In its obituary on Crazy Joe, *Time* magazine said: "Gallo had been counted among the walking dead ever since he aroused the anger of the biggest boss of them all,

Carlo Gambino. Told to stop muscling into Gambino's operations, including the lucrative narcotics traffic in East Harlem, cocky Gallo hurled the ultimate Mafia insult at Gambino: he spit at him."

(Federal, police, and underworld sources interviewed for this book doubt such an incident occurred. Not even Crazy Joe was that crazy.)

Later, after more bodies turned up, *Time* concluded: "Much of the bloodshed was part of a clever and brutal drive by the nation's most powerful Mafia commander, Carlo Gambino, to seize firm control over all the New York clans to establish himself as undisputed Boss of Bosses."

Six months after the Gallo murder, *New York* magazine devoted a special issue to the Mafia. It reported: "Naturally, the Colombo family wanted Joey Gallo killed, but, as authorities have now learned, it was actually Gambino who issued a contract at the Colombo's urging for Joe Gallo's death.

"When the real fighting erupted between the Gallos and Colombos in the spring of 1972, the Gambino family eagerly provided both sides with guns and ammunition. Evidently the more men killed on each side, the better. Those left will be in a much weakened position, more easily controlled by Gambino."

CHAPTER 14

LITTLE LAMB OF THE CROSS

WHILE GANGLAND GUNS WERE THINNING the ranks of the Colombo and Gallo gangs, the old Genovese group was undergoing a much more peaceful upheaval.

It's co-chairman, Jerry Catena, was sent to prison in March 1970 for refusing to answer questions put to him by the New Jersey State Investigation Commission. He was then 68 and in poor health. He had been talking about retiring to Florida.

With Jerry in jail, Thomas (Tommy Ryan) Eboli became the family boss. He had long aspired to this post, but now it seemed to be more trouble than it was worth. Since Vito Genovese's death in 1969, several valuable lieutenants and soldiers had defected to other gangs and at least two of these gangs had moved into territory formerly controlled by Don Vito.

Adding insult to injury, one of Eboli's captains was taking over racquets that Tom had run for years. An arrogant, violent man who often used his fists instead of his head to settle an argument, Eboli must have considered drastic measures to stop these incursions. But other factors restrained him from making any sudden moves.

Too many eyes were watching. In the summer of 1972, he was under intensive investigation by the Federal Bureau of Narcotics and Dangerous Drugs, the New Jersey State Investigation Commission, the Waterfront Commission, the Joint Federal State Task Force on Organized Crime, and the New York City Police Department Organized Crime Control Bureau. It was no time to do anything drastic. Tommy had no intention of joining Jerry in jail.

Born in a small town near Naples in 1911, Eboli was a baby when his parents brought him to New York. He grew up on the pushcart-crowded streets of the Italian section of bohemian Greenwich Village. He became a professional pugilist, taking the name Tommy Ryan in that era of Irish boxers, and later made a name for himself as a fight manager.

His stable of sluggers included such top-ranking contenders as Tony Pellone and Rocky Castellani. When Rocky was knocked out in Madison Square Garden in 1952, Eboli jumped into the ring and attacked the referee and the matchmaker. He was arrested, charged with assault, fined $3,500, and barred forever from the fight game in New York State.

But it wasn't a total loss. His reputation as a hot-tempered head-basher got him a job as a strong-arm goon for Anthony (Tony Bender) Strollo, rackets ruler of Greenwich Village and the West Side docks. Eventually he became a *caporegime* under Bender in the Genovese army, then an underboss when Genovese went to prison, then co-administrator with Catena when Strollo disappeared. And, finally, the ex-pug was the family champ.

Despite the body blows delt some of his underworld enterprises, he still had a lot of clout. He ran Bender's old rackets in Greenwich Village and on the Manhattan waterfront. He was a secret partner in several nightclubs, discotheques, after-hours joints, and homosexual hangouts. He owned one of the city's biggest vending machine and jukebox businesses. He had several other legitimate fronts plus a piece of the gambling action in Las Vegas. And he was negotiating to buy a hotel in the Catskill Mountain resort area, hoping to set up a casino there when and if the state legalized this form of gambling. Legislators had already been approached about passing such a law.

Although he was getting on in years, Eboli was still handsome and physically tough. He spent at least two or three nights a week at nightclubs and dimly-lit East Side cocktail lounges and when these places closed he lingered until dawn with shapely showgirls and $100-a-trick call girls.

He had at least three mistresses—one in Greenwich Village, one in Brooklyn, one in New Jersey. One of these, Mary Carcella, an abundantly endowed brunette, shared his luxurious $800-a-month apartment in Horizon House, on the Jersey Palisades in Fort Lee, N.J., overlooking the Hudson River and the Manhattan skyline.

From his terrace and picture windows, Tommy Ryan had one of the most magnificent views in the world, but he gave it up abruptly and without notice. A moving van pulled up to Horizon House on July 11, 1972. Four men got out, entered Eboli's apartment, and began clearing out the furniture and furnishings.

Eboli's lease was not up until August 1 and his sudden departure caught the management by surprise. The Fort Lee Police Department does not concern itself with the comings and goings of its several affluent, Mafia-connected citizens. But other lawmen got wind of Tommy's "disappearance" and started looking for him. They learned that on Thursday, July 13, a young man had removed Eboli's Cadillac from the Horizon House garage.

The mystery was quickly solved. Tom and Mary had simply moved into a $150,000 mansion he had purchased a few blocks from the apartment house. They spent the first couple of days in their new home supervising the laying of rugs, hanging of drapes, arrangement of furniture, and other chores. Then Tom decided he had earned a little recreation.

He shaved, showered, powdered, sprayed and cologned himself on Saturday July 15. He put on a blue sport shirt and matching slacks, instead of the silk or mohair suits he usually wore on business trips, and stuck a thick wad of bills in a pants pocket. When he was satisfied with his appearance, he climbed into his air-conditioned 1972 Cadillac and was driven over the river by his longtime chauffeur and bodyguard, Joseph Sternfeld.

Sternfeld, then 53, ran the G.I. Joe Frankfurter Service, a pushcart hotdog business with headquarters in Greenwich Village, and he had been with Tommy enough years to know all his habits, good and bad. He took his boss to the Crown Heights section of Brooklyn and stopped the Caddy near the intersection of Lefferts and New York avenues, in a formerly Italian neighborhood that was now mostly black and Puerto Rican.

It was a few minutes after 6 p.m. when Eboli left the car. "Pick me up at one o'clock," he told Sternfeld. As the Caddy pulled away from the curb, Eboli entered a three-story, yellow-brick apartment building that was the home of an old friend, Mrs. Elvira (Dolly) Lenzo.

Dolly, a pretty, brown-eyed, brown-haired divorcee or widow, had met Eboli several years earlier while she was supporting herself and her three children as superintendent of an apartment house in his old Greenwich Village neighborhood. Their romance continued when she moved to Brooklyn. Tommy never phoned or made a date in advance, but he expected her to be home when he called.

He spent seven hours in her comfortable apartment that last Saturday night. Around 10 o'clock, she served him one of his favorite meals—stuffed peppers and beans.

He kissed her goodbye at one a.m., walked through the gate in the four-foot-high wire fence in front of her home at 400 Lefferts Ave. and started toward his black Cadillac, parked about 60 feet away. He didn't notice the yellow-and-red truck moving slowly along the street behind him.

Eboli was directly under the street lamp when the truck pulled alongside. A man leaned out of the open window on the passenger side of the truck cab and pumped five .32-caliber slugs into Tommy Ryan's head. The gunman also pegged a shot at Sternfeld as the truck sped away, smashing the left front window of the Cadillac.

Unhurt, the burly bodyguard got out of the Caddy and ran to Eboli's side. One glance at the bloody mess on the sidewalk convinced Sternfeld there was nothing he could do. So he hurried back to the Caddy and drove home to New Jersey. He later explained to the authorities that he didn't leave the car there because he was afraid someone would steal it.

One of the first theories police picked up from underworld informers was that Eboli was killed by some of his young soldiers who had disobeyed his orders to get out of narcotics. As the Genovese gang had been dealing in junk for at least 25 years, this seemed implausible.

Detectives and federal agents later received reports that Eboli, far from shunning the dope trade, actually was the middleman in a huge heroine deal that cost the New York Mafia about $3 million.

A key figure in this project was Louis Cirillo, a Bronx bagel baker who was not listed on any crime family report but had become the biggest dope wholesaler in the United States. The Federal Government charged that Cirillo was the American head of an international narcotics syndicate that smuggled nearly $300 million worth of heroin (the estimated street value) into the U.S. from France.

Cirillo was convicted of narcotics trafficking in April 1972 and sentenced to 25 years in prison. His trial lasted seven days but it took the jury only an hour to decide he was guilty. As he passed sentence, Federal Judge Edward Weinfeld described Cirillo as the supplier of "one-sixth of the six tons of heroin consumed each year by addicts in the United States."

One shipment for Cirillo arrived in the Port of New York concealed in the paneling of a red car. The car arrived on a Manhattan waterfront aboard a freighter. It cleared customs on August 23, 1971, and was driven over the

George Washington Bridge to a mansion in Fort Lee, N.J., where it was dismantled in the garage.

Five men removed the door handles, panels, and seats from the car and took out 180 pounds of heroin packed in plastic bags. Each of the bags contained 500 grams. One bag accidentally fell on the floor, burst open, and spilled nearly a quarter of its contents.

"There's enough there (on the floor) to kill a regiment in the Air Force," one of the smugglers remarked.

Cirillo paid $300,000 dollars cash for the heroin haul. The money, in crisp new $100 bills, was delivered in a brown suitcase. Two of the smugglers gave James a $1,500 gold watch when the deal was completed. He was wearing the watch on his left wrist when he was arrested five months later.

One of the smugglers, Roger Preiss, a Paris interior decorator, became a key prosecution witness at Cirillo's trial and lead narcotics agents to the Fort Lee mansion where particles of heroin were found on the garage floor. The inquiry then turned to a prominent Fort Lee resident, Tommy Eboli.

Although his name was not mentioned officially in the Cirillo case, investigators said privately that Eboli introduced Cirillo to the Cosa Nostra establishment and vouched for his reliability. On Eboli's word, Carlo Gambino and other mob leaders invested $3 million in Cirillo's smuggling ventures. The bagel baker still had their dough when the feds grabbed him.

On April 29, two days after Cirillo was convicted, the narcs invaded his modest Bronx home with a search warrant, crowbars, and shovels. They found $978,100 cash, mostly in $100 dollar bills, buried in his backyard and $100,000 dollars more behind the wood paneling in his basement recreation room.

The $1,078,100 was one of the biggest cash seizures ever made in a narcotics investigation, but the agents weren't satisfied. They had reliable information that Cirillo had about $4 million more stashed away. Hunting this buried treasure, agents virtually tore down the $65,000 home of Cirillo's brother-in-law in Massapequa, L.I., and dug up the front and back yards. But they didn't find what they were looking for.

Wherever Cirillo hid the money, the mob was searching just as hard as Uncle Sam. And it was reported that Gambino held Eboli responsible for the loss.

Four months before Eboli was hit, his captains held a meeting and voted to remove him from his command—an extremely unusual action that could not be accomplished peacefully unless Eboli agreed to resign or the Mafia Commission backed up the captains. The captains wanted to replace Eboli and the incarcerated Catena with one of their own—*Caporegime* Francesco Alphonse Tieri.

Tieri, then 68, was the gang's senior captain and most popular leader. He was much closer to Don Carlo and Gambino underboss Aniello Dellacroce then he had ever been to Eboli or Catena. Called Frank, Funzi, and Frenchy, also Francois and The Frenchman, he was born in Naples and had more than his share of the fabled Neapolitan charm.

He owned several garment manufacturing firms and was a vice-president of an interstate frozen-food trucking firm. He had been arrested for assault, robbery, bookmaking, and conspiracy to violate federal tax laws, but had never been convicted. He was reputed to be very powerful on the New Jersey waterfront where he supervised gambling and loansharking.

After the captains' conference in late March, James had a sitdown with Gambino and Dellacroce. What was said has not been recorded, but immediately thereafter Tieri began taking over some of Tommy Ryan's rackets. Tieri has been in the pool a long time without making any waves. He certainly would not have antagonized the terrible-tempered Tommy without the knowledge that Gambino was behind him. And Eboli certainly would not have allowed such gross insubordination had he not seen Don Carlo's dark shadow.

Investigators spotted other signs of the don's disfavor. One was the mass defection of Eboli troops to the Gambino camp. Another was the fact that Gambino encouraged these men to bring their racquets with them whenever possible. He also encouraged Phillip Rastelli, a leader of the former Joe Bananas bunch, to invade Eboli territory in Bergen County, N.J.

The people who keep an underworld body count noted that Eboli was the ninth gangland murder victim in New York City since Crazy Joe Gallo was executed and the 18th since Joe Colombo was shot.

And Don Carlo was now in firm control of all five families.

His Godson, Vinnie Aloi, was running the Colombo outfit. His old friends, Phil Rastelli and Natale Evola, were running the old Bonanno group since the semi-retirement of ailing Paul Sciacca. Another old friend and protégé, Carmine (Mr. Gribbs) Tramunti, was handling the affairs of the former Lucchese mob. And an even older pal, cheerful

Funzi Tieri, had succeeded Tommy Ryan, a man Gambino had never really trusted.

None of the new mob leaders had the stature or strength of such awesome predecessors as Joe Profaci, Joe Bananas, Albert Anastasia, Three-Finger Brown, or Vito Genovese. They were all good captains, born to obey orders, but each lacked one or more of the qualities that make a great Mafia boss—intelligence, shrewdness, aggressiveness, ruthlessness, an ability to get along with the troops and people outside the mobs, a brain that works like an IBM computer and a heart that can appear warm or cold, depending on the occasion. Don Carlo completely dominated them all.

He had merged the five forces into One Man's Family, something the other great dons had been unable to accomplish. But there was still the bothersome problem of what to do with the surviving Gallo gangsters.

The youngest brother, Albert (Kid Blast) Gallo, was still around, though he had neither Larry's brains nor Joey's ferocity. At least two other members, Punchy Illiano and John Cutrone, were seasoned veterans of the mob wars and were considered a threat to peace.

The Gallos were down but no one counted them out. Then they made a horrendous blunder that brought the full forces of the law and the Mafia down on them.

A Gallo associate was sitting in the Neapolitan Noodle restaurant on Manhattan's E. 79th St. on the evening of August 11, 1972, when three Colombo lieutenants walked in and parked on bar stools. The Gallo man ducked into the restaurant's phone booth, made a short call and then departed. A few minutes later, the Colombo gangsters were assigned a table. Their places at the bar were taken by three businessmen, all kosher meat executives.

As they sipped their drinks, a Gallo gunman entered the restaurant and shot the businessmen, killing two and wounding the third, in the mistaken belief that they were Colombos. This senseless slaughter was denounced publicly by Mayor Lindsay and privately by Don Carlo.

The next night, August 12, the city's Mafia bosses met in emergency session at a private home on Staten Island. Gambino presided over the meeting with his underboss, Aniello Dellacroce, and his new *consigliere*, Joe N. Gallo, at his side. The other four families were represented by their acting administrators—Vincent Aloi, Natale Evola, Carmine Tramunti, Frank Tieri. Their underbosses and counselors also were present.

The bosses voted to break up the Gallo gang and distribute its approximately 100 members and associates among the five families. Each family would select the men it wanted. It was like the National Football League's player draft, except that in this case the strongest team got first pick.

Tom Renner, investigative reporter for the Long Island newspaper *Newsday*, quoted federal sources as saying Gambino chose John Cutrone, senior *caporegime* of the Gallo gang.

Gambino reportedly commented that if Cutrone didn't want to serve on his team, "his first play is for two yards." Asked what he meant by his remark, "Gambino turned his thumb down and gestured toward the ground, answering: 'Six feet.' "

The Newsday article said the bosses decided that the

Gallo brothers' still-active father, Umberto Gallo, would be assigned to Natale Evola and his sole surviving son, Kid Blast, would go to Carmine Tramunti. When Umberto was informed of this arrangement, he gave a two-word reply. The second word was "you." Joey would have been proud of his old man.

The bosses decreed that the Gallo-Profaci War, which had become the Gallo-Colombo War, was now officially over. Whether the cease-fire would be obeyed remained to be seen. 10 days after the Staten Island sitdown, a Manhattan grand jury began probing the mistaken-identity killings in the Neapolitan Noodle. And Gambino's underboss went to jail.

Little Lamb of the Cross, which is the literal translation of Aniello Dellacroce, was convicted in March 1971 of criminal contempt for refusing to answer grand jury questions about his underworld activities. Six months later, he was sentenced to one year in jail. But he managed to avoid going there for almost a year while his conviction was appealed all the way to the U.S. Supreme Court. This legal maneuvering cost him an estimated $20,000.

His appeals were finally exhausted, and he may have heaved a secret sigh of relief when a Corrections Department van whisked him to the city's prison complex on Rikers Island. Considering the recent excitement, a rest might do him good.

Only three weeks before, he had narrowly escaped a bizarre assassination attempt at his Little Italy headquarters, the Ravenite Social Club.

The Ravenite occupies a former store on the ground floor of an old, five-story tenement at 247 Mulberry St.

It's heavy wooden door is usually closed and it's two large windows are covered with green curtains so no one can look in—or fire in—from the street. It has no sign to announce its presence. Strangers pass it by without a second glance and neighborhood residents pretend not to know it is there, although all Little Italy realizes it is the *sanctum sanctorum* of Don Carlo's field commander.

Dellacroce lives across the street at 232 Mulberry in a tenement flat as lavishly furnished as a millionaire's mansion. When he is at home or in the club, his Cadillac Eldorado, fire engine red with a white top and dazzling white interior, usually is parked at the curb. Unlike Don Carlo, the Little Lamb believes that if you have it, flaunt it. He is a throwback to the Roaring 20s.

The Mulberry St. block between Spring and Prince Sts., where Dellacroce lives, is only a stone's throw from Police Headquarters but he relies on his own for protection. Every adult male stranger who enters the block on foot or by car is observed and reported. On the night of August 1, 1972, however, a car stopped outside the Ravenite so suddenly that the watchers were caught off-guard.

Carlo Anthony Lombardi, 29, a hotheaded Brooklyn thug suspected of at least two murders, stormed out of the car and into the club. As he was neither a member nor an invited guest, this was an extremely dangerous thing to do. Lombardi had a revolver stuck in his waistband and he was looking for Carmine Consalvo, brother of Dellacroce's chauffeur–bodyguard, Frank Consalvo.

Carmine and a half-dozen other members were playing cards when Lombardi barged in. There were a few angry words. Then Lombardi drew his gun and fired four shots in the general direction of Carmine. No one was hit. The Ravenites disarmed Lombardi and clubbed him with fists, feet, and his own firearm. He fought free, ran outside, and drove to Beekman-Downtown Hospital for treatment, but left when doctors inquired how he received a deep wound over his right eye.

When Gambino gunmen went hunting next day, they couldn't find Lombardi at any of his customary haunts. He had gone upstate to practice firing an M-1 automatic rifle he had recently acquired.

Ravenite members learned about the greasegun a week later when Lombardi returned and tried to use it on them. He burst into the club, which was the last place anyone would have looked for him, and squeezed the trigger as horrified hoods dived under tables and chairs. But the gun jammed.

Cursing, Lombardi backed out the door and took off in a car driven by another man. Before his intended victims were up off the floor, he was out of the neighborhood. Dellacroce was in the club on at least one of Lombardi's visits and he notified Gambino that he had another Crazy Joe on his hands.

Instead of heading for South America or some other far-off land, Lombardi holed up in the Catskill Mountains with a bosomy 22-year-old brunette. Around midnight on August 9, two young gunmen crashed into their motel room and ordered them to get dressed. They were taken for a ride that ended on lonely Old Route 17 near the Sullivan County hamlet of Thompson, between the resort towns of Liberty and Monticello, N.Y.

There, Lombardi and the girl got out of the car and the gunmen used them for target practice.

Shot twice in the head, Lombardi fell dead beside the road. His curvaceous companion was hit in the neck and the bullet blow knocked her to the ground a few feet from him. She lay still, held her breath and played dead.

One of the gunmen walked towards her, raising his pistol to administer the *coup de grace*. At that moment a frightened squirrel, awakened by the shots, began chattering in the bushes. The nervous hoods fired a volley at the sound, killing the squirrel. Then they jumped into their beige convertible and roared away.

A passing truck driver spotted the splattered figures alongside the road about 30 minutes later and called police. The girl was taken to Community General Hospital in Liberty and later held under heavy police guard as a material witness in the murder.

Around the same time that Lombardi and his friend were shot, the two nephews of Gambino gangster JoJo Manfredi—Phil D. and Phil J.—were executed in the Bronx. Detectives considered the two double hits an interesting but unconnected coincidence.

There was a definite connection, however, between the Lombardi snuffout and the subsequent slaying of his lifelong friend, Joseph Fucillo, a city water meter reader. Two marksmen planted five slugs in Fucillo's head on October 17, 1972, as he backed his 1968 Dodge down the driveway of his Brooklyn home. Police said he was the wheelman who drove Lombardi to and from the Ravenite Social Club.

Two days later, state police sent out a wanted-for-murder alarm for two Ravenite members. They were described as "armed and extremely dangerous."

By this time, Aniello Dellacroce was safely tucked away

on Rikers Island, far from the gunsmoke–polluted air of Mulberry St. And Carlo Gambino was in a Columbus Hospital oxygen tent, giving rise to rumors that his next breath might be his last.

CHAPTER 15

SIC SEMPER MAFIA

THE FEDERAL GOVERNMENT'S EFFORTS TO deport Gambino, begun in 1940 and renewed after the 1957 Apalachin conference, accelerated in 1966.

After nine years of legal battles, the Immigration Service ordered Gambino to enter the U.S. Public Health Service Hospital on Staten Island so that government doctors could determine exactly how serious his heart condition was.

While he was there, a deportation hearing was held at the hospital. Those present included an Immigration Service hearing officer, a prosecutor, Gambino, his lawyer, a hospital doctor, a nurse, three or four witnesses, and an FBI agent who was there as a spectator.

The agent had been following Don Carlo's career for years and knew the details of many of his Byzantine intrigues. Gambino looked a bit thin and pale, but otherwise healthy. Speaking so softly that it was difficult to hear him, he answered the first few questions put to him by the prosecutor. Then he looked up and saw the FBI man.

Gambino gasped. "I've got a pain," he said, placing his right hand over his heart. He popped some heart-stimulant pills into his mouth while the doctor and nurse fiddled with an oxygen tank. He was given oxygen and morphine. Then he was carried out on a stretcher and the hearing was adjourned.

By now, the sight of Gambino in an oxygen mask or stretcher-borne had become familiar to the weary Immigration officers. But they still kept plugging away. Public Health Service doctors said he was indeed a sick man, but not as sick as he sometimes seemed. Their diagnosis was "arteriosclerotic heart disease."

The hearing officer found: "He was able, despite poor health, to attend various family functions... travel to the barber shop... visit his business operations..."

If he could do all of this, the Immigration Service decided, he was well enough for an air or sea trip. An order for his deportation was issued Dec. 30, 1966. "COSA BIG TOLD TO GO BACK TO SICILY AND STAY THERE," a *Daily News* headline announced on New Year's Eve. But telling him was one thing; getting him there was something else.

"I love this country," Don Carlo had said at one of the deportation hearings. "It would break my heart to leave."

Another five years passed while his lawyer appealed the deportation order up to the Supreme Court, which upheld it. Meanwhile, several of Gambino's seemingly healthier acquaintances, including a half-dozen mob leaders, a doctor who treated his heart ailment, and one of the FBI men who arrested him in 1970, had died of heart attacks.

His wife, Katherine, who had been expected to outlive him, also died in August 1971 following a long illness that canceled the Fourth of July celebration at the "summer house" that year. Hundreds of mourners attended the Mass of Resurrection offered for her at Our Lady of Grace Catholic Church in Brooklyn, where she had attended Sunday services most of her life. She died as quietly as she had lived and her death was announced simply by paid advertisements in the daily newspapers.

Three months later, the Government made a final effort to send Don Carlo home. All his appeals had been used up. The Italian government didn't want him back but reluctantly agreed to accept him. The Immigration Service booked him on a TWA flight to Rome and also reserved a cabin on the passenger liner *Christoforo Colombo* in case he missed the plane. It looked as if he had lost the long deportation battle.

Two days before he was scheduled to leave, Gambino was admitted to Victory Memorial Hospital in Brooklyn. His doctor said he was too ill to go anywhere. Other sources close to the don said his heart ailment was aggravated by his wife's death, worry over the deportation order, and fear of flying. He had never taken an air trip.

Public Health Service cardiologists examined him and reported he was suffering from heart disease, congenital heart failure, severe chest pains, arteriosclerosis, and diabetes. His heart condition, they said, was "permanent, deteriorating, and cannot improve."

They added that Gambino cannot travel without risk

to his life. So the Immigration Service, which had been trying for 30 years to get rid of him, issued an indefinite stay of deportation. Sol Marks, chief of the New York office of Immigration and Naturalization, claimed it wasn't a total surrender.

"Because the doctors state that to move Gambino at this time would be a definite gamble with his life, we have temporarily brought our efforts to a halt," Marks said. "We are not saying we have given up, only that we'll see what the future holds."

The Justice Department also called a "temporary" halt in its efforts to bring Gambino to trial in the alleged armored car plot. It began to look as if Gambino could coast downhill from now on. But he would have to coast very cautiously.

Aware that the feds are watching him to make the slightest wrong move, Don Carlo has become a virtual recluse, running his empire from his large second-floor flat at 2230 Ocean Parkway. He is cared for by his wife's sister and her husband, Providencia and Phil Villano, who live on the first floor and have never concerned themselves with mob affairs. Gambino does not keep a single bodyguard on the premises.

He has a listed telephone, but he uses it only to talk to his sons, grandchildren, and other relatives about personal family affairs. "How are you feeling?" "How is the weather out there?" Nothing important is ever discussed over the phone.

As no outsiders are ever admitted to his second-floor sanctum, he is reasonably certain the rooms have not been bugged. Once a week, a Cadillac or Lincoln driven by one of his brothers or cousins takes him to a small barber shop where his white hair is trimmed. Sometimes, when the weather is good, he is driven out to his Long Island home, but the barbecues and Fourth of July parties he used to host for his Mafia peers are over. No more boats are tied to his dock and the only sounds heard there on most days are the cries of seagulls.

He is seldom seen at Ferrara's or Angelo's or any of the other cafes or restaurants he patronized for many years, not even at the tiny Brooklyn places he preferred to the gourmet palaces of Manhattan. His simple meals are prepared and eaten at home.

On rare occasions he ventures out for an emergency gathering of the Mafia hierarchy. He prefers to conduct as much business as possible in his Ocean Parkway retreat, surrounded by the familiar things he gathered over half a century. But this isolation does not mean that he is cut off from his realm. Gambino pals and protégés run all the families. And beneath them, as captains and soldiers, are other Gambino men ready to make their move in the event of a sudden vacancy at the top.

There are men in every clan who owe their comfortable positions to Don Carlo. They watch their bosses carefully and report the slightest signs of dissatisfaction or disloyalty. There are even one or two such men in the Ravenite Social Club, keeping tabs on the Little Lamb of the Cross. This spy system works so well that none of the bosses know Papa is watching him.

These men report to Don Carlo's most trusted captains—brothers Joe and Paul and cousin Paul Castellano—and client counselor Joe N. Gallo, a shadowy figure with far more influence than his police files indicate.

Though Gambino lives alone, he is seldom lonely. He receives daily visits from his children, brothers, and cousins. He discusses mob matters with Dellacroce when the underboss is out of jail; with Gallo and with his old soldiers James (Jimmy Brown) Failla, Tom Masotto, and Salvatore Guglielmini, another cousin.

When Dellacroce went away to Rikers Island, the mob continued to function as smoothly as ever. The don's brothers and cousins made daily checks on Aniello's Mulberry St. minions to make sure they were doing their jobs.

Shortly before noon on Saturday, September 30, 1972, a private ambulance stopped outside Gambino's Brooklyn home. Two white-uniformed attendants entered the house and wheeled him out on a stretcher. Although several hospitals were nearby, the ambulance took him to Columbus Hospital in Manhattan.

His previous hospital sojourns seemed to coincide with the grand jury inquiries or official hearings. But this attack apparently was not triggered by a subpoena. A Columbus Hospital spokesman reported: "Mr. Gambino is suffering from a severe heart condition. He's not allowed visitors or phone calls. There is nothing more we are at liberty to talk about at this time."

Two weeks later, while Gambino was still in the hospital, Brooklyn District Attorney Eugene Gold announced what he modestly called "the most massive investigation of organized crime in the history of the country."

He disclosed that an electronic bug had been planted in the office ceiling of the Brooklyn auto junkyard that was the headquarters of Paul Vario, a captain in the Mafia family now bossed by Carmine Tramunti. The "Gold Bug," as the newspapers immediately called it, enabled detectives to listen in on mob conversations for six months. Gold claimed that every mob leader in the city visited the junkyard, although it was later learned that Gambino was never seen there. But Don Carlo was talked about often, just as he was in the Big S garage and at Sam the Plumber's place, and his name was on a list of 677 persons Gold planned to subpoena.

The subpoena barrage was fired on October 16, hitting hundreds of mobsters and policemen suspected of protecting gang rendezvous. Gambino's subpoena could not be served, however, because he was in the sanctuary of a hospital bed.

Some skeptical lawmen suggested that Gambino was tipped off to Gold's impending fireworks and therefore checked into the hospital before the big explosion. Stranger things have happened in mobland, though in this case nothing was proved except that Don Carlo's health was still delicate.

When he left the hospital on October 21, the *Daily News* confidently predicted that he was "headed for the witness stand before a Brooklyn rackets jury." This forecast was as accurate as the one that had him heading home to Sicily.

Or the doctors that told him years ago that he had only a short while to live. But Don Carlo is well aware that he has been living on borrowed time.

So he is taking steps to perpetuate his works. None of his sons or brothers or cousins can do it. His sons are not even in the crime family. And other mobsters' sons who have chosen their fathers' profession are too soft or too weak or too stupid. Except for a few like Vinnie Aloi, they are all too American.

Consequently, Vinnie is the only young boss in the five families. Funzi Tieri was born in 1904; Natale Evola was born in 1907; Carmine Tramunti was born in 1910; Aniello Dellacroce was born in 1915.

Of these, Dellacroce is the strongest although the others outrank him as family heads. An underworld mastermind of security thefts had this to say about Dellacroce in testimony before the Senate crime committee:

"His influence is enormous. His power is incredible."

But whether he will succeed Don Carlo as boss of bosses is anybody's guess. Some underworld sources insist that even if he assumes control of the Gambino mob, he will never have Gambino's influence over the other families because he has too many enemies.

Edward J. McLaughlin, General counsel of the New York State Joint Legislative Committee on Crime accused Dellacroce in 1970 of plotting against Gambino. He said Dellacroce had tried to disguise his own ambitions by suggesting to other underworld leaders that the ailing Don Carlo be replaced by the clan counselor, Joe N. Gallo. Actually, McLaughlin said, Dellacroce wanted the job for himself.

"Weren't you trying to push Gambino out and lining up support for Joe N. Gallo?" McLaughlin asked Dellacroce on the witness stand. Not surprisingly, the Little Lamb refused to say even baaa. McLaughlin also claimed Dellacroce had sought the Mafia Commission's approval of his plan to dump Carlo. As Gambino controls the Commission, this seems highly unlikely. Gambino apparently did not believe McLaughlin's charges. But he kept an eye on his underboss and beefed up his own private army, just in case.

The old dons were dying off and their young lieutenants were not fit to succeed them, so Carlo turned to the Mafia homeland for replacements. He had learned the alien-smuggling game from the biggest smuggler of them all, Little Caesar Maranzano. And Gambino himself had helped thousands of Italians enter the United States illegally, as he had done over the years.

Now thanks to Don Carlo, the alien tide is rising again. They are slipping across the Canadian and Mexican borders and jumping ship in U.S. seaports and flying in with forged passports and visas. Some of them are unskilled laborers who go to work on the Brooklyn docks or a Queens construction project or a Bronx pizza parlor. Others are skilled craftsmen for which the mob has many uses. Still others are strong-arm thugs, thieves and professional killers.

You can see them any day in Little Italy, swaggering around Mulberry St. with their hair a little longer and their clothes a little sharper than the young men who were born in the neighborhood. The American-born residents resent them and call them "greasers," but not to their faces for many of the foreigners are quick with a knife or gun. And they have moved into many of the local rackets.

For example, they tried to extort money from a Little Italy restaurant-owner, and when he refused to pay they set his place on fire. Then they came back and he still said no, so they torched it again. Finally, the owner sought and received protection from an old-time mobster strong enough to keep the newcomers away. But there aren't many old-timers left and the imports are coming on fast.

They are driving the cops and feds frantic because they don't have any police records in this country and nobody in authority knows who they are or what they are up to. And what they are up to is everything.

One group of Gambino-imported aliens has become so big and so diversified that it could be considered a separate crime family. Its specialties include counterfeit watches, hijacking, safecracking, armed robbery, arson, extortion and a complete line of services for illegal aliens, from identification papers to rooms and job placement.

This gang formerly operated the Garofalo Swiss Watch & Movements Import Co. A police raid on the firm's offices turned up thousands of counterfeit watch faces bearing the names of well-known manufacturers like Omega, cheap watch works from Switzerland, phony industrial diamonds, and a stamping machine to imprint brand names on watching dials.

Detectives said the gang would produce a replica of a $200 watch for around $10 dollars or $15 and sell it to a sucker who thought he was getting a bargain for $50 or $100.

In the company warehouse in Little Italy, the cops found thousands of stolen identification papers, including blank Social Security cards and New York State driver licenses. Other items included a stamping device stolen from the Motor Vehicle Department, stacks of stolen airline tickets, pornographic magazines, obscene movies, thousands of slugs for use in vending machines, and 20 cases of cosmetics taken from a hijacked truck.

When police disclosed what was found in the raids, mobsters who owned vending machine firms (such as Tommy Eboli's Tryan, Inc., one of the biggest distributors of jukeboxes, cigarette machines, coffee and soft drink machines, etc.) roared with rage. For many slugs sold by the Swiss Watch gang had wound up in their machines. A sitdown with Carlo Gambino was required to straighten out this sticky situation.

The gang's watches also were widely distributed. A U.S. Border Patrol intelligence report on this operation states:

"The Chicago office is investigating a group of Italian aliens who have been posing as Alitalia Airline pilots and crew personnel with the appropriate identification. They allegedly frequent bars and other business places in groups of three to eight, claiming they are just in from an overseas flight and short of money. They offer to sell allegedly valuable Omega watches for a fraction of their value. The watches are cheap imitations. If arrested, they post bond and abscond. They have operated in Atlanta, New York, Miami, Los Angeles, and Chicago. Some are suspected narcotics couriers."

The phony pilots, their identity papers, and counterfeit watches all came from the Swiss Watch gang. The head of this gang, Bruno Pennisi, a swarthy Sicilian born in 1939, already acts like a Mafia don although his name does not appear on any of the official lists of underworld overlords. He drives from his New Jersey home to Little Italy every day in a chauffeured Continental and as soon as he appears in his favorite coffee shop, bar, or restaurant he is surrounded by 10 or more young Sicilian-speaking hoods who have been awaiting his orders.

"Bruno Pennisi is a leading figure in Carlo Gambino's new Sicilian Secret Society," a police Intelligence officer says. "Gambino is a master at mixing criminal activities with legitimate businesses and labor unions. Now he is adding hundreds of aliens, with no criminal records in this country, to this mix, making it almost impossible to determine who's running what rackets."

He pointed out that many law enforcement agencies are still using the Mafia family charts prepared by the Senate crime committee in 1963 and 1964. Most of the mobsters named on these charts are now dead, retired, or in prison. Even the Gambino family tree prepared by the Justice Department in 1969 is out of date.

To most investigators, Gambino's new recruits are faceless shadows.

"Say we pick up a suspect near the scene of a crime and he turns out to be an illegal alien," a detective commander says. "He gives us a name which is probably phony. He claims he can't speak English, although he understands all our questions. His fingerprints aren't in our files. Neither is his picture. So, unless we catch him in the act, we have to let him go and we still don't know who he is and who he works for.

"We can't contact Interpol (the international police organization) every time we collar a no-speak-English."

The identity of one Sicilian import, Tomaso Buscetta, was so well-known that he couldn't hope to keep it secret indefinitely. But the nefarious Buscetta had managed to elude the police of many nations, including his own.

Chief executioner of the Sicilian Mafia, he was involved in a Palermo shootout that left seven policemen and civilians dead. He skipped to South America and entered the U.S. from Mexico with a forged passport. Then he came to New York, where he reportedly handled several contracts for the Gambino organization.

He was strolling along 42nd St. near the United Nations one humid August day in 1970 when he was suddenly surrounded by heavily-armed federal, state, and local lawmen. Also present was an Italian detective who had pursued him halfway around the globe.

Buscetta was Italy's most wanted criminal. He had been tried there *in absentia*, convicted, and sentenced to a long prison term for the Palermo massacre. Immigration authorities wanted to deport him as soon as possible, but Italy failed to follow up its original request for his extradition. After waiting several months for the extradition papers to arrive from Italy, a federal judge reduced his bail from $75,000 to $40,000 and turned him loose when the necessary collateral was raised.

Immigration agents then escorted him to the border at Nogales, Ariz., and he returned to Mexico. He was later seen in various parts of South America, including Montevideo, Uruguay. In June 1972, a year after he jumped bail, Buscetta was back in New York.

Frank Faso of the daily news reported he was "brought here to lend his lethal expertise to Carlo Gambino" and was "only one of several professional killers imported from Italy by Cosa Nostra chiefs who can no longer count on their own crime family members to run the rackets properly.

"Like the rest of America's 'permissive society,' the Mafia sons are refusing to obey their fathers and godfathers."

Buscetta reportedly was in the dope-smuggling and counterfeit watch rackets, among other things. And he was very close to Rosario Gambino, a cousin of Don Carlo. Rosario first entered the U.S. illegally in 1962. Caught and deported, he returned legally as the husband of a U.S. citizen.

In January 1970, he took Buscetta's mother and sister from their Brooklyn home to prevent their deportation as illegal aliens. Buscetta's son, Antonio, also an illegal alien, was arrested the same day as he was driving a car registered to another Sicilian mobster who had been caught trying to sneak into the U.S. from Canada.

In April 1970, Rosario and three other imported thugs assaulted an off-duty cop who interfered while they were clobbering a Brooklyn coffee shop owner who had refused to pay the Gambino clan for protection. The four were arrested and indicted for assault and extortion.

Rosario pleaded guilty to the assault charge in Brooklyn Supreme Court and was let off with a $100 fine. The federal charge of extortion was still pending as this was written.

In 1972, 10 years after he entered the U.S. illegally and went to work for Don Carlo, Rosario bought three homes for himself, his brother Giuseppe and their father, Tomaso Gambino, at the Tenby Chase development in Delran Township, N.J. Cost of the three-house complex was $103,680. The three also own Father and Sons Pizza, Inc., of Philadelphia, Pa.

Salvatore Inzerillo, one of the men arrested with Rosario in the Brooklyn assault case, also ran a string of pizza parlors where several illegal aliens were arrested by immigration agents.

Carlo Gambino himself is probably the world's biggest pizza pieman. Investigators say he is the secret partner in the metropolitan area's largest pizzeria chain, employing hundreds of aliens.

One apprehended alien told immigration agents his travel itinerary was Palermo-Rome-Montréal-Toronto-Windsor-Detroit-New York. His Palermo contact instructed him to carry a small toy Sicilian donkey cart in his hand when he got off the plane at Montréal International Airport. He was met there by a man who arranged transportation to Toronto and Windsor, Ontario.

Another member of the smuggling ring took him across the river from Windsor to Detroit by motorboat. A car and trailer was waiting on the Detroit side. The smuggler put the boat on the trailer, drove to the airport, and put the Sicilian on a plane to New York, where he was met by a member of the Gambino clan.

Every alien smuggled in by the family is a valuable asset. To start with, he pays $1,000 to $2,000 in transportation fees, above the cost of his plane or ship ticket, and Gambino gets a percentage. Some aliens pay cash; others pay in narcotics, on which the mob makes huge profits. When they reach New York, the aliens go to work for the mob's businesses or rackets, depending on their individual skills. Thus Gambino has a steady supply of professional criminals—gunmen, burglars, counterfeiters, etc.—plus cheap labor for his pizza parlors, meat markets, and fruit stands.

Should an alien complain about low wages or high payoffs to the mob, all it takes is a phone call to get him picked up and deported at the taxpayers' expense. So Gambino even has Uncle Sam working for him on occasion!

Don Carlo always has squeezed every possible penny out of all of his operations. He was the last Mafia boss in New York to collect monthly dues of $25 from each member.

This traditional practice was discontinued a few years ago while he was forming his five-family alliance. As the unofficial boss of all the clans, he couldn't continue collecting dues from his own men without imposing a similar levy on the other gangs. And if he did this, there would surely be a rebellion.

Though he gave up a dues income estimated at $150,000 to $300,000 a year, he more than made up this loss by collection of 10 to 25% of the proceeds from all the waterfront, airport, labor, trucking, produce, carting, smuggling, gambling, shylocking and other rackets in his expanded domain.

Headquarters of his alien-smuggling branch is a Mulberry St. barbershop where seldom is heard an American word. It has a large air-conditioned room in back furnished barracks-style with cots on which illegal immigrants spend their first night in New York. Paul Gambino and Sebastiano Aloi are the official greeters and fee collectors.

The barber shop is the official Port of Entry to Don Carlo's underworld empire. Through it flows a steady stream of Old World crime craftsmen, the kind of carefully trained specialists that affluent America doesn't produce anymore.

The new recruits respect Don Carlo and the Mafia code of conduct. They obey orders and protect their chief from any mutinous members. Remembering what happened to Joe the Boss and Little Caesar, Gambino has surrounded himself with a double layer of loyalty—the inner layer of brothers and cousins, the outer layer of Sicilian imports.

In return for their absolute loyalty, the newcomers are guaranteed jobs that eventually will pay them more in a year than they could earn in Sicily in a lifetime. The wages may be low at first, especially in the legitimate businesses, but Don Carlo always takes good care of his own.

Sicilian triggermen undoubtably have contributed to the recent explosions of underworld violence. Their presence is a warning to all ambitious mobsters who covet Don Carlo's wealth and power.

No one knows how many criminals Gambino has imported, but immigration authorities estimate he has brought in at least 2,000 aliens over the past five years. Federal agents have prepared a master list of more than 100 Mafiosi, all with long criminal records, who have been smuggled into the United States. At least half of them are believed to be working for Don Carlo.

"These guys are animals on a leash," a Justice Department official says of Gambino's foreign legion. "The gang murders show what could happen if that bunch takes over."

Don Carlo holds the leash. No one else—not his brothers or cousins or fellow bosses—is strong enough to control the animals. And when Don Carlo dies, they will be unleashed and the law of the jungle will prevail.

Investigators believe Gambino's underworld legacy will be total terror. His billion-dollar conglomerate will not continue to grow as he had planned but will be torn apart by family feuds. The newcomers brought here to protect the old dons will repeat Lucky Luciano's purge of the Mustache Petes. Then the young immigrants will seize control of the U.S. Crime Syndicate and the cycle will start all over again.

But there will probably never be another underworld genius like Don Carlo Gambino, *Capo di Tutti Capi*.

WHAT GOES UP MUST COME DOWN

THIS CLASSIC EXPOSÉ OF GAMBINO'S rise to power in the Mafia underworld was first published in 1974 by Paul Meskil. Meskil was a reporter and investigative journalist for the *New York Daily News*. When the first edition of this book was published, Carlo Gambino was very much alive. In fact, he was at the height of his power, ensconced as chairman of The Commission, La Cosa Nostra's ruling body. Of course, that is not the case today. Much has changed. For one, Don Carlo has long since passed away. And also, although the Gambino family is still in existence, it is but a shell of its former self.

At its peak in the 1970s, the Gambino family possessed over 800 sworn soldiers as well as 2,000-plus associates, spread across the nation's 50 states. Back then, the Gambino family also had critical ties to key Mafia factions on the island of Sicily, as well as Italy at large. Today, the family only has 100 sworn members and less than 800 associates. And it has virtually no links to any international crime organizations. The remaining four New York crime families—the Genovese, Lucchese, Colombo, and Bonanno outfits—have also seen their ranks weakened since the heydays of the '70s. This decline in the Mafia's powerbase can be attributed to three factors. First, the passage of the R.I.C.O Act in 1970. Second, the legal and skillful implementation of wiretaps in law enforcement investigations. And third, the widespread violation of *omerta* (the Mafia's code of silence) by its own members and associates.

Let us begin with La Cosa Nostra's most venerable enemy: RICO. The acronym stands for Racketeer Influenced and Corrupt Organizations act. The act was passed and made law in 1970. RICO is a legal weapon specifically designed by the federal government to combat organized crime in the United States. It allows for prosecution for racketeering activities performed as part of an ongoing criminal enterprise. To convict a defendant under RICO, the government must prove that the defendant either invested in, or maintained an interest in, a criminal enterprise that impacts interstate commerce.

As it were, in order to secure a successful conviction prior to the RICO Act, law enforcement had to prove that a defendant *personally* took part in the commission of a designated crime. But after the codification of the RICO Act, law enforcement merely had to show that the hoodlum was either invested in, or had an interest in, an ongoing criminal business. Therefore, a mob boss like Carlo Gambino could no longer hide behind the pretext that he had not personally, or directly, committed a crime. For if the government could prove that others had committed crimes on his behalf, and that he had benefitted from said criminal activities, then Gambino himself could be indicted and prosecuted. In short, another way to describe the RICO Act is *guilty by association*.

Perhaps no other law enforcement official in this country's history used the RICO statute so efficiently as Rudolph "Rudy" Giuliani. From 1983 to 1989, Giuliani served as the U.S. Attorney General for the Southern District of New York. And his prime objective—from the first day he took office until his last day in the big chair—was to take down New York's Mafia element.

As a whole.

Where his predecessors (like, for example, notable New York District Attorney Thomas Dewey) had only been able to target *individuals* within the Mafia (due to limitations in prohibition-era statutory codes), Giuliani, now armed with RICO, could take on La Cosa Nostra—*collectively*. From the bosses who sat atop the Commission, right on down to the minions who carried out their treacherous orders. Giuliani now had the means to wage war against the entire machine, all together.

And that's exactly what he did.

But before we delve into Giuliani's crime-fighting exploits, let us take a look at the state-of-affairs of the Gambino family following Don Carlo's passing.

Gambino died on October 15, 1976 of congenital heart failure. He was at home watching a New York Yankees game on T.V. when his heart gave out. He was 74-years-old.

Right before his death, Gambino appointed his cousin

Paul "Big Paulie" Castellano as his successor, though not everyone agreed with this appointment (as we'll discuss later).

In the years leading up to his death, Carlo Gambino—whether deliberately or inadvertently—had divided the Gambino family into two factions. A white-collar division, and a blue-collar division.

The white-collar group generated income for the family through subtle and sophisticated crimes such as transatlantic labor-racketeering; large-scale money-laundering; mail-and-wire fraud; insurance scams; embezzlement; cyber-crime; copyright infringement; identity theft and conversion; and multi-million dollar stock market fraud on Wall Street. These crimes were associated with high finance, and thus were more "corporate" in nature. The *capo* in charge of the white-collar operations was the aforementioned Paul Castellano.

Then there was the blue-collar wing of the family. This group generated money for the family through the more traditional "street" rackets. Such as extortion; loan sharking; illegal gambling; drug-trafficking; theft; fencing; and contract-murder, to name a few. This division of the family was headed by Neil "Mr. Neil" Dellacroce. Dellacroce was a soldier whom Gambino had inherited from his former boss, the ultraviolent and bloodthirsty Albert Anastasia.

After murdering Anastasia in 1956 and taking over the family reigns, Gambino had been faced with two options. The first option was to wage war with Dellacroce and the remaining Anastasia loyalist. The second option was to broker for peace. Gambino, ever the diplomat, chose the latter alternative. A war with Dellacroce would have devastated the family. Mr. Neil and his cronies were killers of the highest order. As Anastasia's henchmen, they had once formed the elite assassination squad known as Murder, Incorporated. Headed by Anastasia, Murder, Inc. had once served as the enforcement arm for the entire National Crime Syndicate. From 1930 to 1941, this infernal brotherhood of assassins had committed hundreds upon hundreds of barbaric homicides, the majority of which remained unsolved by law enforcement.

Carlo Gambino despised bloodshed. It was bad for business. And Gambino *loved* business. And so to that end, he smartly sued for peace with Neil Dellacroce. And to further show his good intentions, Don Carlo promoted Dellacroce to supreme *capo* of the then newly-formed Gambino family. Gambino placed Dellacroce specifically in charge of the family's street rackets. By default, Dellacroce became the nominal leader of the deadly soldiers who plied the family's more barbaric criminal trades.

One of Dellacroce's most loyal protégés at the time was one John Gotti. A Bronx-born ruffian, Gotti would later rise to prominence within the family after heading the hit squad that avenged the death of Carlo Gambino's nephew, Emanuel "Manny" Gambino. An aging Don Carlo took Gotti into his confidence, and gave the young mobster the contract on one James McBratney. A member of the Kidnap, Inc. crew, McBratney was the individual that was actually responsible for kidnapping Don Carlo's nephew, and killing the latter when the Gambino family failed to pay the required ransom. Gotti and his men tracked McBratney down at Snoop's Bar & Grill (a restaurant on Staten Island) and murdered McBratney in cold blood, on

May 22, 1973. Gotti's star would rise even further, as he would eventually become boss of the entire *fratellanza,* after murdering Paul Castellano in 1985 (which we will discuss a bit later, in detail).

Gotti and the other soldiers in the family were shocked when Gambino appointed Paul Castellano as boss, instead of Neil Dellacroce. Castellano had no street credibility whatsoever, whereas Dellacroce was a street legend. And although a sworn member of the family, Castellano was viewed by the other *mafiosi* as a pompous businessman, instead of a true gangster.

Dellacroce, on the other hand, was a mobster's mobster.

As real as they come.

And this was apparent to everyone. Even outsiders. One federal prosecutor said of Dellacroce, "He likes to peer into a victim's face, like some kind of dark angel, at the moment of death." A reporter once described a brief encounter with Dellacroce by saying, "His eyes had no color... as if his soul was transparent." And a mob investigator once stated, "Dellacroce was one of the scariest individuals I ever met in my life."

Needless to say, friction quickly rose between Castellano's white-collar camp and Dellacroce's blue-collar crew. But the two factions dared not go to war out of respect for their don, Carlo Gambino. And even after Don Carlo's passing, cooler heads prevailed as Castellano and Dellacroce forbade any antagonistic moves by their respective soldiers. Both men had promised Don Carlo that they would always keep the peace, for the betterment of the family. And they kept their promises.

The proverbial poop did not hit the fan until Dellacroce

passed away in December of 1985. With Dellacroce gone, all bets were now off. The young, brash, swashbuckling Gotti took over Dellacroce's position as overseer of the family's street operations. And from the very beginning, Gotti denounced Castellano's appointment as boss of the Gambino family. Gotti credited Castellano's promotion to nepotism, instead of meritocracy. And immediately, Gotti and his men looked for ways to undermine Castellano's authority.

Mutiny was afoot.

"The guy ain't Cosa Nostra," Gotti would say of Castellano to whomever would listen. "I mean, not really, anyway. He's just some buttered-up businessman. He wants to be Howard fuckin' Hughes. And what's more, he don't give a flying fuck about anybody else but himself. The guy's a fuckin' selfish prick, sittin' up on his high horses, lookin' down on the rest of us."

And on the surface, at least, it seemed as though Gotti had a point.

For a man who'd been worth millions upon millions of dollars, Don Carlo Gambino had chosen to live rather modestly. He had lived in a simple, two-story walk-up in a middle-class, Italian-and-Jewish neighborhood in the heart of Brooklyn, New York.

Castellano, not so much.

As soon as Paul Castellano assumed the position of family boss, he built a gargantuan mansion in an elitist section of Staten Island called Todt Hill. The house was so opulent, it garnered the nickname "The White House." The 10,436-square-foot mega-mansion boasted 17 rooms, 12 bathrooms, and an Olympic-size pool. And like its namesake, it featured a pillared portico, as well as a circular front drive surrounding a sprawling fountain. The pharaonic palace also housed a full-fledged, multi-room apartment where the housekeepers lived.

When he'd been alive, Carlo Gambino never allowed his status as the country's most revered mob boss go to his head. He retained the common touch. He would invite everyone—fellow *mafiosi*, civilians, and even law enforcement agents—into his humble abode on Ocean Parkway in Brooklyn. And there he'd serve them coffee and pastries and converse amiably about whatever matter was at hand. Don Carlo would also make frequent trips into Manhattan's Little Italy. There, he'd hold court at Ferrara's, a tiny neighborhood bakery. And there, once more, he'd meet with all of the neighborhood folk. Rich and poor. Young and old. Connected and civilian. The grandfatherly don would meet with everyone, listen to their problems, and provide them with solutions to their troubles.

Paul Castellano, not so much.

As soon as Castellano was through building his colossal fortress, he was seldom seen outside of it. He became a virtual recluse. And by doing so, he severed all ties to the old neighborhood. He lost all of what little ability he had to gauge the pulse of the streets. Which—in Castellano's case—would prove to be a fatal mistake.

During his tenure as boss, Don Carlo did not require huge kickbacks from his underlings. The crew chiefs and soldiers were free to earn, and keep, the majority of their take. Which was how it should be, the soldiers thought. After all, they were the ones out there hustling on the streets, risking their freedom and their lives. Thus, the fact that Don Carlo gave them a long leash to pretty much do as they pleased (within the confines of La Cosa Nostra's rules and guidelines, of course), inspired a sense of allegiance amongst the family's rank and file. In fact, it can even be said that Don Carlo's diplomatic genius in instituting this "live and let live" policy is one of the foremost reasons why—in his 20-plus years as a mob boss—he was never targeted for execution by an underling *within* the family.

But, of course, in this instance as well, Castellano elected to deviate from form.

The minute he became boss, Castellano allowed greed to cloud his reason. All of the family's soldiers were required to kick up almost twice as much as they had in the past. And, as if that weren't enough, Big Paulie began to take business opportunities away from the members of his own family, and started giving them to delegates in other families (namely, the Genovese family). Thus, while Castellano's *personal* bank account was enriched, it damaged the overall prospects of the Gambino family, at large.

"Big Paulie's takin' the bread right out of our fuckin' mouths," Gotti bellowed. "Don't he fuckin' get it? Can't he see that he's makin' the family look weak when he cuts these side deals with the fuckin' Genoveses? Sure, *he* makes a buck. But he's doing it at *our* expense. At the *Gambino family's* expense. All's so he can kiss up to The Chin." (The Chin being Vincent "The Chin" Gigante, the legendary boss of the Genovese family).

As time went on, the other *capos* and *soldati* in the family found it harder and harder to ignore Gotti's reprieves. For they were legitimate in nature. But what ultimately tipped the scale for Gotti and his men, was when Paul Castellano failed to attend Neil Dellacroce's wake and funeral.

"After what Neil did for the family, that fat prick, Paulie, don't show up to the wake *or* the funeral?" Gotti seethed. "Don't Paulie know that, had it not been for Neil, he woulda been dead a long time ago? Neil is the only reason that *stronzo*, Paulie, is still breathin'. Don't he get that?"

And Gotti was right. For no sooner had Neil Dellacroce passed away than Paul Castellano was lying in a pool of his own blood.

Dellacroce died of lung cancer on December 2, 1985.

Castellano, of lead poisoning a mere 14 days later, on December 16.

The Castellano hit was orchestrated by none other than John Gotti and his right-hand man, Sam "Sammy the Bull" Gravano. The gunman alleged to have carried out the order was one John "Johnny Carnegs" Carneglia, a sworn soldier and infamous hitman in the Gambino *borgata*.

It was quite nippy on the night of December 16, 1985 as Castellano and his underboss/bodyguard Thomas "Tommy" Bilotti pulled up to the entrance of Sparks Steakhouse. The five-star restaurant was located on East 46th Street between Second and Third Avenue, a busy thoroughfare in Midtown Manhattan. The street was teeming with honking cars and giddy Christmas shoppers. The atmosphere was exuberantly festive and jovial.

Until it wasn't.

The minute Paul Castellano popped the passenger-side door open and slid his portly frame out of the car, Carneglia emerged from the shadows like the Grim Reaper. Carneglia was not alone though. He was accompanied by three other pistol-packing plug-uglies.

All four men were dressed identically, in white

trench-coats and black Russian hats. Gotti and Gravano had settled on this dress code for the hitmen, in order to confuse any possible witnesses.

Carneglia, the point man, reached Castellano first. He whipped out his handgun and pumped six bullets into the boss' beefy frame. Five pellets found their way into Castellano's chest and abdomen. But the final kill-shot was a headshot. Castellano lay dead on the sidewalk, blood gushing from the gaping wounds in his body.

A shell-shocked and flabbergasted Tommy Bilotti stumbled out of the driver's side door.

Only to meet the same fate.

One of the other shooters (alleged to be Anthony Rampino) decapitated Bilotti with a volley of shots from an automatic pistol. Bilotti—like Castellano—was hit with exactly six bullets, most of which found their way into his skull.

Surprisingly, throughout the entire ordeal, no one heard anything. After the melee, a few pedestrians who happened to be at the scene were interviewed. They all claimed to have heard absolutely nothing. As a result, the police speculated that the killers had used silencers on their weapons. But who knows…

What *is* certain—according to government witness testimony offered a few years later—is that the hitters vanished as quickly as they'd appeared. The gunmen sauntered through the throng of ambling pedestrians and hopped into a car that was parked halfway down the block. Once inside the car, they sped off, leaving the grisly murder scene in their wake.

Another car was also parked half a block away. It was

a Lincoln sedan with tinted windows. In the driver's seat of this car sat John Gotti. In the passenger seat sat Sammy Gravano. Both men had watched the entire hit enfold right before their eyes. And they were pleased. Everything had worked out as they had planned.

Or had it?

That's why they were there. To make sure.

Gravano removed an automatic pistol from his waistband and rested it on his lap. Then he turned and faced Gotti, waiting.

Gotti stared intently through the windshield at the corpses of Paul Castellano and Tommy Bilotti. The two carcasses were strewn on the street like roadkill. They *had* to be dead, Gotti thought. But one could never be sure. Until one was *absolutely* sure.

Gotti turned away from the windshield and faced Gravano. "Okay. I'm gonna drive by slow," Gotti said to Gravano. "And if any of them pricks is still breathin', you hop out the car and finish 'em. *Capisci*?"

"You got it, John," Gravano replied, yanking the slide back on his pistol, readying it for action.

But no further action was needed.

As Gotti and Gravano drove slowly by the cadavers, it was evident that Castellano and Bilotti were as dead as doornails.

John Gotti—who had already drummed up the necessary support from the other members of the *borgata*, prior to making the move on Castellano—was now boss of America's most powerful crime family.

Gotti had made it.

He was now King of the Hill.

But heavy is the head that wears the crown.

Re-enter Rudy Giuliani, U.S. Attorney for the Southern District of New York.

The sweeping advantages that the RICO Act afforded Giuliani in his fight against organized crime have already been discussed. Now let us consider the second factor which played a major role in La Cosa Nostra's downfall in general, and the Gambino family's decline in particular.

The wiretap.

Also known as a "covert listening device," a "bug," or simply a "wire," a wiretap is a particular form of electronic surveillance that secretly monitors telephonic, telegraphic and/or other types of auditory communication.

A bug is usually placed inside a perpetrator's phoneline, or somewhere inside the perpetrator's private residence or place of business. Once the covert transmitter is installed, it functions somewhat like a radio, imparting and recording all sounds within its vicinity.

Including conversations.

Although bugs have been around since the 1890s, the evidence they collected was not admissible in a court of law until the 1960s. In *Katz vs. United States*, the Supreme Court established that where an individual has an expectation of privacy, the government is required to obtain a warrant for wiretapping. Once the court-approved warrant is obtained, however, law enforcement can then proceed with the implementation of a wiretap. And, barring few exceptions, all of the sounds picked up by said wire/bug can then be used as evidence in legal prosecutions.

So now, not only did Giuliani have the platform by which to prosecute La Cosa Nostra as a whole (by way of the RICO Act of 1970), he also had the means to collect the evidence needed to launch said prosecutions (by way of the wiretap).

And Giuliani hit the ground running.

He secured a litany of warrants. And with these warrants, he was able to plant a score of bugs on the phones and premises of La Cosa Nostra's top executives. Like, for example, the Palma Boys Social Club. This was the principle headquarters of Anthony "Fat Tony" Salerno, acting boss of the powerful Genovese family. Giuliani also bugged a Jaguar sedan used by Anthony "Tony Ducks" Corallo, boss of the Lucchese family. Giuliani had informants wear wires that collected incriminating evidence against the likes of Carmine Persico and Gennaro Langella, the boss and underboss of the Colombo family, respectively. Wiretap evidence collected by the famous undercover agent Joseph "Donnie Brasco" Pistone, against the bigwigs of the Bonanno family, decimated that entire *borgata*. And, for the purposes of our story, Giuliani also planted a listening device in Gambino boss, Paul Castellano's, White House mansion.

These bugs gathered endless hours of recordings. And what these recordings proved was that La Cosa Nostra did in fact exist, and that this brotherhood of criminals was governed by the Commission, a sovereign committee consisting of the heads of New York's five families. This committee met, however infrequently, to resolve disputes and/or discuss criminal activities. And these activities included (but were not limited to) extortion, loan sharking, labor-racketeering, drug-trafficking, and contract-murder.

The bug that holds the most relevance, for the purposes of our story, is the one that was placed in Paul Castellano's kitchen. The hidden transmitter captured 600 hours of conversation. And it gave Giuliani all of the impeaching evidence he needed to go after the boss of the Gambino family, as well as other *mafiosi* in the family's rank and file.

Thirty-plus Gambino family members were caught on the Castellano wiretap discussing illegal activities. The bug produced over 3,000 pages of transcripts, and eventually led to more than 300 indictments. The bug also ruined Paul Castellano's reputation amongst his own *capos* and soldiers. By law, everyone against whom the wiretap was used as evidence had the right to hear and review the contents of the recordings. And so, a host of Castellano's subordinates within the family (as well as bosses, *capos*, and soldiers from other crime families) were sent copies of the transcripts.

And they were all *appalled*, to say the least, by the contents within the transcriptions.

Castellano was caught on tape ridiculing Gambino family members, denigrating mob bosses from other *borgatas*, and unwittingly setting sanctions against business associates. The recordings also revealed—what other mobsters deemed to be—dishonorable behavior unbecoming of a Cosa Nostra boss, as they divulged the full-blown affair Castellano was having with his Columbian housekeeper, Gloria Olarte. The tapes showed Castellano professing his love to the housemaid, even while his wife (Nina Castellano) still lived in the residence. The recordings even showed that, due to a diabetes condition, Paul Castellano had not had an erection in many years. And, to better satisfy his Columbian mistress, Castellano underwent a penile implant operation.

Castellano's fellow mobsters within the family—including John Gotti—were stunned by these revelations. Gotti would later use the contents of these recordings to justify whacking Castellano.

Using the evidence gathered from the Castellano bug (as well as other wiretaps) Giuliani was able to indict all of the heads of New York's five families under the Racketeer Influenced and Corrupt Organizations Act. The trial that would determine the fate of La Cosa Nostra's ruling panel was dubbed the Mafia Commission Trial.

Apart from Castellano, 11 other high-ranking Mafia officials were indicted and arrested. They were: Anthony "Fat Tony" Salerno, acting boss of the Genovese family; Anthony "Tony Ducks" Corallo, boss of the Lucchese family; Phillip "Rusty" Rastelli, boss of the Bonanno family; Carmine Persico, boss of the Colombo family; Aniello Dellacroce, then underboss of the Gambino family; Gennaro "Gerry Lang" Langella, underboss of the Colombo family; Salvatore "Tom Mix" Santoro, underboss of the Lucchese family; Christopher "Christy Tick" Furnari, *consigliere* of the Lucchese family; Ralph "Little Ralphie" Scopo, a high-ranking soldier in the Colombo family; Stefano Canone, *consigliere* of the Bonanno family; and Anthony "Bruno" Indelicato, a high-ranking *capo* in the Bonanno family.

Both Dellacroce and Castellano died before the trial could commence. The former of natural causes, the latter by lead poisoning.

Thereby leaving John Gotti in charge of the Gambino family.

But, alas, Gotti would commit the same error as his predecessor. Gotti, too, would fall victim to a wiretap investigation. And his demise would signal the end of the

Gambino family's reign atop America's organized crime sanctorum.

Gotti was not a target of the feds during the Mafia Commission Trial, which eventually sent all of La Cosa Nostra's bosses to the penitentiary for long prison sentences. (Prison bids which, in reality, amounted to death sentences, as all of the Commission patriarchs ended up passing away behind bars).

But it did not take law enforcement a long time to make a target out of John Gotti. Emboldened by their sweeping victory in the Mafia Commission Trial, the feds set out to make an example of Gotti, whom they absolutely loathed.

The feds thought Gotti was an unscrupulous, pompous bigshot.

And Gotti did nothing to dissuade their opinion of him.

In fact, he *welcomed* the feds' disdain.

Whereas Gambino (and even Paul Castellano) had been publicly discreet and self-effacing to a fault, Gotti embraced the spotlight that came with being a boss.

Not since Al Capone had the public seen a more debonair, suave, smooth-talking mob boss. Gotti seemingly appeared straight out of central casting, epitomizing all of the traits of the hot-shot, Hollywood gangster, to a tee. Pepper-salted, slick-backed hair. Thousand-dollar, tailored suits. Multicolored, hand-painted ties. Heavy, silver Rolex watches. Gleaming wingtips. And a million-dollar smile to boot.

Not to mention, one or two charming sound-bites for a devoted press and enchanted public, who followed him everywhere. It was as if he was Christ, and the public his enamored disciples.

To the community and press, Gotti was as rock star. And demigod that he was, the new boss of the Gambino family loved the attention and ate it all up…

… while the feds waited and lurked on the sidelines, seething with resentment.

The media took to calling Gotti "The Dapper Don," due to his stylish appearance and exquisite flair. But this moniker was quickly replaced by another: "The Teflon Don." Law enforcement, enraged at Gotti's celebrity status, began throwing charges at him as fast as they could muster. But the charges never stuck. Hence the sobriquet, "Teflon" don.

Indeed, Gotti spent the late 1980s in and out of courtrooms, dodging prison sentences through a string of highly-publicized acquittals. (It would later be revealed that the Gambino family engaged in incessant witness intimidation and jury tampering tactics to secure these acquittals). Nevertheless, for the time being, Gotti was riding high. He was America's darling gangster (hundreds of fans would camp outside the courthouses where Gotti's trials took place, in order to cheer Gotti on, while protesting Gotti's abuse at the hands of the federal government). He was boss of the most powerful crime family in the nation (the Gambino family, at the time, was La Cosa Nostra's preeminent criminal organization). And he was filthy rich (the Gambinos were raking in close to a billion dollars in annual revenue, a sizeable cut of which went directly into Gotti's pockets, as boss of the *borgata*).

But what goes up must come down.

Eventually.

And Gotti's star—no matter how brightly it shown—could not escape this irrefutable law of nature.

The feds caught a lucky break in 1989. The Ravenite Social Club in Little Italy was John Gotti's primary headquarters. It was where he conducted the majority of his business and held most of his meetings. The feds had bugged the bar and lounge area of The Ravenite a long time ago. But the bugs never generated any incriminating information. The gangsters who fraternized The Ravenite spoke freely, indeed. Just not about their illegal activities. It was as if they knew (or at least, had a hunch) that the feds might be listening in on their conversations. As a result, the only thing the bugs picked up were mob wise-cracks and other useless chatter.

But then the feds, through an informant, got wind of an important tidbit of information. The mobsters who congregated inside The Ravenite were, in fact, aware that the bar area was bugged. Including, of course, John Gotti. As a result, when Gotti (or any other high-ranking officials in the family) wanted to discuss matters of great import, they would exit the bar area through a rear door and climb some steps that led to an apartment located directly above the social club. The apartment belonged to an old lady named Nettie Cirelli. Mrs. Cirelli was the widow of a long-time family soldier, the late Michael Cirelli. Mrs. Cirelli allowed Gotti, and the top echelon of the family, to use her tiny apartment for their private meetings. It was said that even the late Gambino underboss, Neil Dellacroce, had often used the apartment to hold important conferences.

This significant piece of information would prove to be John Gotti's (and the Gambino family's) undoing.

The FBI surveillance team assigned to the John Gotti case waited until Thanksgiving weekend of 1989. At that time, Mrs. Cirelli was in Florida, on vacation, visiting family. Armed with a schematic delineation of the apartment's interior, the feds stealthily entered the flat and planted a well-positioned bug in the sitting room.

After that, it was all she wrote.

The recordings captured John Gotti talking with his underboss, Frank Locascio; his *consigliere* and right-hand man, Sammy Gravano; and a host of other important family members. And these conversations (unlike the ones picked up by the bug one level below) were nothing *but* incriminating.

Gotti's mouth ran like an open faucet. Day in and day out, he incriminated himself on the tapes. He openly admitted to approving the killings of a score of individuals. Both within, and outside, of the family. For example, during one conversation, Gotti justified whacking a high-ranking soldier in the Gambino family by the name of Louis DiBono.

"You know why he is dying?" Gotti's voice rang like cold death on the tapes. "He is gonna die because he refused to come in when I called. He didn't do nothing else wrong."

And not too long after this recording, DiBono's bullet-riddled corpse was found inside his own 1987 Cadillac Deville, in the underground parking garage of the World Trade Center.

In another instant on the tapes, Gotti could be heard putting a hit out on a neighborhood gambler by the name of Jack Zorba. In fact, Gotti even threatened to do the hit *himself.*

"You tell this punk, I, me, John Gotti, will sever your motherfuckin' head off," Gotti snarled on the recording.

Elsewhere on the tapes, Gotti openly confirmed the very existence of the Italian-American Mafia.

"This is going to be La Cosa Nostra 'til I die," Gotti asserted. "Be it an hour from now, or be it tonight, or a hundred years from now when I'm in jail. It's gonna be La Cosa Nostra… It's gonna be the way I say it's gonna be. La Cosa Nostra. La Cosa Nostra. You might, because a guy's nice to you… think that makes him a good guy. It makes him a motherfucker to me. It don't make him a good guy. It makes him a good guy if he's one of us, and he proves he's part of us."

The feds couldn't believe what they were hearing. This was the big break they had been waiting for. Gotti's condemnatory rants were like sweet music to their ears. They licked their chops as the ever loquacious Gotti kept digging himself into a deeper and deeper hole.

And, as if that weren't enough, Gotti supplied the feds with even more leverage.

Just as Paul Castellano had been caught ridiculing his underlings and associates on the White House bug, Gotti, too, was caught deriding his fellow *mafiosi* on The Ravenite transmitter. In particular, his best friend and counselor, Sammy "The Bull" Gravano. As the tapes rolled on, Gotti could be heard bad-mouthing his *consigliere* time and time again. At first, Gotti's admonishments of Gravano had a hint of jealousy to them, as Gravano was the top earner in the family.

Speaking to Frank Locascio at one point, Gotti says of

Gravano's penchant for starting businesses, "And I tell him a million times, Sammy slow it down… Pull it in a notch."

But then, Gotti's tone switched from jaundiced to accusatory, as he began to blame Gravano for a slew of murders within the family. (Murders which John Gotti, as boss of the family, had obviously signed off on.)

"When Di B [Louis DiBono] got whacked," Gotti vented on the tapes, "they told me a story. I was in jail when I whacked him… I done it anyway. I allowed it to be done anyway… I took Sammy's word that he [Louis DiBono] talked behind my back."

As Gotti continued to talk subversively about Gravano on the tapes, the feds sensed that they were being presented with a wonderful opportunity.

The opportunity to, possibly, flip Gravano to their side.

Which brings us to the third and final factor which prompted La Cosa Nostra's (and the Gambino family's) decline: the widespread violation of the code of *omerta* by its sworn members.

The word *omerta* comes from the Italian dialect, and is a variant of another Italian word: *umilita*, which means "humility." The word dates back to pre-16th century times, and is indicative of a code of conduct (or lifestyle) that Sicilians were forced to adopt, as a means to survive the constant invasion of their island by foreign principalities.

In order to ensure their survival and preserve their traditions, Sicilians had to band together. They had to protect one another from their foreign oppressors. And the best way to do this was by erecting a wall of silence around their internal affairs. While these foreign governments might be able to invade their lands *physically*, Sicilians vowed never to allow the foreigners to annex their inner sanctum, or society.

So, Sicilians responded with a show of humility when confronted, head on, by their oppressors.

While at the same time silently scheming and conniving, behind the scenes, to rid themselves of their tyrants.

Thus, cooperation with any foreign government was deemed fatal to the very fabric of Sicilian civilization. And no other institution embodied this way of thinking like La Cosa Nostra.

At least, back then it had.

But times had changed.

In 1963, Joe Valachi became the first sworn member to publicly acknowledge the existence of La Cosa Nostra. Valachi served as a low-ranking soldier in the Genovese family. Facing the death penalty for a murder he committed in 1962, Valachi decided to cooperate with the U.S. government in exchange for his life.

Valachi appeared before Arkansas Senator John L. McClellan's Permanent Subcommittee on Investigations (which would come to be known simply as the "Valachi Hearings"). The hearings were televised nationally and received the utmost press. And before a mesmerized and awe-struck public, Valachi not only admitted to the existence of the Italian-American Mafia, but also laid out all of its inner workings. He spoke in both general terms (for example, explaining the rank-and-file and organizational structure of the Mafia), as well as in specific terms (for example, citing certain *mafiosi* by name, and detailing particular capers and murders these *mafiosi* engaged in).

Though Valachi's testimony did not lead to the

prosecution of any Mafia bosses, it did provide the government and the public with an expansive account of La Cosa Nostra's history, including many of its rituals and undertakings. In fact, Valachi is the individual credited with introducing the term "Cosa Nostra" into the English-speaking vernacular.

And for an organization like the Mafia (whose strength and power lied in the clandestineness of its ways and customs), Valachi's testimony was severely damning, if not near-fatal.

But perhaps no other violation of the Mafia's code of *omerta* was as significant to the demise of New York's five families as a tell-all autobiography entitled *A Man of Honor*, written and published by Mafia boss Joseph Bonanno.

Bonanno was one of the original founding fathers of the American Mafia. He was appointed boss of his own outfit by none other than Salvatore Maranzano—*capo di tutti capi* of the entire Cosa Nostra during prohibition.

Bonanno's appointment took place right after the Castellammarese War of 1930. In that war, Maranzano defeated his arch-rival, Giuseppe "Joe The Boss" Masseria. And in doing so, Maranzano became the single, most powerful *mafioso* in the country. To consolidate his power and increase his wealth even more, Maranzano organized five *borgatas* who were tasked with controlling all of the criminal enterprises in New York City's five boroughs and surrounding areas. These five criminal factions would come to be known as the Five Families. And they all answered—and paid tribute to—Salvatore Maranzano, their chief.

The Bonanno family was one of the five families, with Joseph Bonanno (then only 26-years-old) serving as godfather. The other four families were the Profaci family, headed by Joseph Profaci; the Mangano family, headed Vincent Mangano; the Gagliano family, led by Thomas Gagliano; and the Luciano family, run by Charles "Lucky" Luciano.

As the story goes, Luciano would eventually kill Salvatore Maranzano and abolish the title of *capo di tutti capi* altogether, in favor of a more democratic, committee-like structure. Thus, New York's five families (as well as a few other criminal outfits from adjoining states) became "The Commission." And this Commission (which was essentially a board of directors, whereby each outfit boss had equal voting power) would go on to oversee all of La Cosa Nostra's activities in the United States.

Indeed, Joe Valachi's testimony shed light on La Cosa Nostra's machinations. But Valachi was, at best, a low-ranking figure in the Mafia. And so, his knowledge—even of mob activities—was somewhat limited. Many times during the McClellan hearings, Valachi was forced to answer his interrogators' probing questions with a despondent shrug of the shoulders. Or a listless, "I'm sorry. I don't know the answer to that question, senator." And he did so not to avoid prosecution, but because he truly and honestly did not know the answer to many of the senate committee's questions.

But Joseph Bonanno was a different story entirely.

As a founding father of La Cosa Nostra, Bonanno's insight into the mob's activities was limitless. And while Bonanno never took the witness stand, he did law enforcement one better. He provided the feds (and the public at large) with a detailed, written account of La Cosa Nostra's evolution. Beginning with its roots in Sicily, and ending with its relocation and prodigious growth as a criminal entity in America. Bonanno, godfather and boss, had *experienced* it all. And his story proved it, as the autobiography was replete with specific names, dates, times, and locations.

U.S. Attorney Rudolph Giuliani only commenced his probe into New York's organized crime element *after* reading Bonanno's biographical exposé. The detailed information in *A Man of Honor* gave Giuliani the intel he needed to later investigate, and prosecute, all of New York's Cosa Nostra families.

And prosecute them he did, as the Mafia Commission Trial led to the incarceration of *all* of New York City's Cosa Nostra bosses.

A blow which the Mafia has yet to recover from.

Bonanno's 1983 opus proved that the current rung of *mafiosi* held the code of *omerta* in very little regard. *Omerta* had become a forlorn tradition, no longer adhered to by the very members who had sworn to uphold its edicts. *Omerta* was a thing of the past, replaced now by ego and self-aggrandizement.

And it was with this thought in mind that the feds approached John Gotti's number-two man, Sammy Gravano, with the intent to persuade Gravano to become a federal informant. Like Bonanno, Gravano was a high-ranking member of La Cosa Nostra. As *consigliere* and underboss of the nation's pre-eminent mob family, Gravano—law enforcement knew—possessed a treasure-trove of incriminating information that would not only bring about the Gambino family's demise, but also that of other important mob figures and *borgatas* across the country.

After collecting all of the evidence they needed from the Ravenite bug, the feds decided to shut down the investigation.

As well as the Gambino family, once and for all.

On December 11, 1990, FBI agents raided the Ravenite Social Club and arrested Sammy Gravano, Frank Locascio, and John Gotti. All three were hauled to jail. And due to the extensiveness of the evidence gathered against the trio, all three were denied bail.

The wiretap recordings were played at several pre-trial hearings for all the defendants to hear. As the tapes whirred—the voices and conversations on them echoing loudly off the high-ceilinged walls of the courtroom—the feds paid close attention to Gotti and Gravano's reactions. Gotti maintained his bravado, shaking his head silently and snickering from time to time at the feds. Gravano's face, on the other hand, remained absolutely expressionless. But behind the stoic façade, the feds could tell that Gravano was seething. He *must* be. It was the first time Gravano was hearing the tapes. It was also the first time he was hearing his "best friend," John Gotti, badmouth him extensively behind his back.

Still, Gravano held firm, refusing to break the law of *omerta*. Though he had heard Gotti denigrating him on the tapes, Gravano chalked it up as useless, backroom banter. That is what Gravano *wanted* to believe. And for close to a year, after hearing the tapes, that is what Gravano convinced himself took place.

Until Gotti himself proved Gravano wrong.

Gravano and Gotti were both being held at the same correctional facility. They spent their days hanging out with each other. Chatting. Socializing. But mostly trying to come up with a line of defense for the charges being brought against them in their forthcoming court trial. And it was during these conversations with Gotti that Gravano picked up on something rather peculiar.

Gotti wanted to set Gravano up to take the fall for him.

As time passed, Gotti made this clear as day. He would say to Gravano, "Hey, Sammy. You're gonna have to take the fall on this one. For the family." Or, "Sammy, I can't do a bid. Not now. I'm the boss. The family needs me. My public needs me. You're gonna have to bite the bullet on this one." Or, "You hear this shit the government is saying about you, Sammy? They're making you out to be a fuckin' monster. It's all those fuckin' guys you whacked. I warned you it would come back to bite you in the ass. You were too fuckin' greedy, Sammy. I warned you this would happen. So, now, you gotta take the hit, *amico*. You gotta do the time. You gotta do this, for the family."

Suddenly, it dawned on Gravano that the FBI recordings of Gotti were not useless banter after all. Gotti had, indeed, meant everything he'd said on the tapes regarding Gravano. Gravano was flabbergasted. For he had committed all of those murders on *Gotti's* behalf. In fact, his role as an enforcer had helped Gotti ascend to, and solidify, his position as boss of the family. And what about all of the money Gravano had made for Gotti over the years? All Gotti did was sit on his fat keister all day while he, Sammy, slaved, day in and day out, to acquire businesses that strengthened the family's—and Gotti's—economic position. Hell, Gravano thought, he had made Gotti a multimillionaire damn near overnight! And *this* is how Gotti repaid him? Instead of formulating a plan that would get them *both* out of the jam they were currently in, Gotti (with his oversized ego) *actually* believe that he deserved to go free, while Gravano rotted away in a prison cell? How was that fair? Especially when it was *Gotti's* big mouth that had gotten them into this mess in the first place!

Gravano suddenly realized that the notion of "family" within La Cosa Nostra only applied when things were going well. But when shit hit the fan (at least, these days) it was every man for himself.

And so, rather than be the victim of a double-cross, Gravano decided to be the architect of one. He reached out to the feds behind Gotti's back (in the same manner Gotti had talked behind his) and brokered a deal, formally agreeing to testify on November 13, 1991.

The moment was fraught with undeniable tension as Gravano entered the courtroom that day and took the witness stand. Gravano was visibly nervous. He was about to become the thing he'd hated most during his tenure as a wiseguy: a *rat*. And by doing so, he was about to turn his back on the only life he'd ever known. The only friends he'd ever had.

On that day, the courtroom was packed with those very same friends. Law enforcement authorities, reporters, and spectators rounded out the bunch. Gravano faced them all, holding their gazes (some longer than others). The feds, reporters, and public stared back at him with enthusiastic anticipation. His friends and family, on the other hand, glared at him shamefully. But there was also the slightest glimmer of hope in their eyes. Through their stares, they begged Gravano not to proceed with his testimony. And for a fleeting moment—under the pressure of their sanguine gazes—Gravano actually considered reneging on his deal with the federal government, thereby preserving his honor as a sworn *soldati* of his beloved Cosa Nostra.

That is, until his eyes landed on his friend-turned-nemesis, John Gotti.

If looks could kill, Gravano would have been reduced to a corpse on the courtroom floor. Gotti stared quietly at Gravano, his eyes piercing, like two daggers. Gotti's lips were curled in a tiny snarl. And his breathing was slow and steady, like a lion sizing up his prey from afar.

That's when Gravano realized that there was no going back. He had already reached the point of no return. Even if he elected not to testify today, Gotti would have him killed. Simply for *feigning* betrayal. That's the kind of guy Gotti was. At least if Sammy testified, he'd have the protection of the government. But *without* that protection, he'd be a sitting duck. Good as dead.

So, his mind made up, Gravano proceeded to testify against Gotti and the rest of the *borgata*. And by doing so, he became the highest-ranking *mafioso* (at the time) to become a government witness.

Gravano spent a total of nine arduous days on the witness stand. During this time, he fielded tough questions from both the prosecution, and defense, teams. And in the process, much was unearthed. Like, for example, Gravano's participation in 19 murders (10 of which Gotti was implicated in, including the hit on Paul Castellano in 1985). Plus, a host of other nefarious activities which Gravano, Gotti, and other members of the family engaged in.

Gravano laid it all out for the judge and jury, leaving no

stone unturned. And as a result, the Gambino family was decimated. The jury needed only 14 hours of deliberation to find John Gotti guilty on all the charges of the indictment—thanks largely in part to the FBI tapes, as well as Gravano's trouncing testimony. Gotti was sentenced to life imprisonment without the possibility of parole. He entered the federal penitentiary on December 14, 1992, and died ten years later while still incarcerated, at age 61.

Gravano, on the other hand, spent less than a year in jail following his testimony. The judge considered the time Gravano had already served, as well as Gravano's vital contributions to the government's efforts to take down John Gotti and the Gambino family.

But despite all of his faults, Gotti was a leader of men. There was no doubt about that. His flair, his presence, and his polished—though underlyingly sinister—air had not only ensnared the public's fascination, but also that of his fellow *mafiosi*. Gotti's associates and underlings not only feared and respected him, they also *adored* him. And because of this, Gotti had been able to rise to a position of power within the family. And once he assumed the throne, he'd done a fairly good job of sustaining the Gambino family's dominance over the other four New York crime families.

Therefore, no one was surprised when the Gambino family went from first to last place in La Cosa Nostra's pecking order, following John Gotti's incarceration. Not only did the family not have a suitable replacement for Gotti, but also, any notable or worthy *mafiosi* capable of doing the job did not want the position. For fear that they would become the government's next target. The appeal and prestige that came with being a boss had lost its muster.

Heavy is the head that wears the crown. The government had showcased this with Gotti. And now, as a result, no one wanted to wear the tiara.

But *someone* had to.

And that someone ended up being Peter Gotti, John Gotti's older brother.

Peter Gotti was one year John's senior. But Peter looked up to, and worshipped, his younger brother so much, innocent bystanders would've thought that John was the older of the two. Peter went by several nicknames, such as: "One Eyed Pete," "Petey Boy," and simply "One Eye." But perhaps the most telling nickname of them all was "The Dumbest Don."

John Gotti himself may not have been a criminal genius, but he'd at least been smart enough to surround himself with intelligent and capable men. Also, John Gotti, for all of his faults, had been a staunch visionary with extraordinary ambition. How else could a dirt-poor kid from Queens grow up to become boss of the most storied criminal organization in the country's history? Indeed, John Gotti had made up for his lack of brains with other venerable qualities.

Peter Gotti, not so much.

Not only was Peter stupid, he also lacked vision, toughness, and ambition. In fact, had it not been for his younger brother, John, Peter might never have become a made man in the Mafia. He probably would have remained a two-bit wannabe his entire life.

Upon becoming boss of the family, Peter Gotti wasted no time living up to his reputation as the "Dumbest Don." He was immediately thrown in jail. The reason? Attempting to extort money from the famous film actor, Steven Seagal.

Now, what business the boss of a powerful crime family has extorting funds from a public figure, when his crime organization is already generating millions of dollars per week from its more discreet operations, is beyond anyone's imagination. But where there is a will there is a way. And Peter Gotti found a way to live up to his moniker.

Peter was summarily sentenced to 20 years in prison.

And—as the saying goes—shit rolls downhill. Lacking sound leadership, the Gambino family quickly fell apart. Constant attacks from the government, as well as other criminal organizations (both Italian and non-Italian), proved too much for the now-leaderless and unstable clan. Bit by bit, the family's territories were usurped, and their income streams dried up. They lost all of their political clout, as well as all of their influence over the unions that powered America's industries. Their major ties to international crime organizations (even those in their homeland of Sicily) were cut off. The unencumbered power the family had wielded since Don Carlo's rise to the top of the Mafia food-chain was now defunct.

And nothing serves as a better example of the family's denouement than a most recent incident, which has been splayed all over the tabloids for the world to see.

Franky "Franky Boy" Cali—nominal head of the Gambino family—was gunned down in gory and indiscriminate fashion while standing outside of his Staten Island residence, on March 13, 2019. When the event took place, everyone feared the worst. It was the first noted slaying of a New York mob boss in over 30 years. Not since John Gotti's ousting of Paul Castellano had a mob hit featured so prominently in the newsreels.

Was it a murder-contract?

And if so, who had issued it?

Had the contract come from *within* the family, or from an outside source?

Would there be repercussions?

Would this disparaging hit on Francesco "Franky Boy" Cali—a much-loved and avuncular member of the Gambino family—set the stage for an all-out mob war?

Surely it would. For as sure as day, Cali's death *must* be avenged.

Right?

Yes. Maybe it would have. Back in *Don Carlo's* time. In fact, in Gambino's time, a hit of such magnitude would have never even happened, due to proper security measures. For, as the story enfolded, it turned out that Cali's front-and-center assassination had not been the result of a mutinous uprising within the family ranks. Nor had it been the work of highly-skilled hitmen from a rival criminal organization.

No.

Francesco Cali had been slain by none other than Anthony Comello. A mentally-unstable, 24-year-old kid who was angry with Cali, because Cali forbade Comello from dating his niece.

As mob historian and author, Selwyn Raab, told Rollingstone Magazine in an interview: "This was an erratic, isolated kind of hit… Somebody pulls up and bangs your car and rings your doorbell?… this [was] an ad hoc hit by a screwball kid."

How truly powerful is the President of the United States, if a deranged vagabond can walk up to the front door of the White House, knock, and pump six shots into the president's head without suffering immediate repercussions?

As this is being written, Cali's assassin, Anthony Comello, is alive and well. He is preparing his defense for his murder trial. His attorney plans to enter an insanity plea. And this might just do the trick, seeing as Comello does, in fact, appear to be somewhat crazy. During pre-trial court hearings, Comello has made it clear that his reasons for murdering Don Francesco Cali did not center strictly on his relationship affairs with Cali's niece. No. There was a bigger plot afoot, Comello stated. Cali, Comello argued, was a member of "The Deep State" (a clandestine, anti-government movement); and it was up to him (Comello) to kill Cali, in order to preserve the American president, Donald Trump's, life. Comello professed that he was a believer in "QAnon" (a conspiracy theory claiming that there are secret agents within, and outside of, the federal government who are trying to do away with President Donald Trump). Comello further stated that he was merely doing his duty as a loyal American citizen when he murdered Cali. In fact, Comello added, his initial inclination had been to make a citizen's arrest of Cali, and hand Cali over to the Secret Service or CIA. But, unfortunately, things got out of hand.

Indeed, things have gotten out of hand for the Gambino family since the early 90s. The once-almighty, criminal dynasty has been reduced to nothing more than a rogue street gang, with little power, little influence, and few resources.

At least, that's how it appears on the surface.

But one can never be sure when speaking about the Mafia and its criminal elements. Generations ago, La

Cosa Nostra grew to prominence by tricking the public into thinking that it did not exist. Perhaps the leaders of the Gambino family, today, learned from the Gotti fiasco. Perhaps they are making it a point to "appear" weak and insignificant. In which case, perhaps, they *do* actually wield more power and influence than meets the naked eye.

Whatever the case may be, one thing is certain and beyond speculation: There will never again be a mob chieftain like Carlo Gambino. Never again will the nation's most elite criminal organizations unite under one man's flag, as they did under Don Carlo.

And that, in and of itself, is a legacy that will stand the test of times.

James Pierre
March 2020
Windsor, Connecticut

Printed in Great Britain
by Amazon

26743374R00179